The Hope of Israel

The Hope of Israel

Compiled by Rob Lawson

The Christadelphian
404 Shaftmoor Lane, Hall Green, Birmingham B28 8SZ, UK

2017

First published 2017

© 2017 The Christadelphian Magazine and Publishing Association

ISBN 978 0 85189 379 2 (print edition)
ISBN 978 0 85189 380 8 (electronic edition)

Printed and bound in the UK by
CMP (UK) Limited

Extracts from the Authorised Version of the Bible (The King James Bible), the rights in which are vested in the Crown, are reproduced by permission of the Crown's Patentee, Cambridge University Press.

Scripture quotations marked (ESV) are from the ESV® Bible (The Holy Bible, English Standard Version®), copyright © 2001 by Crossway, a publishing ministry of Good News Publishers. Used by permission. All rights reserved.

Contents

Foreword vii

Part 1: God's purpose with the Jews 1

1. The restoration of the ancient kingdom of Israel 3
2. God's purpose with the Jews (1) 12
3. God's purpose with the Jews (2) 21
4. God's purpose with the Jews (3) 32
5. God's purpose with the Jews (4) 43
6. God's purpose with the Jews (5) 54
7. God's purpose with the Jews (6) 66
8. God's purpose with the Jews (7) 76
9. God's purpose with the Jews (8) 84
10. God's purpose with the Jews (9) 94
11. God's purpose with the Jews (10) 103

Part 2: The hope of Israel – still the Christadelphian hope 115

1. Share certificate for the Jewish Colonial Trust 116
2. The State of Israel 118
3. Israel and the purpose of God 123

4. For the Hope of Israel 140
5. What hope now for Israel? 151
6. The God of Israel 156

Part 3: Zionism – an autobiography (1791-1948) 161
1. Loi relative aux Juifs 162
2. Promoting Christianity amongst the Jews 164
3. Memorandum to Protestant Powers 167
4. A mission of Inquiry 175
5. An extract from the twelfth letter of *Romans und Jerusalem* 178
6. Disraeli's purchase of a stake in the Suez Canal 184
7. The Basel Programme 187
8. Diary entry for January 26, 1904 189
9. The Balfour Declaration 195
10. British policy in Palestine 197
11. Buying the Emek 204
12. Recommendations of the Palestine Royal Commission Report 213
13. An Extract from the speech 'On the Jewish Question' .. 218
14. Extracts from 'UN General Assembly Resolution 181' .. 222
15. The Declaration of the Establishment of the State of Israel 228

Epilogue: Brother John Thomas and *Elpis Israel* 233
1. The final chapter of *Elpis Israel* 235

Scripture index 262

Foreword

THE world generally does not look favourably on the Jewish people or the State of Israel. This is sometimes given as a reason for leaving Israel in the background of our lectures and personal preaching. The New Testament Gospel is, however, inescapably centred on the Jewish nation.

In this book we seek to reaffirm the traditional Christadelphian position on the subject. The first part of the book, written in the 1860s by Brother Robert Roberts, was his response to those in his day who thought the Jews' relationship with God had ended. Our past was his future, and looking back we see the accuracy with which his Bible-based expectations for Israel were fulfilled. The second section is a series of articles from other past editors of *The Christadelphian*, showing their reactions to major world events involving God's people, their work on behalf of impoverished Jews, and their constant commitment to the doctrine of the Hope of Israel. Finally, we see God at work in history through the speeches, diaries and essays of those who, knowingly or not, made the events of 1948 happen.

A danger facing English language publications of this kind is the natural tendency to prioritise the words of English-speaking people. This would be detrimental to any history of modern Zionism, an emphatically international movement. Particularly important were the German-speaking peoples, the most notable being Theodor Herzl, founding President of the

World Zionist Organization, and his Vice-President Max Nordau. For this reason the publishers wish to thank Brother Gabriel & Sister Carolyn Bauer (Rochdale, UK) and Brother Graham Jackman (Reading, UK) for their work in translating the German language documents included herein.

The question of how God views the largely unbelieving Jewish people is not a new one. Working to unite Jews and Gentiles into one body in first-century Rome, the issue was one central to the teaching of the Apostle Paul. Let us then hear his inspired words:

> "I want you to understand this mystery, brothers: a partial hardening has come upon Israel, until the fullness of the Gentiles has come in. And in this way all Israel will be saved, as it is written, 'The Deliverer will come from Zion, he will banish ungodliness from Jacob; and this will be my covenant with them when I take away their sins.'"
>
> (Romans 11:25-27, ESV)

Rob Lawson
Birmingham, March 2017

Part 1: God's purpose with the Jews

(Robert Roberts, 1864-65)

The 1850s saw political tensions rise throughout the United States of America, particularly over the issue of slavery. The election of the abolitionist Abraham Lincoln to the office of President in November 1860 was the spark that lit the fuse of civil war, and in April 1861 the Confederate bombardment of Fort Sumter saw the violence begin in earnest. Although a conscientious objection stance saved the Christadelphian community from some of the harshest griefs of the war, the division of the nation put a variety of strains on the Brotherhood. This was true individually of Brother Thomas, who travelled far and wide to help brethren gain exemption from conscription into the two armies. This was particularly difficult as many of the brethren lived in the Confederate States, where Brother Thomas could be held in suspicion as a resident of the 'Yankee' North. This shift in focus, combined with the issues of distribution, led to the termination of his periodical *The Herald of the Kingdom and the Age to Come*.

There were two Christadelphian magazines that ran after the demise of *The Herald*, but, in the words of Brother Roberts, "they lacked vigour or certainty in the sound they gave out, and received but a very feeble attention" (*My Days and My Ways*, first edition, page 189). Brother Thomas therefore advised Brother Roberts to begin a new publication. This magazine, later to be called *The Christadelphian*, was first published in July 1864 as *The Ambassador of the Coming Age*.

The *Ambassador* was doctrinally hearty from the start, with a heavy emphasis on the 'Hope of Israel'. Evidence of this is the lengthy series on "God's purpose with the Jews" that ran throughout 1864-65, demonstrating that "God has not yet done with the Jews".

1 |

The restoration of the ancient kingdom of Israel

(October 1864)

> *"And I will restore thy judges as at first, and thy counsellors as at the beginning. Afterwards, thou shalt be called, the city of Righteousness, the faithful city". (Isaiah 1:26)*

MANY believe in the doctrine ... that Christ will come to reign on the earth – without perceiving what it involves in relation to that ancient kingdom of God which was established under Moses, perpetuated in the hands of divinely appointed kings for many centuries, and finally scattered to the winds because of iniquity. We shall best see the connection of the two things by considering what is said of Jesus in reference to "the throne of David". Peter, on the day of Pentecost, says:

> "David being a prophet, knew that God had sworn with an oath to him, that of the fruit of his loins according to the flesh, *he would raise up Christ* **to sit upon his throne**."
>
> (Acts 2:30)

If we turn to the record of this oath (Psalm 132), we find words almost parallel to Peter's:

> "The LORD hath sworn in truth unto David; he will not turn from it; *of the fruit of thy body* **will I set upon thy throne**."
>
> (verse 11)

The application of this to Jesus is placed beyond a doubt by Peter's statement, and by the message of the angel to Mary, prior to his birth: "**the Lord God shall give unto him the throne of his father David**" (Luke 1:23), the meaning of which is illustrated in the words of Isaiah: "*The government shall be upon his shoulder* … **upon the throne of David and his kingdom**" (9:6,7).

We deem it unnecessary to argue upon the literality of these statements, for the simple reason that there is nothing in them to suggest or justify, or even admit of figurative interpretation. There once existed a literal throne of David, and Jesus was descended from David's literal family by Mary. This being so, a plain promise with reference to the two things must obviously be accepted in the same plain and literal way. Under the circumstances, it would be taking a most unwarrantable liberty, and doing violence to the most ordinary rules observed in the understanding of language, to explain it away in a mystical sense. To make the words mean anything else than they plainly express, must appear to every thoughtful mind a most arbitrary and unsatisfactory way of dealing with the scriptures, opening the way for unlimited fancy and exposing the Bible to the charge so frequently brought against it, that it can be made to prove anything – a charge which is false in itself, but which only derives too much countenance from a system of interpretation which ignores its plain statements and makes them mean anything that it may be thought they should mean, or which a lively imagination may suggest.

It is impossible for the subtlest ingenuity to get over the simple point established by the testimonies adduced, viz. that the throne of David is bequeathed as an inheritance to Jesus of Nazareth. What this proposition may mean is a point of the greatest importance; for upon the understanding of it, depends our apprehension of the declared purpose in the case. It is to be noted, then, that "the throne of David" is a definite individual subject of discourse. It is no general phrase devoid of local point or application. It is an historic appellative, pointing to a political constitution existing in the past, so that no doubt may be entertained as to its character, and no difficulty experienced in understanding the meaning of the promise concerning it.

The throne of a nation is not the gilded chair on which the king sits; it is *the position, the royal office* of the nation's ruler, of which the throne becomes but **the symbol**. The throne of David, therefore, is not "a wooden seat" as some have called it by way of contempt, but the position David occupied as the king of Israel. No candid mind will dissent from this proposition, in view of the current use of the word "throne". "The throne of England", "the throne of France", "the throne of Russia", are well understood figures of speech representing the royalties of these respective states entirely apart from the mechanical accessories, which are, in every case, matters of individual taste. Why, then, should some novel sense be attached to the same phrase as applied to David in the scriptures?

The evidence that it should be understood in the same way is abundantly furnished in the Bible itself. We select one or two instances. Jeremiah 22:2: "Hear the word of the LORD, O king of Judah, **that sittest upon the throne of David**". These words were addressed to Zedekiah who reigned over the kingdom of Judah upwards of 400 years after David and when therefore the literal seat occupied by David must have long passed into disuse. Zedekiah was a wicked king, and it was not therefore from any spiritual resemblance that he was said to sit on David's throne, but simply and purely because, as a matter of political fact, he occupied the royal position established by God in the person of David his royal ancestor. It is said of Solomon (1 Kings 2:12), "*Then sat Solomon* **on the throne of David his father**", while it is afterwards stated that he made a new throne of ivory and overlaid it with gold (1 Kings 10:18), so that as regards the actual chair of state used by David, Solomon appears to have dispensed with it, and yet, in the sense in which the scriptures use the phrase, he sat "on the throne of David".

The throne of David being the kingly office or position, let us for the better understanding of the matter as affecting Jesus, consider what that position was. It was unlike the position of ordinary kings whose ancestors have at one time or other gratuitously assumed the mastership by the right of conquest or accidental might, and transmitted a title to their posterity valid only by usage, and not by original derivation. David was divinely selected and commissioned. He was a contented shepherd boy when Samuel, by guidance of the Spirit, poured the anointing oil upon his head, in typification of the qualification by Spirit-anointing of which "the root and offspring of David" – the real anointed or Christ – was to be the subject. He was elected to the position by God, and held it of "Divine right" in the most absolute sense. He was not king from fancy, from liking, from natural masterhood, but by appointment; neither was he king for his own purposes. His office was a representative one. He was God's vicegerent. He ruled as *"King for God"*, as was said of Solomon after him (2 Chronicles 9:8). God was originally the king of Israel, communicating with the nation through the testimony in the tabernacle. That this is the light in which God regarded Himself is evident from what he said to Samuel when the people desired to have a king, to go in and out among them like other nations (1 Samuel 8:7). "They have not rejected thee, but *they have rejected* **me** *that I should reign over them*", and still more so in the declaration of Samuel, when delivering God's message to them: "Ye said unto me, Nay, but a king shall reign over us *when the* LORD *God was your King*" (1 Samuel 12:12). The people, however, were unable to appreciate the privileged government they were under, and were weak enough to wish to be like other nations around them in having a human head. God yielded to their wishes in the matter, but did not surrender His prerogative as the nation's ruler; he gave them a king, but only as a deputy. He was to rule – not for his own magnification, but "for God". Hence he was said to be but "captain over God's people", and the throne he occupied was styled "the throne of the LORD" (1 Chronicles 29:23). This was David's position, this is the primary and distinguishing character of "the throne of David", *a God-constituted and God-representative royalty, occupied vicegerently for God.*

The nation over whom this exalted jurisdiction was exercised demands consideration as the next important element of "the throne of David". Historically, it presents a contrast to every other nation on earth. It does not owe its existence like other peoples, to the chances of war or migration, but had a distinct selective origin with an individual man; and the peculiarity of the origin is that that man – Abraham – had nothing to do with it. He was a dweller in Mesopotamia, following the occupation and conforming himself to the quiet policy of his fathers, and left to himself, would probably have lived and died among his kindred, unnoted and unknown; but God commanded him to leave his father's house, and go into a strange country which should be shown him, telling him he would there become a great nation. He obeyed the commandment, "not knowing whither he went", and came into the land of Canaan. The rest of the story is too familiar to the scripture reader, to require recapitulation. From Abraham – an old man – past the time of life, sprang there even of one (and that a "child of promise", begotten of divine energy, when nature's power had waned, viz.: Isaac) as many as the stars of the sky for multitude (Hebrews 11:12). The result was, the children of Israel – a nation of God's creation, and of God's rearing; who forgets the fostering care with which its infancy was watched, the corn of Egypt, the raising up of Joseph, the mission of Moses, the plagues of Pharaoh, the deliverance from bondage, the triumph of the Red Sea, the provision of the wilderness, the destruction of the Canaanitish nations, and the settlement in the land of promise? God through the prophets repeatedly reminded them of these things, and speaks of them as His vineyard which He tended (Isaiah 5:7), His "children" whom he brought up (Isaiah 1:2), His wife whom He espoused in early youth (Jeremiah 2:2). He claims them as His own:

"Israel is my firstborn." (Exodus 4:22)

"Thou art an holy people unto the LORD thy God ... *a* **peculiar people unto himself** *above all people that are on the face of the earth.*" (Deuteronomy 14:2)

"*You only have I known of all the nations of the earth*, therefore will I punish you for your iniquity." (Amos 3:2)

Then if we consider the laws by which this nation was governed, and which David as king for God was called upon to enforce, we find the same divine speciality of feature. They were not the product of human legislation; they were not devised in human wisdom; they were the direct prescriptions of God, communicated by the hand of Moses, amid the visible terrors of Sinai. They were not open to human amendment; they were to be preserved with scrupulous sanctity, as the unalterable dictates of the Almighty:

"Ye shall not add unto the word which I command you, neither shall ye diminish aught from it". (Deuteronomy 4:2)

The king was to study and observe them:

"*He shall write him a copy of this law* in a book out of that which is before the priests, the Levites; and it shall be with him, and *he shall read therein all the days of his life* that he may learn to fear the LORD his God to keep all the words of this law, and these statutes, to do them" (Deuteronomy 17:18,19)

The divine character of the kingdom as a body politic is further evident in the selection of the territory it occupied. This was not capriciously chosen by the leaders of the nation, nor accidentally acquired in the chances of war, but was covenanted to Abraham, about 500 years before the nation existed; and the subsequent allusions to it evinces the speciality of it: "The land is mine" (Leviticus 25:23), "My mountains" (Ezekiel 38:21). The land of Palestine, as the fundamental element of the kingdom of David, is of God's selection and allotment. "A land" said Moses, "that the LORD thy God careth for. The eyes of the LORD are always upon it from the beginning of the year, even unto the end of the year" (Deuteronomy 11:12).

Thus the throne of David when analysed turns out to be *a divinely appointed jurisdiction over a divinely constituted arrangement of things political*. The throne of David was in fact the throne of the Lord, and the kingdom of David the kingdom of God. How comes it to have no existence now? Because of the wickedness of the people who were related to it. It was an arrangement based upon and hedged in by contingencies. It was founded upon the Law of Moses, and the condition of stability under that law was perfect obedience to its requirements. Disobedience was threatened from the beginning with national retributions (Deuteronomy 28:15-68). The national existence depended upon conformity to the national constitution; and when this national constitution was violated beyond all hope of amendment, the national organization was broken up, the royal family abolished, the people scattered in dispersion, and the land given to the enemy. This result was predicted by the prophets with the greatest reiteration and emphasis; and we see the warranty of their words in the present prostrated condition of the kingdom of David. Where is it? The land exists, but in a state of hopeless sterility and indefence, infested with "the worst of the heathen" (Ezekiel 7:24). The people exists, but in a state of universal degradation and powerlessness. The royal family is extinct, its only living representative being Jesus Christ at the right hand of the majesty in the heavens; the Mosaic constitution is abolished both by force of irrepressible events and the decree of its divine framer. The kingdom of David in the emphatic metaphor of the spirit is "in the dust".

> "Thou hast cut off and abhorred; thou hast been wroth with thine anointed. Thou hast made void the covenant of thy servant: *thou hast profaned his crown by casting it to the ground.* **Thou hast made his glory to cease, and cast his throne down to the ground**." (Psalm 89:38,39,44)

So the words of Ezekiel have been verified:

> "I will *overturn, overturn, overturn it*, and it shall be no more *until he come whose right it is, and I will give it him*." (21:27)

The kingdom *has been overturned and* **is no more**. The Jews have fallen by the edge of the sword and been led captive among nations, and Jerusalem is trodden under feet of the Gentiles (Luke 21:24). This is as far as events have sustained the prophetic forecast. The question powerfully presses itself – what next? "*He comes whose right it is.*" "*The time of the Gentiles be fulfilled.*" These are the two divinely indicated limits of the present prostration. This is incontestably evident from the use of the word "until": "It shall be no more **until** he come"; "Jerusalem shall be trodden down of the Gentiles **until** the times of the Gentiles be fulfilled". What is this but saying, that **when** "he comes whose right it is", and **when** "the times of the Gentiles have expired", the non-existing and the down treading of the kingdom of David shall come to an end? This is in exact accordance with Hosea's prophecy (9:11), quoted by James (Acts 15:16): "After this **I will return** *and build again the tabernacle of David* that is fallen down, and I will build again the ruins thereof." And this connects us with the starting point: "*The Lord God shall give unto Jesus the throne of his father David.*" If Jesus is to receive a throne which has not existed for more than twenty centuries, obviously something must occur to bring it into existence. This "something" it is evident, is the second advent of the Christ, to do the work of reorganisation, to build again the fallen tabernacle, to "restore the kingdom again to Israel" in accordance with the request of the apostles after his resurrection (Acts 1:6). In doing this, he will reclaim his country – the land of promise – from the desolation which now reigns over it, and gather to it the scattered Jews from the countries of their dispersion, rebuild Jerusalem, re-enact the laws, and generally restore the ancient kingdom of Israel, "upon the throne of David, and his kingdom to order it, and establish it with justice and judgment, from henceforth even forever. *The zeal of the* LORD *of Hosts will perform this*" (Isaiah 9:7).

But the more systematic demonstration of these propositions must be reserved till next month. Meanwhile we briefly summarise the conclusions to which every honest mind must arrive in view of the evidence adduced:

1. *The throne of David was* **a God-constituted royalty** *erected as a delegated administration of His authority in a*

nation formed by Himself, and settled in a land of His own choosing (Palestine).

2. *This throne does not now exist,* but
3. *It will be re-erected in the same country at the coming of Jesus the Christ and occupied by him when he reigns "over all the earth" as "King of kings and Lord of lords".*

2 |

God's purpose with the Jews (1)

(November 1864)

GOD has not yet done with the Jews. They are His nation, though dyed in iniquity and scattered among the Gentiles in disgrace. "God hath not cast away his people whom he foreknew (or knew beforetime)." This is Paul's testimony (Romans 11:1) which is but a re-echo of the divine declaration placed on record ages before:

"Though I make a full end of all nations whither I have scattered you, *yet will I not make a full end of you*, but will correct thee in measure." (Jeremiah 30:11)

Their prolonged national adversity, therefore, is no token of divine abandonment, but the very reverse, on the principle supplied in Amos:

"You only have I known of all the families of the earth, **therefore** *will I punish you for all your iniquities.*" (3:2)

The national tribulation, rightly interpreted, is a guarantee of the national election, and a pledge of national restitution under the promises made through the prophets, which we shall presently consider.

There be many which look upon the Jews as an abandoned race, finally and forever dissevered from special divine regard and degraded to the level of the uncovenanted and accursed Gentiles among whom they are dispersed. Many do this from a sincere but perverted conscience, created within them as the result of partial information and indiscriminating contemplation of certain apostolic statements. Ignorant of those future national movements and national blessings which come within the scope of God's purposes prophetically and apostolically declared, they cannot see but that the abrogation of "the middle wall of partition" between Jew and Gentile in the matter of *individual salvation*, involves the divine repudiation of the national relationship which He established in former days between Himself and the Jews: and equally unacquainted with the fact that "salvation is of the Jews" (John 4:22), and is to the very end to be developed like a kernel from their midst, they naturally feel the doctrine of Jewish restoration to be a spiritual anomaly which they reject altogether. How ill-advised they are, we shall presently see.

It is evident from the proposition demonstrated in our last article concerning Christ's future occupancy of David's throne, that the restoration of the ancient kingdom of Israel is necessitated as a logical sequence thereto. We mean that if there were no other testimony in the whole of the Bible, the restoration of the Jews could be deduced from the simple statement that Jesus is to ascend the throne of his father David, since that throne comprises the Jews as its fundamental element. But the grounds of the belief are not restricted to this inferential kind of evidence. The Bible is luminous from beginning to end with the glory of a purpose which involves the blessing of universal man. The glory commences to glow in the promises made to Abraham, wherein is covenanted the blessing of all nations **in** Abraham and **in** his seed at a time when Abraham occupies the Promised Land with a seed numerous as the stars of the sky. But the specific and indisputable testimony may be said to commence with the declaration of Moses:

> "*The* LORD *thy God will raise up unto thee a prophet from the midst of thee, of thy brethren like unto me*; **unto him ye shall hearken**." (Deuteronomy 18:15)

This statement was addressed to Israel after the flesh; this will not be disputed. It was an intimation concerning themselves; this will not be disputed in view of the emphasis on the pronoun "**thee**" as applied to those whom he was addressing. It concerned them *as a nation*, and not as scattered individuals. This is evident from several considerations. It was not fulfilled to the generation who heard the words; therefore it was not addressed to them as individuals but as constituents of the national "**thee**" which has survived the vicissitudes of all ages since then, and lives in its scattered modern representatives. The prophet was to be "like unto Moses". Moses was a national lawgiver, and not an individual moral preceptor; therefore the second Moses must bear a like relationship to the nation addressed in the pronoun "**thee**". Who is this "prophet like unto Moses?" No New Testament reader will hesitate to answer. The point is set authoritatively at rest in the following quotation from a discourse by Peter to the Jews shortly after Pentecost:

> "**God shall send Jesus Christ** who before was preached unto you whom the heavens must receive **until** *the times of restitution of all things*, which God hath spoken to all his holy prophets since the world began. *For Moses truly said unto the fathers, A prophet shall the Lord your God raise up unto you of your brethren like unto me; him shall ye hear in all things whatsoever he shall say unto you.*"　　　　　　(Acts 3:20-22)

Jesus, then, is "the prophet like unto Moses". This is an important conclusion as throwing light on the future of Israel; because the statement is that Israel shall "**hear him**" in his capacity as a national leader like Moses – that as a nation, they will one day put themselves submissively under his direction. It is superfluous to say that this has never come to pass. "Jesus came to his own, but his own received him not" (John 1:11). He came to look after the lost sheep of the house of Israel (Matthew 10:6), but they knew him not, and in ignorance that he was indeed "that prophet" they put him to death; and he departed, leaving them with the words:

"*Ye shall not see me henceforth* **until the time come that ye shall say, Blessed is he that cometh in the name of the Lord**." (Matthew 23:39)

Ever since, during a long period of eighteen centuries, in the midst of the bitterest adversity, the Jews have been the malignant rejecters of Jesus, and at the present time, show no signs of relaxing the asperity of their opposition. With the blindness of the undestroyed veil which Moses symbolically assumed on coming down from the mount, they cling to a system which though divinely originated, was but representative and provisional; and with an almost incomprehensible infatuation reject that of which their first dispensation was but the shadowy typification. Obviously then, in no sense has the prediction of Moses been fulfilled. Nationally, Israel continues to follow Moses, and boast in him, and continues to be unbelieving in the prophet like unto him. But God's purpose will be carried out. The time will come when they shall say, "Blessed is he that cometh in the name of the Lord". The prophecy under consideration not only predicts the national acceptance of Jesus as lawgiver and king, but indicates the inexorable stringency of his *regime* when established. "It shall come to pass that that soul which shall not hear that prophet *shall be cut off from the people*." There is no such individual adjudication now and never has been. The hard-hearted Jew blasphemes the name of Jesus and goes scot free, and instead of being "cut off from the people", he continues prosperously connected with the unbelieving and corrupt mass of the nation. Most obviously, the time contemplated in the prediction of Moses is yet future, when the nation recognising Jesus, will be established in their land under his judicial administration, and subjected to a discipline which, with more unyielding severity than the law of Moses itself, will infallibly destroy every rebel and extirpate every germ of disaffection.

Peter connects the inauguration of this, with the coming again of Jesus at "the times of restitution spoken by all the holy prophets". His words are "He shall send Jesus Christ unto you

… For Moses truly said unto the fathers, a prophet", etc. He makes the second coming of Christ to the Jews *the fulfilment of what Moses said about the prophet like unto himself.* This is strictly in harmony with the obvious facts of the case; for the words of Moses have not yet had their fulfilment; and if they are to be fulfilled at all it must be in connection with a future manifestation of the Prophet; and when more appropriate than at the times of restitution of all things spoken by the prophets? Whereof we shall see a little more by and bye. That this is the time when the Jews are to receive the Messiah and submit to him is further evident from the words of Zechariah 12 where it is said:

> "They shall look upon me whom they have pierced, and mourn for him as one mourneth for his firstborn." (verse 10)

Taking a step forward in the progress of the specific evidence of God's purpose with the Jews, we come to the prediction of the present national ruin recorded in Leviticus 26:

> "I will make your cities waste and bring your sanctuaries into desolation. And I will not smell the savour of your sweet odours; and I will bring your land into desolation and your enemies that dwell therein shall be astonished at it. And I will scatter you among the heathen, and I will draw out a sword after you, and your land shall be desolate and your cities waste … and they that are left of you shall pine away in their iniquity in your enemies' land." (verse 31)

This gloomy picture is relieved by the prospect of ultimate restitution put in the form of a hypothesis, and afterwards prophetically foretold:

> "If they confess their iniquity and the iniquity of their fathers with their trespass which they have trespassed against me; if their uncircumcised hearts be humbled and they then accept the punishment of their iniquity, *then will I remember my covenant with Jacob, and my covenant with Isaac, and my covenant with Abraham will I remember, and I will remember the land."* (Leviticus 26:40-42)

That this remembrance of covenant obligations results in the execution of them, is more evident from a further prediction by Moses, recorded in Deuteronomy 30:

> "*The* LORD *thy God will turn thy captivity and have compassion upon thee, and will return and gather thee from all the nations whither the* LORD *thy God hath scattered thee* … The LORD thy God will make thee plenteous in every work of thine hand, in the fruit of thy body and in the fruit of thy cattle, and in the fruit of thy land for good, *for the* LORD *will again rejoice over thee for good as he rejoiced over thy fathers*, if that thou shalt hearken unto the voice of the LORD thy God …" (verses 3,9)

It may be objected that these predictions of national restoration are contingent upon national repentance and reformation; and prove nothing apart from the likelihood of reformation or otherwise. This is true, and the objection would be a fatal one if we were without testimony as to the fate of the contingency, that is, if we were left without information as to whether or not the nation would reform; but we are not without information. We do not require to go out of Moses to get the point conclusively settled. In the very same chapter from which the above quotation is made, we read "*and the* LORD *thy God will circumcise thine heart, and the heart of thy seed to love the* LORD *thy God with all thine heart and with all thy soul, that thou mayest live*" (verse 6). The prophets who succeeded Moses threw great light on this point. They tell us with great clearness and amplitude of expression that one of the most notable features of God's purpose with the Jews is to reclaim them from their present state of perversity and unbelief, and beget in them nationally that state of mind which is becoming and essential in a people holding such a close relationship to God. Listen, for instance, to the declaration by the hand of the prophet Ezekiel:

> "I will take you from among the heathen and gather you out of all countries, and will bring you into your own land. *Then will I sprinkle clean water upon you and ye shall be clean from all your filthiness and all your idols will I cleanse you, and a new heart also*

will I give you, and a new spirit will I put within you, and I will take away the stony heart out of your flesh, and I will give you a heart of flesh, and I will put my spirit within you and cause you to walk in my statutes, and ye shall keep my judgments and do them, and ye shall dwell in the land that I gave unto your fathers, and ye shall be my people and I will be your God." (36:24-28)

The result of this divinely induced change is indicated in the following testimony from the same chapter:

"Then shall ye remember your own evil ways, and your doings that were not good, and ye shall loath yourselves in your own sight for your own iniquities and your abominations." (verse 31)

But while the restoration of the Jews to their own land is accompanied by the most thorough national renovation, yet it is obvious that the one is not the result of the other. That is, God will not restore Israel in consideration of Israel's righteousness. This is obvious from the twice repeated statement of the Almighty through Ezekiel, "*Not for your sakes do I this*, saith the Lord GOD, be it known unto you: *be ashamed and confounded for your own ways, O house of Israel*". The consideration which prompts Jehovah to the work of restoration is set forth in the following words:

"I do not this for your sakes, O house of Israel, *but for mine own holy name's sake which ye have profaned among the heathen* whither ye went. And I will sanctify my great name which was profaned among the heathen, which ye have profaned in the midst of them. *And the heathen shall know that I am the LORD, saith the Lord GOD, when I shall be sanctified in you before their eyes.*" (Ezekiel 36:22,23)

The strength of this motive on the part of God is apparent in the prophetic song of Moses in which the destinies of the nation were portrayed for the national remembrance:

"I will heap mischief upon them. I will spend mine arrows upon them. They shall be burnt with hunger and devoured with burning heat, and with bitter destruction ... I said I would scatter them into corners; *I would make the remembrance of them to cease from among men* **were it not that I feared the wrath of the enemy**, *lest their adversaries should behave themselves strangely, and lest they should say, Our hand is high, and the* LORD *hath not done all this."* (Deuteronomy 32:23-27)

To prevent this triumph of boasting, judgment is to fall upon the enemy and salvation to come to Israel:

"To me belongeth vengeance and recompence; their (the enemy's) foot shall slide in due time, for the day of their calamity is at hand, and all things that shall come upon them make haste. For the LORD shall judge his people, and repent himself for his servants, *when he seeth that their power is gone* and that there is none shut up or left ... Rejoice O ye nations with his people, *for he will avenge the blood of his servants, and will render vengeance to his adversaries* **and will be merciful unto his land and to his people**."

(Deuteronomy 32:35,36,43)

God cannot brook the triumph of the heathen, which involves His own defame and the insensate boast of the ignorant and the foolish. Therefore He proposes the reclamation of his ancient people that through their national restitution by the hands of Christ whom he has raised up for the purpose (Isaiah 49:6), His name in the full plenitude of its multiform significance may become known and revered over all the earth. There may appear to be a little contradiction between this view and the aspect of the case put forward in the earlier quotations from Moses, in which the recovery of Israel from judicial disaster is made to depend upon their recognition of God's justice in punishing them, and their full resolution to amend their ways. In reality, however, there is none. The restoration is a foregone conclusion in the divine mind for reasons already indicated; but the restoration will not be carried out in violation of God's righteous laws. He does all things in righteousness, order, and peace, and will not restore a nation in wickedness to prosperity. Hence in the second instance, the execution of the purpose will be strictly subjected to the conditions indicated in the first announcement. No reprobate Jew will enter the land of promise to participate in the blessings of Messiah's reign. The whole nation will be subjected to an ordeal of discipline which will effectuate the work of purification, and realize the statement by Isaiah, "Thy people shall be all righteous" (60:21). But more of this in our next.

3 |

God's purpose with the Jews (2)

(December 1864)

THIS purpose is so very important, and constitutes so prominent a feature of the plan of mercy by which God is to recover our hapless race from the dilemma in which it is involved – nay, we would say it forms such an essential element of the truth of the gospel which men must know to be saved, that we wish to supplement what has already been advanced, for the purpose of showing that "the restoration of the kingdom again to Israel" is no far-fetched inference from doubtful data, but the emphatically enunciated and voluminously attested purpose of Jehovah which no one with the Bible in his hand can be ignorant of, and be acceptable in His presence.

An acquaintance with Israelitish history is necessary to a comprehension of this subject. We do not refer to the superficial information acquired in juvenile days, but to that intimate familiarity with Jewish antecedents, Jewish institutions, and Jewish relationships which is only to be obtained by the constant application of the maturer faculties to the study of the scriptures, and this not to any one department, but to the whole Bible from beginning to end, for the whole Bible relates to the Jews, to whom all God's past transactions have referred and in whom all future purposes centre. We would, however, for present purposes, limit the observation to the past as developed in the historical writings, and may lay it down as an invulnerable proposition that a minute and comprehensive knowledge of Bible history, is absolutely necessary to an understanding both of Old Testament prophecy and New Testament revelations. The reason of this appears on reflection; God's dealings with the earth have been but the progressive unfolding of one harmonious plan from the beginning. Every successive act has been but the consistent sequel of what has gone before. Nothing has been done of caprice, nothing without deliberate plan. Later dispensations are but continuations of the scheme which commenced with the promise to the mother of all living, and will end in the perfection of the ages to come. Hence no one part can be comprehended by itself. Knowledge of the whole is necessary to the understanding of any part. A distinct knowledge of the past is necessary to a correct and satisfactory faith in the future. Ignorance of the history of the Jews as comprehensively delineated in the sacred writings involves inability to appreciate the arguments arising from prophetic announcement. On this principle, the man anxious to be "wise unto salvation" will strive to master the historical part of the word of God, and in doing this, he will not confine himself to the nominally historical books of the Bible, but will extend his researches to the prophetic records in which is to be found the inner history of Israel, the unveiling of God's mind in reference to the transactions of the nation, and their position as affected thereby. Here, to read what God thought of them, and intends with them, is to ascend as it were from the arena of human strife to the cool and elevated pinnacle of God's Almighty scan: to step in fact out of the finite and the fallible, and lay hold of God's unerring and all-compassing discernment. This altitude is so much above the natural grasp of the human mind that we have to go often there to become accustomed to it. At first the height makes a man mentally dizzy, but in time he feels at home and enjoys the extended survey. Away from that height, we see not with God's eyes, but regard things from a carnal point of view – that is, with the views formed by the unassisted mind of the flesh on subjects which, apart from dogmatic revelation, i.e., divine instruction, it is unable to apprehend. An occasional visit to the exalted summit of which we speak is not adequate

3 – God's purpose with the Jews (2)

to our spiritual wants. The natural tendency of the mind is so entirely contrary to that which is divine, that the corrective must be constantly applied. The knowledge of God must be constantly kept streaming through the mind. The study of the word of God must be incessant. An acquaintance with the history of God's doings in the past is not to be acquired like profane history, as a mere educational accomplishment, to be once mastered, and then neglected and allowed to decay under secular engrossments. It is too important and too easily forgotten to be thus lightly dealt with. It must be constantly renewed like our daily bread. Only thus is the mind so thoroughly affinitized to the divine purpose as to be able instinctively to apprehend it accurately in all its remote and immediate bearings, and eschew those quagmires of error which the sincere are constantly falling into from partial information.

The Mosaic argument in favour of the future restoration of Israel presented in our last article must be admitted to be conclusive; but the doctrine does not rest on grounds so limited. The evidence takes a wider range, it is more abundant than the ordinary reader may imagine. In fact, it is so extensive, so multiform in its character, so complex in its ramifications so in-woven with the very structure of prophetic writing that the attempt to systematise it or to present anything like a comprehensive view of it is bewildering. This task, however, we shall essay under a full and solemn conviction that no one who is ignorant or unbelieving of the doctrine of Jewish restoration can have any comprehension of the gospel promulgated by Jesus and his apostles. This conviction we hope to justify in the course of these articles.

A convenient starting point in the consideration of the subject is obtained by reflecting on the national position of the Jewish nation, which was slightly dwelt upon in a previous article. The essential character of that position is *divine election*; **the Jews are God's nation**. They are not necessarily God's *children*; but they are His **nation**. They are His because He chose them. Their election was a sovereign act prompted by ulterior considerations having reference to His purposes, and not to their moral qualifications. If one doubts this, he has only to remember the mission of Moses, which was delegated to him in these words:

"Come now therefore, and I will send thee unto Pharaoh that thou mayest bring forth **my people** Israel out of Egypt."

(Exodus 3:10)

When these words were addressed to him, Israel was a nation of untutored idolatrous slaves, among whom the God of their fathers had degenerated to a dim tradition, and whose national hopes had vanished under the severe discipline of the Egyptian taskmaster. They were not a nation of God's knowing – of God-fearing, God-hoping men, such as God would naturally (speaking humanly) be drawn to in plans of favour, but a nation of ignorant and brutish servants, content with the flesh-pots, and only regretting the task-rod of their masters. What then is the explanation of the apparent violation of moral law in God's proceeding towards them? The answer is to be found in Exodus 2:

"And God heard their groaning, **and God remembered his covenant with Abraham, with Isaac and with Jacob**."

(verses 23,24)

If God's interposition on their behalf had depended upon their fitness to receive divine favour, that interposition would never have taken place; but this was not the case. God had formed a purpose of election irrespective of the nation's deserts. This election we shall see in its final causes to have been in strict harmony with the eternal laws of the moral universe; but this we reserve to the proper occasion; Israel's unconditional election as God's nation is all we are meanwhile concerned to establish; and we submit the message of Moses to Pharaoh as a further proof of it:

"Thus saith the LORD, Israel is **my son**, even **my firstborn**, and I say unto thee, Let **my son** go that he may serve me."

(Exodus 4:22,23)

"Let **my people** go that they may serve me."   (Exodus 5:1)

Why are they said to be "**his**" people? Simply because they *are* His: and if it be asked on what principle they became His, the answer is, because He chose them. He set them nationally apart for Himself as part of a plan which is to ultimate in the redemption of the world. His choice was not regulated by the merits of the nation, but determined upon with sovereign regard to His own schemes. It may be thought to be a contradiction of this that He always punished them for their transgression; but it is the very reverse. Chastisement is evidence of paternity. It is only the fatherless child that does as it likes without interference. This is the position of the Gentile nations. As Gentiles, they are beyond the pale of God's regards. They are the unredeemed descendants of the first Adam, and are left to do as they like, and to perish under the unrepealed law of Eden which sends them to the dust, except in so far as individually, they may separate themselves from Gentile stock and place themselves under the bond of the Israelitish covenant in Christ. It is very different with Israel. God has made them his own. Moses tells them:

"The LORD thy God hath chosen thee to be a special people unto himself above all people that are upon the face of the earth." (Deuteronomy 7:6)

David adds to the testimony in the following words:

"What one nation in the earth is like thy people, even like Israel, *whom God went to redeem for a people unto himself? ... For thou hast confirmed unto thyself thy people Israel to be a people unto thee for ever.*" (2 Samuel 7:23,24)

God's property in the national Israel is therefore a foregone conclusion. It is a settled point that God is their God and that they are His whether they behave themselves or not. It is a question that cannot be affected by their misbehaviour. They are under law to the Almighty and cannot shake off the divine yoke by any amount of rebellion. This is the explanation of their long and bitter history since the rejection of Jesus.

"*You only have I known of all the families of the earth*; **therefore will I punish you for all your iniquities**." (Amos 3:2)

It is a principle in the divine economy that "the gifts and calling of God are without repentance". Applying this principle to the proposition before us, the question may be raised, how it is that while enjoying the privilege of a national election, Israel have been so long in a state of national alienation and adversity. We cannot better answer the question than by quoting the following testimony:

> "Who gave Jacob for a spoil and Israel to the robbers? *Did not the* LORD, *he against whom we have sinned? For they would not walk in his ways, neither were they obedient unto his law. Therefore he hath poured upon him the fury of his anger and the strength of battle ...*" (Isaiah 42:24)

Israel is now and often has been under the rod. Their election did not mean unconditional blessing, but simply *divine national relationship which can never be abrogated*. Blessing is a question of obedience. Ages ago, Moses called heaven and earth to witness that curses would descend upon them if they were disobedient, and history has verified his words. Times without number has Israel been the prey of the robber and the butt of reproaches, and never more so than now when the enemy has had their land in possession and their persons in servitude for a long unbroken night of eighteen centuries. But there is to be an end to this changeful chapter of events. The history of God's nation is not always to be a monotonous alternation of prosperity and catastrophe. There is a consummation which God has in his eye, and has had in view all along – a glorious ending in which God's supremacy will be placed on the secure basis of the nation's gladsome allegiance, and the nation's weal on the sure foundation of the nation's God developed righteousness. But to the mind unfamiliar with the word of God, it is hard to believe this. It is contrary to the present appearance of things, Israel is in weakness, exile, and disgrace. The Gentile star is in the ascendant. On sea and land, the sword of Gentile power is gleaming. The hand of Gentile dominion is lifted high and secure. The daughter of Zion is prostrate and lifeless under the heel of the great giant of Nebuchadnezzar's vision, and it seems as if the times would never change – as if the vision of the ancient seers would always remain dumb – as if the enemy would always triumph. But there is consolation if there is also trial in waiting:

> "The vision is yet for an appointed time. *At the end it shall speak. Though it tarry wait for it,* **because it will surely come, it will not** (always) **tarry**." (Habakkuk 2:3)

God has declared, "*This people have I formed for myself;* **they shall show forth all my praise**" (Isaiah 43:21). Here is a guarantee of Israel's restoration; they have never shown forth His praise yet but rather on the contrary, have, in the words of Ezekiel, profaned His name among the heathen wherever they have gone (36:21). But some may say that this statement does not refer to Israel after the flesh. Struck with the apparent incongruity of making a people so mean and sinister and grovelling (as the Jews appear as a whole to be in their present state) instrumental in developing the praise of Jehovah in the earth, they come to the conclusion that it is applicable to some sort of spiritual antitype in whom they conceive God's original intention with Israel will be realised. The reasoning is plausible, but the mistake is evident. The context conclusively shows that it is the national Jew that is spoken of.

> "But thou hast not called upon me O Jacob; thou hast been weary of me O Israel. Thou hast not brought me the small cattle of thy burnt offerings, neither hast thou honoured me with thy sacrifices … Thou hast made me to serve with thy sins. Thou hast wearied me with thine iniquities."
>
> (Isaiah 43:22-24)

It is the people against whom these complaints are made, that are ultimately to "show forth all Jehovah's praise". Could such things be said of a spiritually perfect antitype? But the argument is clinched and closed beyond all dispute by the statement with which the chapter closes: "Therefore I have profaned the princes of the sanctuary, *and have given Jacob to the curse and Israel to reproaches.*"

How then is Israel to show forth all Jehovah's praise? The reply, which we shall give in the words of scripture, is an unanswerable demonstration of the future restoration of the Jews:

> "Moreover the word of the LORD came unto me, saying, Son of man, when the house of Israel dwelt in their own land, they defiled it by their own way, and by their own doings; their way was before me as the uncleanness of a removed woman. Wherefore I poured my fury upon them for the blood that they had shed upon the land, and for their idols wherewith they had polluted it: and I scattered them among the heathen, and they were dispersed through the countries: according to their way and according to their doings I judged them. And when they entered unto the heathen, whither they went, they profaned my holy name, when they said to them, These are the people of the LORD, and are gone forth out of his land. But I had pity for mine holy name, which the house of Israel had profaned among the heathen, whither they went. Therefore say unto the house of Israel, Thus saith the Lord GOD; I do not this for your sakes, O house of Israel, but for mine holy name's sake, which ye have profaned among the heathen, whither ye went. *And I will sanctify my great name, which was profaned among the heathen, which ye have profaned in the midst of them; and the heathen shall know that I am the LORD, saith the Lord GOD,* **when I shall be sanctified in you before their eyes**. For I will take you from among the heathen, and gather you out of all countries, and will bring you into your own land." (Ezekiel 36:16-24)

The answer then is, *the Jews are to show forth the praise of God by being restored.* This is the proposition of the testimony quoted, and cannot be gainsaid if the word of God is true; but lest a single testimony should be considered a doubtful settlement of the point, we shall make a few other quotations:

> "And say unto them, Thus saith the Lord GOD; Behold I will take the children of Israel from among the heathen, whither

they be gone, and will gather them on every side, and bring them into their own land: and I will make them one nation in the land upon the mountains of Israel; and one king shall be king to them all; and they shall be no more two nations, neither shall they be divided into two kingdoms any more at all; neither shall they defile themselves any more with their idols, nor with their detestable things, nor with any of their transgressions: but I will save them out of all their dwelling places, wherein they have sinned, and will cleanse them: so shall they be my people, and I will be their God. And David my servant shall be king over them; and then all shall have one shepherd; they shall also walk in my judgments, and observe my statutes, and do them. And they shall dwell in the land that I have given unto Jacob my servant, wherein your fathers have dwelt; and they shall dwell therein, even they, and their children, and their children's children for ever; and my servant David shall be their prince forever. Moreover I will make a covenant of peace with them; it shall be an everlasting covenant with them; and I will place them, and multiply them, and will set my sanctuary in the midst of them for evermore. My tabernacle also shall be with them; yea, I will be their God and they shall be my people. *And the heathen shall know that I the* LORD *do sanctify Israel*, when my sanctuary shall be in the midst of them for evermore." (Ezekiel 37:21-28)

"So the house of Israel shall know that I am the LORD their God from that day and forward. *And the heathen shall know that the house of Israel went into captivity for their iniquity*: because they trespassed against me, therefore hid I my face from them, and gave them into the hand of their enemies; so fell they all by the sword. According to their uncleanness and according to their transgressions have I done unto them, and hid my face from them. Therefore thus saith the Lord GOD; Now will I bring again the captivity of Jacob, and have mercy upon the whole house of Israel and will be jealous for my holy name; after that they have borne their shame, and all their trespasses whereby they have trespassed against me, when they dwelt safely in their land, and none made them afraid. *When I have brought them again from the people, and gathered them out of their enemies' lands,* **and am sanctified in them in the sight of many nations**; then shall they know that I am the LORD their God, which caused them to be led into captivity among the heathen: but I have gathered them unto their own land, and have left none of them any more there. Neither will I hide my face any more from them: for I have poured out my spirit upon the house of Israel, saith the Lord GOD." (Ezekiel 39:22-29)

Let the following testimonies be read in connection with the foregoing:

"The word that Isaiah, the son of Amoz, saw concerning Judah and Jerusalem. And it shall come to pass in the last days, that the mountain of the LORD's house shall be established in the top of the mountains, and shall be exalted above the hills; and all nations shall flow unto it. And many people shall go and say, *Come ye, and let us go up to the mountain of the LORD, to the house of the God of Jacob;* and he will teach us of his ways, and we will walk in his paths; for out of Zion shall go forth the law, and the word of the LORD from Jerusalem. And he shall judge among the nations, and shall rebuke many people: and they shall beat their swords into ploughshares, and their spears into pruning hooks: nation shall not lift up sword against nation neither shall they learn war anymore." (Isaiah 2:1-4)

'Thus saith the LORD of hosts; It shall yet come to pass, that there shall come people, and the inhabitants of many cities: and the inhabitants of one city shall go to another, saying, Let us go speedily to pray before the LORD, and to seek the LORD of hosts: I will go also. *Yea, many people and strong nations shall come to seek the LORD of hosts in Jerusalem, and to pray before the LORD.* Thus saith the LORD of hosts; In those days it shall come to pass, that ten men shall take hold out of all languages of the nations, even shall take hold of the skirt of him that is a Jew, saying, *We will go with you; for we have heard that God is with you.*" (Zechariah 8:20-23)

"In that day it shall be said to Jerusalem, Fear thou not; and to Zion, Let not thine hands be slack. The LORD thy God in the midst of thee is mighty; he will save, he will rejoice over thee with joy; he will joy over thee with singing. I will gather them that are sorrowful for the solemn assembly, who are of thee, to whom the approach of it was a burden. Behold at that time I will undo all that afflict thee: and I will save her that halteth, and gather her that was driven out; and I will get them praise and fame in every land where they have been put to shame. At that time will I bring you again, even in the time that I gather you: for *I will make you a name and a praise among all people of the earth, when I turn back your captivity before your eyes saith the LORD.*" (Zephaniah 3:16-20)

It is scarcely necessary to say, after the reading of these testimonies, that God will make Himself known among the nations by interfering among them for the recovery of His people the Jews, and by afterwards settling them in righteousness in their own ancient land, under Christ, as a great nation and as the instructors and illuminators of all the earth. A few other features of the subject will be considered in future articles.

4 |

God's purpose with the Jews (3)

(January 1865)

IT is evident from the testimony already adduced that God's purpose with the Jews is one of national restitution and blessing. This purpose is necessitated by a variety of considerations. The first is one to which we have already given a little prominence namely, that the Jews are God's nation. A full recognition of this fact will infallibly lead to the conclusion that a time of national recovery is in store for them, else were God's proprietorship invalidated and His supremacy subverted by the obstinacy of rebels. A few admit the fact without coming to the conclusion.

A second class admit the fact in such a qualified form that it vanishes into nothing, when subjected to the test of logical examination – that is, it turns out to be a vague sentimental notion, convenient for platform use when the "Society for the Conversion of the Jews", is putting forth its claims, or for pulpit flourish when funds are needed for the society's coffers; but which has no body, or substance in it, and which will not bear the honest strain of an inference one way or other. A third party boldly and at once deny that there is any relationship now existing between Jehovah and the Jews, other than what exists between Him and all mankind, which though true in one aspect of the case, is entirely untrue in the sense in which the assertion is made by those who advance it.

On one point all are bound to agree who believe the Bible, and that is, that in the early part of their history, the Jews were unquestionably God's nation in a special and peculiar sense. This inevitable admission is of great importance in helping us to decide what their present position is. We do not mean in the matter of their dispersion and degradation, for there cannot be two opinions that their dispersion is a condition of punishment in which they are for the time being alienated from divine favour – but, their position as respects fundamental relationship to the great Being who first called them into national existence. Its value arises from the repeated declarations to be found in the Prophets, that the original divine relationship of Israel is to be perpetual, though at present temporarily obscured under a cloud of displeasure. Those declarations are made with an emphasis and with an explicitness, which leave no room of doubt or misapprehension. If for instance we take Jeremiah 33:24-26, we find a lesson which has almost a special applicability to the last class of Bible readers to which we have referred. The words are:

> "Considerest thou not what this people have spoken, saying, the two families which the LORD hath chosen *he hath even cast them off*. Thus they have despised my people that they should be no more a nation before them. Thus saith the LORD; **If** *my covenant be not with day and night, and* **if** *I have not appointed the ordinances of Heaven and Earth,* **then** *will I cast away the seed of Jacob and David my servant* … For I will cause their captivity to return and have mercy on them."

If, again, we consider the statement of Jeremiah 30, it is impossible conscientiously to maintain the doctrine of Israel's final reprobation:

> "I will save thee from afar, and thy seed from the land of their captivity, and Jacob shall return and be in rest, and be quiet, and none shall make him afraid … Though *I make a full end of all the nations whither I have scattered thee* **yet will I not make a full end of thee**, but will correct thee in measure and will not leave thee altogether unpunished." (verses 10,11)

The teaching of this statement is in complete harmony with Paul's assertion in Romans 11:2, that "God hath not cast away his people whom he foreknew", and in verses 25 and 26, that when the fullness of the Gentiles is come in, "all Israel shall be saved, for out of Zion shall come a Deliverer". And these combined testimonies would throw light on Christ's statement concerning himself that he was sent to "the lost sheep of the house of Israel".

And this introduces us to the second consideration which necessitates the restitution and blessing of Israel, viz. the mission of Christ. This mission though comprehensively related to the human race as a whole, has in its details, a specific bearing upon Israel. The statement quoted from Matthew 15:24 establishes this point; and to remove any doubt which might exist as to the "**Israel**" to which it refers, it is only necessary to quote the words addressed by Jesus to his disciples on another occasion, which are to be found in Matthew 10:5, "Go not into the way of the Gentiles, and into any city of the Samaritans, enter ye not, but *go rather to the lost sheep of the House of Israel*". The contrast drawn in these words conclusively shows that it was *Israel after the flesh* whom Jesus regarded as the special object of his mission. But this is made more abundantly evident in those scriptures of the prophets from which after his resurrection, he "expounded the things concerning himself" (Luke 24:27,44). In Isaiah 49 we have a disquisition upon this mission, and in verse 5, we find Christ in the spirit of prophecy saying, "The LORD formed me from the womb to be his servant **to bring Jacob again to him**", and in verse 6, he is described as Jehovah's servant *"to raise up the tribes of Jacob and to restore the preserved of Israel"*. These statements no doubt are made incidentally and in connection with the announcement of other objects in Christ commission. Still they retain the full force of a declaration of fact, the point of which will be evident to the reader. We may be profoundly thankful that the words are added, "I will also give Thee for a light to the Gentiles that thou mayest be my salvation unto the ends of the earth". But this extension of his mission does not displace that primary part which relates to God's own nation, but rather forms a graceful supplement to it. "I will preserve thee", continues the prophetic record (verse 8), "and give thee for a covenant of the people", that is the Jews, to whom the phrase "the people" is almost exclusively appropriated in the scriptures. A little light is thrown on this statement by the remark of Caiaphas, the High Priest, during Christ's sojourn in the flesh, of which remark it is said, "He spake not this of himself, but being High Priest that year, *he prophesied that Jesus should die for that nation*" (John 11:51). The remark itself which was addressed to a council of Chief Priests and Pharisees, is as follows: "Ye know nothing at all, nor consider that it is expedient for us that one man should die for the people and that the whole nation perish not." True, it is added (and we Gentiles may be devoutly grateful for the addition) that his death should be "not for that nation only, but that also he should gather together in one the children of God that were scattered abroad". But as in the other case this does not in validate the primary Jewish speciality of what Christ came to do but rather makes it obvious by contrast. This speciality is further apparent in the following testimony from Isaiah 61:

> "The Spirit of the Lord GOD is upon me because he hath anointed me ... *To appoint unto them that mourn* **in Zion**, to give unto them beauty for ashes, the oil of joy for mourning, the garment of praise for the spirit of heaviness, that they may be called trees of righteousness, the planting of the LORD, that he might be glorified. *And they shall build the old wastes; they shall raise up the former desolations, and they shall repair the waste cities, and the desolation of many generations, and strangers shall stand and feed your flocks, and the sons of the alien shall be your ploughmen, and your vinedressers, but ye shall be named the Priests of the Lord; men shall call you the Ministers of our God.* **Ye shall eat the riches of the Gentiles**, and in their glory shall ye boast yourselves. For your shame, ye shall have double, and for confusion they shall rejoice in their portion. Therefore *in their land they shall possess the double*. Everlasting joy shall be unto them for I the LORD love

judgment, I hate robbery, for burnt offering; and I will direct their work in truth, *and I will make an everlasting covenant with them. And their seed shall be known among the* **Gentiles**, *and their offspring among the people: all that see them shall acknowledge them, that they are the seed which the* LORD *hath blessed."* (verses 1-9)

The intimate connection of Christ's mission with the national salvation of Israel is made more abundantly evident in the scriptures of the prophets than we can afford space to show, but we cannot leave this part of the subject without presenting the reader with some of the more conclusive illustrations of it. If, for instance, we go to Ezekiel chapter 34, in which the leaders of the nation are inveighed against as false shepherds, it is stated:

"As a shepherd seeketh out his flock in the day that he is among his sheep that are scattered *will I seek out my sheep, and will deliver them out of all places where they have been scattered in the cloudy and dark day,* and I will bring them out from the people, and will gather them from the countries and *will bring them to their own land* and feed them upon the mountains of Israel, by the rivers and in all the inhabited places of the country. And **I will set up one shepherd over them**, and he shall feed them, even my servant David (or him who is the root and offspring of David), he shall feed them, and he shall be their shepherd. And I the LORD will be their God, and my servant David, a prince among them." (verses 12,13,23,24)

In Jeremiah 33 a promise is made (verse 5) that God will raise unto David "**a righteous branch**" who as King shall reign and prosper, and execute judgment and justice in the earth, and it is added "**in his days**, *Judah shall be saved, and Israel shall dwell safely*". To the same import is the statement in Isaiah 11:

"There shall come forth a rod out of the stem of Jesse and a branch shall grow up out of his roots ... *And it shall come to pass in that day, that the* LORD *shall set his hand again the second time to recover the remnant of his people, which shall be left* from Assyria, and from Egypt, and from Pathros, and from Cush, and from Elam, and from Shinar; and from Hamath, and from the islands of the sea. *And he shall set up an ensign for the nations, and shall assemble the outcasts of Israel, and gather together the dispersed of Judah from the four corners of the earth."* (verses 1-12)

There are others which we may have occasion to quote hereafter. These establish the point in hand, that the mission of Christ involves the ultimate restitution of the Jewish nation, its reinstatement in Palestine, and its exaltation to a position of supremacy in the earth.

The necessity of this event being accomplished is further apparent in the designation of Christ as "king of the Jews". Christ is of the house of David, which, as we have seen in a previous article, was divinely appointed to be the ruling family of the Jewish nation. As "son of David", he is therefore heir to "the throne of David", on which Peter testifies he was raised up according to the flesh of David to sit. He is therefore the king of the Jews, since the *throne of David* is but the verbal symbol of divinely-sanctioned royal authority over that nation. This is none the less true because the nation reject him. The time will come when they shall say, "Blessed is he that cometh in the name of the Lord" (Luke 13:35). Then shall they "look upon him whom they have pierced, and mourn for him as one mourneth for his only son" (Zechariah 12:10). Meanwhile, he is in the position indicated in Psalm 110: "Sit thou on my right hand till I make thy foes thy footstool" (verse 1).

If Christ is king of the Jews and is to enforce that character by "raising up the tabernacle of David that is fallen down, and restoring the ruins thereof" (Amos 9:11) and by presiding "on the throne of David and his kingdom, to order it, and establish it with judgment and justice", is it not obvious that the Jews must be restored? When has Christ ever reigned over the Jews? Never. They rejected him when he came, saying, "This is the heir; come let us kill him, and the inheritance shall be ours", and ever since have been his malignant calumniators. To this day, they blaspheme when his name is mentioned, though it is not a great wonder they do, considering the caricature of a Christ that is paraded before them by the zealots of apostate Christendom. The conclusion remains that the restoration of Israel to their own land, is a necessity before Christ can appear in the character which he claimed while on earth, and which the prophets with one voice ascribe to him, viz., king of the Jews, and (in Jerusalem) Lord of all the earth. If this event do not occur, his claims will be frustrated, and the word of God falsified.

The event is necessitated by the covenant which God made with David, the consideration of which almost drags us into a repetition of what has already been said, so uniform and unvarying is the testimony of the scriptures on this point. David "being a prophet, knew that *God had sworn with an oath unto him*, that of the fruit of his loins according to the flesh, *he would raise up Christ* **to sit upon his throne**". This is Peter's testimony (Acts 2:30) and is conclusive of itself, but a glance at the covenant itself will make its bearing on the subject in hand more apparent. It is to be found in 2 Samuel 7. It is contended by some to have reference to Solomon, and though it may have been incipiently realised in Solomon's reign, it is evident from the application of the terms to Christ by Paul, in Hebrews 1 and from the very nature of the statements it contains, that it related fundamentally to the greater than Solomon. David had purposed building a temple to God, but his warlike career was held to be a disqualification for the task, and Nathan was sent to him to turn him away from his purpose, and to inform him that God would give him a son, who should build a temple, and whose throne should be established forever:

> "I will be his Father and **he shall be my Son**. If he commit iniquity, I will chasten him with the rod of men, and with the stripes of the children of men; but my mercy shall not depart away him as I took it away Saul, whom I put away before thee. *And thine house, and thy kingdom shall be established for ever*

before thee; thy throne shall be established for ever."

(verses 14-16)

That David recognised in this, a prediction relating to something more remote than the reign of Solomon, which immediately succeeded his own, is evident in the words of the prayer which he uttered, on the reception of it, "Thou hast spoken also of thy servant's house **for a great while to come**". If the reader will take the trouble to read Psalm 89:19-37, Psalm 132, and 2 Samuel 23:1-7, he will find abundant evidence that it related to the days of Christ, in whom "the horn of David" shall be mightily and permanently exalted upon the earth. Now, in this covenant made with David, there occurs the following statement, which the Biblical unbelievers of Jewish restoration would do well to consider:

> "Moreover I will appoint a place for my people Israel, and will plant them that they may dwell in a place of their own, and move no more, *neither shall the children of wickedness afflict them any more as beforetime."* (2 Samuel 7:10)

What are we to say to this statement in view of the present afflicted and unsettled condition of the Jews? Simply that it has not yet had a fulfilment, and that therefore a time is yet to come when it will be fulfilled in the permanent resettlement of the Jews in their land on such a footing as that they shall never be removed again nor subject any more to adversity. This is so obvious as not to require argument, that is, if it be admitted that the "Israel" of the statement refers to the Jews, and this cannot be denied in view of David's commentary on the covenant: "Thou hast confirmed to thyself thy people Israel **which thou redeemedst unto thee from Egypt** to be a people unto thee for ever" (verses 23,24). The covenant made with David then requires that God recover the Jews from their dispersion, and re-establish them in prosperity and favour in His visible presence again actively among them; and is not this the picture presented in the eight closing chapters of Ezekiel? In the five and twentieth year of the Babylonish captivity, the hand of God upon Ezekiel took him in spirit into the land of Israel and there showed him the vision of a restored city and temple which are described at length in the chapters mentioned. That this vision did not have its fulfilment in the Babylonish restoration under Nehemiah is certain, as will be evident to any one attentively perusing the description given. Of the eastern gate of the temple, for instance, it is said, "The gate shall be shut; it shall not be opened, and no man shall enter in by it; *because the* LORD, *the God of Israel, hath entered in by it*" (Ezekiel 44:2). This could not apply to the temple restored by Ezra and Nehemiah and enlarged and adorned by Herod: because the glory which dwelt between the cherubim in Solomon's temple, and which took its departure before the destruction of the temple by Nebuchadnezzar, never returned. God never manifested Himself in the second temple. It was visited by Jesus during his sojourn upon earth, but this could not be regarded as the official manifestation of Jehovah's glory, since in the first place, the Father was veiled in the human person of Jesus, and in the second, He formed no part of the temple institution. Certainly we are not informed of any gate in that temple which had been at any time consecrated by a divine entrance, and thereafter closed against human use. The fact is, that no such event as is contemplated in Ezekiel, took place in the history of that or any temple that ever existed on earth. That event is described in the following terms:

> "*And behold the glory of the God of Israel came from the way of the east and his voice was like the voice of many waters, and the earth shined with his glory … And the glory of the* LORD *came into the house by the way of the gate, whose prospect is towards the east.*" (Ezekiel 43:2-4)

After witnessing this spectacle, Ezekiel was taken by the spirit into the inner sanctuary, in which the divine presence had taken up his abode; and this inner court was described to him as "**the place of my throne and the place of the soles of my feet** *where I will dwell in the midst of the children of Israel* **for ever**, *and my holy name shall the House of Israel* **no more** *defile, neither they* *nor their kings by their whoredom, nor by the carcasses of their kings, in their high places*" (verse 7). This is a complete identification of the vision with the period depicted in testimonies already quoted, when Jesus as the bearer of Jehovah's glory, shall return to "sit and rule upon his throne, and be a priest upon his throne" (Zechariah 6:12,13) in Jerusalem restored, which is "the city of the Great King" (Matthew 5:35) in which he shall "reign before his ancients gloriously" (Isaiah 34:34). If any further proof of this were needed, reference has only to be made to the concluding declaration of the vision, that *"The name of the city* **from that day** *shall be* **the LORD is there**". It is supererogation to say that this is inapplicable to Jerusalem in her present state. Not God, but Mahomet is there, in the Mosque of Omar, which desecrates the ground made sacred by the divine manifestation of former days. Therefore, it is obvious that this vision of Ezekiel can only find its fulfilment in some future dispensation of God's presence and favour. This is made still more evident by the fact that under the state of things described in the vision, a section of the country, about forty-three miles in length, and eighteen in breadth, in the form of a parallelogram, is to be allotted to the exclusive service of the sanctuary, which is to be situated in the centre of this extensive tract of country. This consecrated territory is called an "oblation to the LORD" (Ezekiel 45:1). Now such a thing has never occurred in the history of the Holy Land and must therefore be realised in that future period of which we are speaking. It is in connection with this aspect of the question that we find the strongest argument for the restoration of Israel. Ezekiel is informed that contemporaneously with the remarkable apportionment of territory in question, the Land is to be divided among the twelve tribes of Israel. The words are:

> "Thus saith the Lord GOD; This shall be the border whereby *ye shall inherit the land according* **to the twelve tribes of Israel** ... And ye shall inherit one as well as another *concerning the which, I lifted up mine hand to give it unto your fathers*."
> (47:13,14)

Then the borders of the land are defined, after which the record continues, "So shall ye divide this land unto you, *according to the Tribes of Israel*". Then follows the enumeration of the Tribes, in the order in which the land (cut into parallel strips) is to be distributed amongst them, after which we find the words, *"This is the land which ye shall divide by lot* **unto the tribes of Israel** *for inheritance*, and these are their portions saith the Lord God" (Ezekiel 47:13,21; 48:29). Now such a division of the land of Palestine has never taken place. The ten Tribes who are included in the distribution of Ezekiel have never returned from the exile to which they were banished by the hand of Shalmaneser more than twenty centuries ago, and probably they are ignorant to this day, wherever God may have hid them, that such a vision as Ezekiel's is in existence. What remains to be said, then, but that if the words of God by Ezekiel are true, the Jews must return to the country which God has chosen for them, and for the manifestation of His own glory. Even as He has said by Jeremiah (31:10): "*He that scattered Israel* **will gather them** *and keep them as a shepherd doth his flock.*"

But time would fail to cite all the evidences of this purpose, and in the attempt we should find ourselves engaged in an almost monotonous iteration of testimony, affirming in varied phrase, but with uniform emphasis and intent, the one purpose which stands forth in brilliant prominence throughout the writings of the Prophets, viz. "the blessing of all nations, and the consummation of redemption itself, in connection with the restoration of the kingdom again to Israel". The further elaboration of the subject must be reserved for future numbers.

5 |

God's purpose with the Jews (4)

(February 1865)

SOME may be disposed to ask why so much should be said about this subject of the Jews. The most direct answer to this question is, that God's purpose with the Jews is one of those "first principles of the doctrine of Christ", without a knowledge of which it is impossible to comprehend the whole counsel of God, or indeed any part of it correctly. A more general answer is to be found in the fact that the whole Bible is filled with the subject. It is impossible to open any part of the book of God that is not in some way connected with the Jews. The Old Testament "begins, continues, and ends", in this one subject, giving us at great length their history, their laws and their oracles. The New Testament tells us of doings among the Jewish people by "the King of the Jews"; of Jewish ambassadors sent by the King of the Jews to attract a people to himself from the heathen, by the exhibition of "the hope of Israel" as developed through his sacrificial accomplishments. It is all of the Jews. To crown the matter, Jesus says, "*Salvation is* **of the Jews**" (John 4:22). It must be so, for "*to them pertain* the **adoption and the glory and the covenants**, the service of God *and the promises*" (Romans 9:4). God has never dealt with the Gentiles. All his intercourse with men, since the call of Abraham, has been with the Jews; and nearly all he has said through the prophets refers to them, in rebuke, in instruction, in imprecation, or in prediction of blessing. The Gentiles come in incidentally and only as they are related to God's nation. Since, then, God has given such prominence to this people – since the Bible is so greatly taken up with them as to be all about them, it surely cannot be a mistake to be concerned in the subject, and to give a good deal of time and space to its consideration.

The history of the Jews is the alphabet of Christianity, and their future, its more advanced lessons. With the former, the majority of Bible readers are somewhat acquainted, though only in a dim traditional way, too superficial to be serviceable. Of the latter, they are, with but few exceptions, entirely ignorant There is no excuse for this ignorance. The future of Israel is as plainly written as their past. As the basis of what we have to say further on the subject, we select the following as an example of what we affirm:

> "Behold the days come, saith the LORD, that *I will make* **a new covenant** *with the house of Israel, and with the house of Judah, not according to the covenant that I made with their fathers in the day that I took them by the hand to bring them out of the land of Egypt, which my covenant* **they brake**, although I was an husband unto them, saith the LORD. But this shall be the covenant that I will make with the house of Israel: after those days saith the LORD, *I will put my law in their inward parts, and write it in their hearts*, and will be their God, and they shall be my people. And they shall teach no more every man his neighbour, and every man his brother, saying, Know the LORD; for they shall all know me from the least of them unto the greatest of them, saith the LORD, for I will forgive their iniquity, and I will remember their sin no more."
>
> (Jeremiah 31:31-34)

This is plain, but there is nothing so plain as not to require some previous knowledge to understand it. So to apprehend the full significance of this clear and comprehensive statement concerning the future of Israel, it is necessary to appreciate the historical allusion in the words, "Not according to the covenant that I made with your fathers".

The first consideration that strikes the thoughtful reader on reading these words is, *that the people with whom the old covenant was made, are those racially with whom the new covenant is to be made.* The new covenant is to be made with the descendants of those who broke the first. This is an inevitable conclusion in view of the testimony, and is of the greatest importance, as it enables us to decide with great positiveness that the prediction has never yet had a fulfilment.

God has never made a second covenant with the Jews. He made a covenant with their fathers "in the day that they came out of the land of Egypt", and under that, by their own blind adhesion, they continue to this day. The Law of Moses continues to hang on the nation's neck like a millstone. It is a rigorous dispensation of death to all continuing not in all its requirements. Peter describes it as a yoke which neither they nor their fathers were able to bear (Acts 15:10) – and Paul as "a handwriting of ordinances which was against them" (Colossians 2:14). The covenant-proper is to be found in the ten commandments (Deuteronomy 4:13) divinely uttered, from the top of Sinai in the ears of the people (Exodus 20); but it also comprehends those numerous 'statutes and judgments' relating to national and individual life, which were privately communicated to Moses on the top of the mount – the people having in great terror requested that God would speak no longer to *them*, but to Moses as their mediator. The whole having been written, the writing was styled "the book of the covenant", (Exodus 14:7) and was ratified or enforced by the sprinkling of blood upon it, and upon all the people, a transaction which Paul informs us, was entirely symbolical of Christ. Now, if we look into this book of the covenant, we shall find how stringent and burdensome it was in its requirements, and shall be prepared to appreciate the prophetic declaration that the second covenant is to be different. First, it arbitrarily constituted a great variety of acts of ceremonial uncleanness before unknown. A man touching a dead body; touching a creeping thing; touching a man having an issue, or anything sat upon or used by such a man; or using any utensil in a tent where a man had died or that was ceremonially unclean, was by the law pronounced unclean, and for the time being was precluded from approach to the sanctuary, or from intercourse with his people; and if he refused to purify himself in the ceremonial manner prescribed, he was liable to death which in the faithful administration of the law was sure to be inflicted. Then it established a rigorous system of exactions for all manner of damage caused to others, in person or property, whether intentional or otherwise – "an eye for an eye, a tooth for a tooth" – which was justice in a very severe form. Then it attached the penalty of death to a long variety of offences which men were liable to commit, such as the cursing of father or mother, the touching of the holy things of the sanctuary, the offering of sacrifice anywhere but at the door of the tabernacle, the possessing of a notoriously dangerous animal which had killed a man, the accidental killing of a man, unless escape was made to the city of refuge; and so on. Then the positive enactments were of a burdensome nature. They were to stay within their tents on the seventh day, and light no fires, and speak no words of their own, at the risk of death. They were to write the law on their doorposts, and talk about it going out and coming in all the days of their life. They were three times a year (when settled in their country) to leave their houses with their families, and appear before God at the place He should appoint with offerings of their substance to His service, and to hold feasts of considerable duration in His honour. All the first fruits and the best of their flocks and herds were to be given up to God. The gleanings of their fields and vineyards they were to leave to the poor, whom they were not to forbid entrance. Every seventh year, they were to leave the land untilled, and every fiftieth year, all property in house or land that they had purchased was to be given back, (with certain slight exceptions) without compensation to its original owner under the allotment of Joshua.

The angel under whom these regulations were appointed to be carried out was rigid in his enforcement of them. God had said to Moses, "Beware of him; obey his voice and provoke him not, for he will not pardon your transgressions" (Exodus 23:23).

And Paul in evident allusion to this says, "The word spoken by angels was steadfast, and every transgression of disobedience received a just recompense of reward" (Hebrews 2:2).

The covenant administered under this "disposition of angels" (Acts 7:53) was entirely conditional in its nature. This is abundantly evident in the following words:

> "**If** *ye walk in my statutes and keep my commandments to do them*, **then** I will give you the rain in due season, and the land will yield her increase, and the trees of the field shall yield their fruit (and so on, describing other blessings that would follow), but *if ye will not hearken to me, and will not do all these commandments*, and if ye shall despise my statutes, or if your soul abhor my judgments, so that ye will not do all my commands but that ye break my covenant, *I also will do this unto you*; I will even appoint over you terror, consumption and the burning ague, that shall consume the eyes, and cause sorrow of heart." [and the record proceeds with the enumeration of bitter curses] (Leviticus 26:3,4,14,16)

In Deuteronomy 30 Moses says to Israel:

> "See, I have set before thee this day *life and good* and *death and evil*, in that I command thee this day to love the LORD thy God, to walk in his ways and to keep his commandments, and his statutes and his judgments, that thou mayest live and multiply, and the LORD thy God shall bless thee in the land whither thou goest to possess it. *But if thine heart turn away*, so that thou wilt not hear, but shall be drawn away and worship other gods and serve them, *I denounce unto you this day that ye shall surely perish*." (verses 15-18)

Thus, the covenant made with Israel "in the day that they came out of the land of Egypt", was one under which the national well-being was made dependent on a law which was too stringent for the capabilities of human nature. It was a yoke which they were unable to bear, and therefore proved inefficacious for the development of the blessing. It was "weak through the flesh", because the flesh was unequal to that unflagging circumspection requisite for perfect obedience in all things. Obedience in ninety-nine points was invalidated by failure in one, for he that offended in one point was guilty of all (James 2:10). If there could have been a law that could have given life, Paul says that life would have been by the law (Galatians 3:21). But it was impossible, for though the law was "holy and just and good", human nature of purely Adamic origin was unable to keep it. We may then ask in the words of Galatians 3:19, "Wherefore then serveth the law?" It had a purpose, though never intended as the permanent basis of relationship between God and man. Paul says "It was added because of transgressions, till the seed should come to whom the (Abrahamic) promise was made". But why because of transgressions? Evidently because of the tendency to transgression in human nature which in the absence of the law, in antediluvian times, developed itself to the filling of the earth with wickedness, and brought upon mankind the ruin of the flood. It was necessary that the recurrence of this catastrophe should be prevented, and therefore the law was established as a schoolmaster (Galatians 3:24) to enforce those preliminary lessons of God's supremacy and man's subordination, and incapacity in the matter of his salvation which were necessary to pave the way for the higher development of grace and truth which came by Christ Jesus. But while the law fulfilled this purpose, it was also "the form of knowledge and the truth" (Romans 2:20). Upon its stringent statutory exterior was impressed the allegory of the mysteries which are developed in the Christ. It is not our present purpose to trace out this allegory, but simply to note the fact in passing, that like all God's arrangements it was multiform in its purposes and bearings. While affording to God's nation a magnificent constitution, which if faithfully carried out, would have promoted the highest form of political freedom, and the best phase of social existence and individual well-being, it also generated those ideas of God on which as a foundation, Christ upreared the higher aspects of the truth he came to unfold, while it constituted a skilful enigma of the truth to be unlocked by his children who delight to search out his hidden wisdom.

But having served its purpose, this first covenant waxed old, and vanished away in the destruction of Jerusalem. The Jews still cling to its skeleton: but for the last eighteen centuries, God has made it impossible for them to obey it, by permitting the establishment of Mohammedan abomination in the city, and in the country, where alone its requirements can be complied with.

In view of God's purpose to restore again the kingdom to Israel, it is interesting to know from the testimony quoted at the commencement of this article, that the old covenant will not be restored with it, but that a new dispensation more accordant with the blessedness of the times of him who was only typified by the first covenant will be brought into force. Under this new dispensation, Israel's obedience will not be dependent upon their apprehension of statutes externally administered merely, but will spring from an indwelling knowledge unknown in the previous history of the nation. "They shall all know the LORD, from the least of them unto the greatest of them." This knowledge results from a process described as a divine writing in their hearts. God's first covenant was written on stones and parchment, and was only morally operative as the ideas were apprehended and treasured.

This could only be done by reading and meditation – a process of mental absorption which in those rude times was precarious, and subject to impairment from the want of ready access to the oracles. All were invited to write copies of the law and thus make themselves familiar with the letter of its requirements, but there was a liability to neglect this injunction to which the thousands of Israel gave way, and thus isolated themselves from the source of divine influence, in consequence of which, the natural mind obtained the mastery, and led to those incessant national apostasies with which the history of Israel is marked. The mere outward manifestation of God's power did not seem sufficient to repress this tendency in the absence of the thorough spiritual perception engendered by the study of the law itself. Again, there were many who were naturally "sons of

Belial" – men of hard unimpressible heart, whom even judgment could not teach righteousness. These the history of Israel has proved to have been in the majority. With this class, the study of the law, even with all the facilities of a modern cheap press, would have been powerless for good, and powerless even for the repression of those grosser outbreaks into which they continually fell away. Human nature is the same as it was then. The Jews under the Mosaic Law would be no better in the nineteenth century, or in the Millennium itself, than they were in the days of the prophets. Therefore, God proposes a better arrangement than the establishment of a system of things "which made nothing perfect". He will restore His people under a constitution which will secure their permanent obedience, and admit of the bestowal of those constant and unqualified blessings of which the prosperity of the nation under David and Solomon was but the faint foreshadowing. God will put His law *"in their minds"*. To regenerate the nation's heart, so that they will be no longer stiff necked, self-willed, and unbelieving in relation to God and His Christ, and no longer rapacious, unprincipled, and grovelling in relation to man, will indeed be a glorious transformation. How is it to be effected? This is an important question, and capable of a clear answer from the word of God. It will not be done in any sudden or incomprehensible manner. The world will not wake up some morning to find the Jews changed in a night, from low moneygrubbers, to high souled God-fearing men. The Jews will be gathered *as they are*, even as they were taken out of Egypt *as they were*. This is evident from the following testimony of Ezekiel 20:

> "I will bring you out from the people and will gather you out of the countries wherein ye are scattered, with a mighty hand and a stretched out arm, and with fury poured out. *And I will bring you into the wilderness of the people, and* **there will I plead with you face to face**, *like as I pleaded with your fathers in the wilderness of the land of Egypt. So will I plead with you, saith the Lord* GOD. *And I will cause you to pass under the rod, and I will bring you into the bond of the covenant.* **and I will**

purge out from among you the rebels, and them that transgress against me. *I will bring them forth out of the country where they sojourn* **and they shall not enter into the land of Israel.**" (verses 34-38)

This is an important phase in the restoration of the Jews, and meets the moral difficulties suggested by some who are only partially acquainted with the subject. The restoration of the Jews will not be an indiscriminate deportation of the race of Abraham from the countries to Palestine. Before it commences, the Lord of the country – Jesus of Nazareth, whom they crucified – will be master of the country, having returned to redeem the inheritance, and will bar the way against unlicensed admission. The Jews as they are, are totally unfit to enter the land, They are, as they have been for ages, the blasphemous rejecters of God's Anointed, and the contumacious breakers of his law, and morally, are in a state of utter reprobation, obnoxious even to man, and abominable in the sight of God. It is therefore necessary, that the national purification described in the testimony we have quoted should take place. Thousands of them, perhaps the whole generation that commences the exodus eastward, will perish in the wilderness, like their ancestors under Moses, and never see the land. "I will come near to you to judgment", says Jehovah of this time, "*and I will be a swift witness against the sorcerers and against the adulterers, and against false swearers, and against those that oppress the hireling in his wages, the widow and the fatherless, and turn aside the stranger from his right*" (Malachi 3:5). To the same purport is the following testimony: "Then I will **take away out of the midst of thee**, *them that rejoice in thy pride*, and thou shalt no more be haughty, because of my holy mountain" (Zephaniah 3:2). This is done in the wilderness to which the nation is gathered before entering the land. The length of time it will take to accomplish the work, seems to be hinted at in Micah 7:15: "*According to* **the days of thy coming out of the land of Egypt** *will I shew unto him marvellous things.*" Forty years would not be too long to effect the moral transformation of which the Jews must be subject before entering the land, even with the exhibition of Jehovah's marvels a second time in their midst; for the behaviour of Israel under Moses shows that the mere working of wonders is not in itself sufficient to bring them into subjection. The "marvellous things" will include supernatural chastisement among themselves: for their gathering is to be "with fury poured out", and with a stretched out arm holding the rod, which he will cause them to pass under by way of preliminary to, and bringing them into the bond of the covenant. The fact that the rebels, and the transgressors are purged out, while the remainder enter the land in the bond of the (new or Abrahamic, Christ-ratified) covenant, shows that before the outpouring of the spirit upon the nation, the national purification is to be accomplished by national discipline, and not by a miraculous spirit-induced metamorphosis of the national mind. Just as in apostolic days, the spirit was never bestowed till the word preached had been received in meekness, so the acceptance of Jesus of Nazareth by the Jews and their acknowledgment of the justice of their long adversities, are preliminary to the glorious effusion of divine blessing which takes place under the new covenant. This change of mind will result from the pleading process; but many of them will remain unchanged, including probably, the bulk of the hard-headed conscience-seared business Jew of the present generation. These will be "purged out". That is, they will be destroyed from among their people: "for whosoever shall not hear that prophet (like unto Moses), that soul shall be cut off from his people." That will be the time for the enforcement of this decree, which will be done with unsparing severity. The result will be the fulfilment of the prediction: "Him shall ye hear." The nation, sobered and enlightened by judgment, and delivered from the modern Korahs, Dathans and Abirams, who will emulate their forefathers in the spirit of rebellion, will gladly receive "the prophet like unto Moses", and enter the bond of the new covenant, ratified by his blood, shed by their ancestors. The following predictions will then have their full accomplishment:

"I will leave in the midst of thee, *an afflicted and poor people*, and they shall trust in the name of the LORD (of which Jesus is the embodiment and bearer). *The remnant of Israel shall not do iniquity, nor speak lies, neither shall a deceitful tongue be found in their mouth*, for they shall feed and lie down and none shall make them afraid. Sing O Daughter of Zion, shout, O Israel, be glad and rejoice with all thy heart, O Daughter of Jerusalem. The LORD hath taken away thy judgments; he hath cast out thine enemy. *The king of Israel, even the LORD, is in the midst of thee: thou shalt not see evil any more."* (Zephaniah 3:12-15)

"I shall bring you into the land of Israel, into the country for the which I lifted up mine hand to give it to your fathers: *and there shall ye remember your ways, and all your doings wherein ye have been defiled; and ye shall loathe yourselves in your own sight for all your evils that ye have committed*. And ye shall know that I am the LORD, when I have wrought with you for my name's sake and *not according to your corrupt doings*, O ye house of Israel." (Ezekiel 20:42-44)

Read also Ezekiel 36:25-31; 39:21-29. The nation of Israel having, by long chastisement been brought into a repentant state of mind, and having accepted their long-rejected Messiah, they will be admitted to the land of promise which Ezekiel says will then have become like the garden of Eden as regards the culture and beauty of the soil. They will then be prepared for the great outpouring of the Spirit which will stereotype, so to speak, their morally-induced submissiveness, and make it a part of the national instinct as it were to know God and obey His commandments. Backsliding will then be unknown. For a thousand years, the nation will rejoice in Messiah, "the Holy One of Israel in the midst of them", and in the apostle-princes (Matthew 19) who will co-operate with him in his rule of righteousness. In the words of Isaiah:

"*The people also shall be **all righteous**; they shall inherit the land for ever; the branch of my planting, the work of my hands, that I may be glorified.*" (60:21)

6 |

God's purpose with the Jews (5)

(March 1865)

IN view of the evidence adduced, it is not too great a liberty to lead off the present article with the proposition that God's purpose with the Jews is to restore them from their universal dispersion, and reconstitute them a great nation in Palestine, under Jesus, the Messiah, returned from heaven; and to subjugate all nations to their new government centralised in Judaea. In our last article, we gave a little consideration to the bearings of this event on the Jews themselves; in the present, we propose to consider its moral and political relations to the nations of the earth at large. In estimating these, it will aid us greatly to recall the incidents of the exodus from Egypt under Moses, since we shall find the objects in both cases pretty similar in character, though differing in the means employed and in the extent of the operations.

The Hebrews were in bondage to Pharaoh. Standing in the position of aliens, exactions were laid upon them from which the citizens of the country were exempt. They were employed in the menial offices of the country, and more particularly in the production of bricks for the Egyptians to use in the construction of their buildings. Pharaoh did not know God and was equally ignorant of the illustrious character of the race he held as bondsmen. It is not therefore to be wondered at that when summoned by Moses and Aaron to let them go he peremptorily refused. The services of the best part of a million of men were valuable to him, while the natural love of supremacy, unsoftened by the high principles which emanating from the word of God, have in later times directly and indirectly ennobled other minds, made it pleasant for him to hold his heel upon a vassal race. Besides, there was an imperiousness about the briefly-worded demand of Moses which must have been exceedingly distasteful to royal ears. The message would have been unpleasant even if couched in the oily words of modern diplomacy, but to be forced upon him in such a blunt and authoritative way, was intolerable. He would not let them go. It was part of God's plan that he should not. God hardened his heart that he might have the infatuation to enter into contest with the Almighty for the possession of His people, and thus give the Almighty an opportunity of revealing his existence by acts of power which should strike deep into the hearts of Israel, and create a fame which should perpetuate the memory and the faith of Him to all generations. The sequel is too well known to need recapitulation. Plagues of appalling magnitude and severity attested God's hand in the operations of Moses, and temporarily persuading the insensate monarch of the futility of the struggle, impelled him to hurry Israel from his coasts, only, however, with returning induration of heart, to pursue them to the Red Sea there to contribute the crowning evidence of Jehovah's power in the fearful catastrophe of a whole army's destruction, with himself at their head, in the heart of the sea. The prolonged struggle ultimating in this event was not necessary as a question of power on the part of God to release His people. He could have decimated the Egyptians in a single night, like the Assyrians in later times, and delivered His people without a ruffle of the elements. But this would not have answered His purpose, which was to make His existence and power known to mankind, in the only way mankind could appreciate them, viz. *by the manifestation of intelligently-directed force in the accomplishment of a specific object*. This purpose was so thoroughly realised that a nation of comparative barbarians surrendered themselves to a leader who boasted no military prowess and offered no inducements that would attract a people, but instead, invited them to a divine servitude which was afterwards characterised as a burden, which they were not able to bear (Acts 15). The completeness of the result is also to be noted in the tenacious faith their descendants have maintained in Moses throughout all their generations, and in the tradition of God throughout the world, which primarily rests on the fame of the transactions attending the deliverance of Israel from Egypt, and their settlement in the land of Canaan. That these remarks may not appear to be mere ingenious theorising, we quote the following scriptures which show that the nature and objects of the Egyptian deliverance were veritably as we have described:

"Thus saith the LORD God of the Hebrews, in very deed, *for this cause have I raised thee* (Pharaoh) *up* **for to shew in thee my power, and that my name may be declared throughout all the earth**." (Exodus 9:16)

"Ask now of the days that are past which were before thee, since the day that God created man upon the earth, and ask from the one side of heaven, unto the other whether there hath been any such thing as this great thing is, or hath been like it heard? Did ever people hear the voice of God speaking in the midst of the fire as thou hast heard and live, or, *hath God assayed to go and take him a nation, from the midst of another nation, by temptations, by signs and by wonders, and by war, and by a mighty hand, and by a stretched out arm, and by great terror according to all that the LORD your God did for you in Egypt, before your eyes*? **Unto thee it was shewed that thou mightest know that the LORD he is God, there is none else beside him**." (Deuteronomy 4:32-35)

"For the LORD your God dried up the waters of Jordan from before you until ye were passed over, as the LORD your God did to the Red Sea, which he dried up from before us until we were gone over **that all the people of the earth might know the hand of the LORD, that it is mighty: that ye might fear the LORD your God for ever**." (Joshua 4:23,24)

"And know ye this day, for I speak not with your children which have not known and which have not seen the chastisement of the LORD your God, his greatness, his mighty hand and his stretched out arm, and his miracles and his acts which he did in the midst of Egypt unto Pharaoh the king of Egypt and unto all his land, and what he did unto the army of Egypt, and to their horses, and to their chariots, how he made the water of the Red Sea to overflow them as they pursued after you and how the Lord hath destroyed them unto this day … *But your eyes have seen all the great acts of the LORD which he did,* **therefore shall ye keep all the commandments which I command you this day**." (Deuteronomy 11:2-4,7,8)

In this later stage of the world's history, we have reached a time in which the moral results of the Egyptian signs and wonders have nearly worn out through the lapse of time and the triumph of the enemy. Belief in God and faith in His word are dim and dying sentiments from which men are everywhere releasing themselves. Intellectual conceit is raising a vigorous front and wrapping itself in theories which would exclude God from the universe and throw discredit on His word as an ancient fable. This is to be attributed to a variety of causes. The natural pride and stupidity of the human heart are doubtless the main sources of this tendency to unbelief. It is by no means a new manifestation. So far back as David's time, there were "**fools**" who said in their heart there was no God, and Paul speaks of those who "not liking to retain God in their knowledge", were judicially given over to the unrestrained dominion of their propensities. The human mind untutored by the knowledge that comes from God through the written words of His servants of past times, inevitably becomes heady and masterful, and hates the submission that God demands. This no doubt explains much of the scepticism that characterises the present times. But much of it is doubtless also owing to the fact that all the knowledge men have of God and His ways is derived from a system of religion which, though universally accredited, is the baldest caricature of the truth that could be palmed upon mankind, bearing as little resemblance to the teachings of the holy oracles, as the most inferior species of the ape does to the noblest specimen of man. At all events, there is the fact to be recognised that the tradition of God, Mosaically-originated, and Messianically-confirmed and propagated, becomes weaker as the world gets older and busier, and that despite the prevalence of scientific light and social culture, the world in relation to God is tending deeper and deeper to that darkness, seen by prophetic forecast (Isaiah 60:2), which should cover the earth and gross darkness the people; and hence may be understood the philosophy, as it may be termed, of the second great postdiluvian outburst of judgment upon the nations foretold in the testimonies accessible by the following references: – Jeremiah 25:15-33; 30:23,24; Isaiah 30:27,28; 66:15,16; Psalm 11:6; 21:9; 50:3-6; Malachi 4:1,2; 2 Thessalonians 1:7-9; Revelation 11:17,18; 19:11,16. Mankind can only be sobered and brought to their senses in relation to God by the exhibition of judgment. They have ever shown themselves in the mass unamenable to other influences. The sense of responsibility to God, which begins with the recognition of His existence, can only be revived by such a demonstration as created it at first in the heart of the Jewish nation; and such a demonstration God has resolved upon, as may be seen by consulting the testimonies we have referred to.

The next consideration leading to the subject in hand is that this demonstration will have shape and occasion. It will not be a mere objectless nature-wrecking outburst of power after the fashion of a thunderstorm. God never has operated in this clumsy way. He waits the opportunity. He selects such a "situation" as gives effect to His doings. He did not destroy Pharaoh suddenly, and without notice, but raised a direct and intelligible issue to which the subsequent plagues had a logical relation. So will it be in the judgments that are coming. They will not descend after the manner of popular expectation, suddenly convulsing the earth in the throes of ruin, and wrapping the world in universal blaze, for the simple reason that His object is not to destroy the world, as in the case of Sodom, but to teach the world righteousness;

"When thy judgments are in the earth, then will the inhabitants of the world learn righteousness" (Isaiah 26:9).

Our object is to show that the manifestation of these judgments, as in the case of those in Egypt, will be connected with the redemption of Israel, this time from a universal vassalage. The first general testimony to be cited on the point is from Joel 3:

> "Behold in those days and at that time *when I shall bring again the captivity of Judah and Jerusalem*, I will also gather all nations, and will bring them down unto the valley of Jehoshaphat, **and will plead with them there for my heritage Israel whom they have scattered among the nations and parted my land.**" (verses 1,2)

That this refers to the period of general judgment spoken of in the other passages alluded to, will at once be made evident by a reading of the chapter from which it is quoted, more especially such verses as the following:

> "Proclaim ye this among the Gentiles; prepare war; wake up the mighty men; let all the men of war draw near, let them come up. Beat your ploughshares into swords and your pruning hooks into spears; let the weak say, I am strong. Assemble yourselves and come, all ye heathen, and gather yourselves together round about; thither cause thy mighty ones to come down, O LORD. Let the heathen be wakened and come up to the valley of Jehoshaphat: for there will I sit to judge all the heathen round about. Put ye in the sickle; for the harvest is ripe: come get you down; for the press is full, the fats overflow; for their wickedness is great. Multitudes, multitudes in the valley of decision: for the day of the LORD is near in the valley of decision. The sun and the moon shall be darkened, and the stars shall withdraw their shining …" (verses 9-15)

The coincidence of the restoration of Israel with judgment upon the nations being obvious, it is for us to find out the connection, if connection exist, between the two things. In attempting to do this, it will help us if we glance for a moment at the present position of the Jews. We behold them scattered up and down the earth as strangers wherever civilised man is to found, sojourning as isolated individuals, subject to the authority that may exist where they are, unconnected by any political tie, without a national polity, without any organisation, except the organisation of the synagogue. How shall a nation so powerless be redeemed? What force shall be brought to bear to gather them from their scattered homes, and re-unite them as one nation? A voluntary movement in times of peace might be effective enough as regards England and America, but even that would be prohibited in other countries where the Jews, only recently admitted to the barest privileges of citizenship, are held as a sort of national property to be utilised in various ways for the national benefit. If there would be a difficulty in times of peace, there would be an absolute impossibility in times of war. Recent events in the freest country on the face of the earth show that the liberty of even the privileged citizen vanishes before the exigencies of a government at war. The waste of warfare calls for men, and the tardiness of voluntary enlistment necessitates conscription, and conscription compels the interdiction of departure from the country on the part of the inhabitants liable to the conscription. Now it is certain that the approaching redemption of Israel occurs at a time when war is rife throughout the earth, and when therefore the Jews will universally be held in the grasp of military necessity just the time when a humanly-originated scheme for their restoration would be impracticable. This is said to be the time of Jacob's trouble:

> "Alas! for the day is great. It is even the time of Jacob's trouble; but he shall be saved out of it; for it shall come to pass in that day, saith the LORD of Hosts, that *I will break his yoke from off thy neck, and will burst thy bands, and strangers shall no more serve themselves of him.*" (Jeremiah 30:7,8)

This being so, it is interesting to enquire what steps will be taken to affect their release? Doubtless the summons will go forth a second time, "Let my people go that they may serve me".

This would appear from the statement, "I will say to the south **give up**, and to the north **keep not back**; *bring my sons from far, and my daughters from the ends of the earth*" (Isaiah 48:6). This message to the nations is substantially identical with the proclamation mentioned in Revelation 14:7 which issues by an agency there symbolised as an angel: "Fear God and give him glory, *for the hour of his judgment is come.*" Those that fear God will give him glory by hasting to deliver His people, and facilitating their transport to the Holy Land, by every means in their power; but this will not be the immediate result. The nations will not respond to the call before the hand of God's judgment is laid heavily upon them. They will ask like Pharaoh of old, "Who is the Lord that we should obey him?" The religious education that the royal personages of the present order of things receive, will be no bar to this attitude, because that education is not of a kind to prepare them for the political development of Jehovah's purposes in the latter days. They are taught to associate God and religion with ghostly regions unknown to which they also confine the jurisdiction of Jesus. Hence when he returns to the earth and interferes in the "temporal" affairs of men, they will never dream that God is in it, but will suppose that the demand addressed to them is the impertinence of some fanatical religious faction, bent upon realising the crotchet of Jewish restoration, and they will doubtless reject it resentfully. The sequel is brought before us in the following portions of scripture:

> "Shall the prey be taken from the mighty, or the lawful captive delivered? Thus saith the Lord, *Even the captives of the mighty ones shall be taken away and the prey of the terrible shall be delivered*: for **I will contend with him that contendeth with thee and I will save thy children; and I will feed them that oppress thee with their own blood** *and they shall be drunken with their own blood as with sweet wine* **and all flesh shall know that I the Lord am thy Saviour and thy Redeemer, the mighty One of Jacob**." (Isaiah 49:24-26)

This reveals a severity in the judgments which fall upon the latter day oppressors of Israel quite equalling, nay, surpassing those inflicted upon Egypt. Only by such crushing visitations could the besotted nations of these Gentile times be brought to perceive the hand of God in the operations of the time, and to promote readily the restoration of His people. The result of the judgment is depicted in the following testimonies:

"*The nations shall see and be confounded at all their might*: they shall lay their hand upon their mouth, their ears shall be deaf. They shall lick the dust like a serpent, they shall move out of their holes like worms of the earth: *they shall be afraid of the L*ORD *our God, and shall fear because of thee.*" (Micah 7:16,17)

"Thus saith the Lord GOD, Behold, I will lift up mine hand to the Gentiles, and set up my standard to the people: *and they shall bring thy sons in their arms, and thy daughters shall be carried upon their shoulders*. And kings shall be thy nursing fathers, and their queens thy nursing mothers: **they shall bow down to thee with their face toward the earth and lick up the dust of thy feet**." (Isaiah 49:22,23)

"It shall come that I will gather all nations and tongues (that is, by representation) and they shall come and see my glory. And I will set a sign among them, and I will send those that escape of them unto the nations (Tarshish, Pul, and Lud) that draw the bow, Tubal and Javan and the isles afar off, that have not heard my fame, neither have seen my glory: and they shall declare my glory among the Gentiles, *and they shall bring all your brethren for an offering unto the L*ORD*, out of all nations upon horses, and in chariots, and in litters, and upon mules, and upon swift beasts*, **to my holy mountain, Jerusalem**." (Isaiah 66:18-20)

The glorious results delineated in these testimonies will not be developed in an instant. It will take time; and it will involve the employment of agency on the part of God; for the trite saying that God works by means is emphatically true in this instance. The question is, by whom will the operations be conducted which results in the deliverance of the Jews? Moses and Aaron were the channel of God's communications with Pharaoh; who will stand between God and the nations at the crisis of the grander second exodus? The question seems to be met in one of the passages last quoted: "I **will send them that escape of the nations**." Who are these? The answer is suggested by the words of Jesus (Luke 21:36): "Pray that ye may be accounted **worthy to escape all these things**, *and to stand before the Son of man*." Those who are adjudged worthy, "out of every kindred, tongue and nation", to be made the companions of Jesus at his coming, will "escape" the judgments which will descend upon the world. As indicated in the following words:

> "Come my people, enter thou unto thy chambers and shut thy doors about thee. *Hide thyself as it were for a little moment*, **until the indignation be over past**; *for behold the* LORD *cometh out of his place to punish the inhabitants of the earth for their iniquity.*" (Isaiah 26:20,21)

In Revelation 17:14, the class thus secreted in divine protection, are said to be **with** the Lamb (called, chosen, and faithful) at the very crisis of national judgment described in Isaiah 66. In Revelation 4 they are said to "follow the Lamb whithersoever he goeth", which in the language of Apocalyptic symbol, can only mean that they are associated with him in everything he does. Hence, that they should be called upon to co-operate with him in the subordinate capacity of ambassadorship in the manner described in Isaiah 66:19, is extremely probable. The principle of co-operation has been observed from the beginning of Christ's connection with his people. At his first coming, he came to seek "the lost sheep of the house of Israel" and in carrying out this work, he employed his disciples – the seventy and the twelve – as agents, saying to them, "Go not into the way of the Gentiles, and into any city of the Samaritans, enter ye not, but go rather to the lost sheep of the house of Israel" (Matthew 10:5,6). On the point of his departure to heaven, he commissioned them to go unto all nations to do the work he was sent to accomplish, viz. to ingather his chosen ones by turning them from darkness to light; and at the death of the apostles, he signified his wish through Paul, that the work should be continued by faithful men, able to teach others (2 Timothy 2:2) so that the work of co-operation in Christ's present office now goes on, "the Spirit and **the bride** saying, Come". When he comes to "be glorified in his saints, and admired in all them that believe (2 Thessalonians 2) the work of co-operation is extended to the higher sphere of operations then inaugurated. He comes *"to raise up the tribes of Jacob, and restore the preserved of Israel"* (Isaiah 49:6), and in this work they are made to share. The mode in which they do so, as it seems to us, is set forth in the testimony from Isaiah under consideration. They are sent as his messengers throughout the world, to be agents in accomplishing it. There are several obstacles to the work which they have to remove. There is first the unbelief of the Jews. How will this be got over? Doubtless in the way in which it was overcome in the case of Moses. He was employed to work miracles in attestation of his mission, in case they should disbelieve him; and his exhibition of them had the desired effect. So the saints will be able to convince the Jews by signs and wonders, that they are messengers from the God of their fathers, and induce them to entrust themselves to their guidance. Having effected an understanding with the Jews in the several localities to which they may be sent; for while Moses and Aaron were sufficient for the work of deliverance from one country – Egypt, in which the whole nation was centred, it will take many messengers to accomplish a similar work extending over the entire surface of the globe. Not a Jew will be left ungathered. The testimony of Moses is:

> *"If any of thine be driven out unto the utmost parts of heaven, from thence will the* LORD *thy God gather thee, and from thence will he fetch thee."* (Deuteronomy 30:4)

And the testimony of Isaiah is:

> *"Ye shall be gathered* **one by one***, O ye children of Israel."* (27:12)

Having effected the understanding referred to, the next step will be to demand the consent of the powers holding them in servitude, to their departure for the land which by that time will have become the centre of events unparalleled in history.

But the want of space prevents the completion of the subject in the present article.

7 |

God's purpose with the Jews (6)

(April 1865)

CHRIST'S messengers having convinced Israel (as Moses convinced their forefathers in Egypt) that they have been sent by the God of their fathers in remembrance of the covenant with Abraham, Isaac and Jacob, and in remembrance of the land (Leviticus 26:42), the powers holding the Jews in vassalage will be summoned to let them go. That they will refuse is not only probable in view of the disposition of those in power, both now and in past times, but certain from the testimonies quoted last month which represent the deliverance of Israel as the result of compulsion brought to bear on their oppressors. But their refusal will avail no more than Pharaoh's:

"*The captives of the mighty shall be* **taken**, *and the prey of the terrible ones* **delivered**: *for I will contend with him that contendeth with thee, and I will save thy children."*

(Isaiah 49:25)

The mighty and the terrible of the earth can only be coerced. They are not open to suasion, especially where the thing they are desired to do is contrary to their likings. They will not be induced to let Israel go by argument; and therefore will be compelled by judgment. What form this judgment will take is not revealed; but that it is administered by the saints, and effective in its results, is certain from various testimonies. Daniel observed that at this crisis – the Ancient of days having come – "judgment was given to the saints of the most High" (Daniel 7:22); and that judgment is to be "given" to them in the executive sense, is manifest from David's description of the functions they will be called upon to perform:

> "To *execute vengeance upon the heathen*, and punishments upon the people, and to bind their kings with chains, and their nobles with fetters of iron; **to execute upon them the judgment written**; this honour have all the saints."
>
> (Psalm 149:7-9)

It is further made apparent by Christ's promise in Revelation 2:

> "To him that overcometh and keepeth my works unto the end, will I give *power over the nations*; and he shall rule them with a rod of iron; as the vessels of a potter shall they be broken to shivers, even as I have received of my father." (verses 26,27)

The point is further strengthened by the fact that when Christ is apocalyptically represented in collision with the beast and the kings of the earth and their armies, he is said to be accompanied by his "called and chosen and faithful" ones, showing that they are actively associated with him in the work of judgment; and also by such general statements as the prophecy of Enoch, recorded by Jude 14,15: "Behold the Lord cometh with **ten thousands of his saints**, *to execute judgment upon all*" and the statement of Joel and Zechariah, that at the crisis of the enemy's discomfiture at Jerusalem, which inaugurates God's coming interference in the affairs of men, and precedes the embassage of which we have been speaking, "the saints" accompany and form part of the manifestation of Yahweh's power in the descent of Jesus.

Whatever the saints, as the delegated representatives of a returned and wrath-executing Messiah, may do upon the refusal of the Gentile powers to let Israel go, the result is unequivocal. A display of power takes place which overawes the foe and exalts the saints to a position of dreaded authority. "Confounded at all their might" the nations quail before them and "creep out of their holes like worms of the earth" in great fear of "the Lord their God", and fearing because of a nation so "terrible from their beginning" (when the Canaanitish nations trembled at the report of their deeds) to that time, when the arm of God will again be bared throughout the earth on their behalf in the sight of the terrified nations of modern Gentiledom, in the judgments he will cause to be manifested in their midst for the chastisement and subjugation of a wicked and rebellious world as a preliminary to the outshine of that universal glory which shall enswathe the globe in the age of righteousness. In the terror of the time, the opposition to Israel melts away. They no longer refuse the demand of Israel's leaders, but sanction their departure, and not only sanction it, but extend assistance to it throughout the world. The movement does not take the shape of a flight. Israel does not hurry precipitately from their coasts as if beholden to a momentary panic among their enemies for the accomplishment of their deliverance. They leave with the dignified deliberation inspired by the fact that God is with them, and that no hostility can circumvent their procedure. This is evident from the following testimony:

> "Depart ye, depart ye, go ye out from thence; touch no unclean thing; go ye out of the midst of her; be ye clean that bear the vessels of the LORD (that is, the saints, the leaders of Israel at the coming of Christ, who are the antitypical priests or vessel bearers of Jehovah), **for ye shall not go out with haste, nor go by flight**; *for the* LORD *shall go before you, and the God of Israel will be your reward."* (Isaiah 52:11,12)

The nations co-operate in this movement:

> "Surely *the isles shall wait for me*, the ships of Tarshish first (by which there is reason to believe is meant the English and American marine) *to bring thy sons from far*, their silver and their gold with them unto the name of the LORD thy God, and to the Holy One of Israel, because he hath glorified thee." (Isaiah 60:9)

> "In that time shall the present be brought unto the LORD of Hosts of a people scattered and peeled, and from a people

terrible from their beginning hitherto, a nation meted out and trodden down, whose lands the river have spoiled, to the place of the name of the LORD of Hosts, the Mount Zion."

(Isaiah 18:7)

But there are stages in the work. The events we have described are not accomplished in a moment. The judgment on the nations will be progressive, as were those on Pharaoh. The departure of Israel for the land of the covenant will only take place when the steps taken by the king's messengers have created a universal recognition of the fact that Jehovah is working; and developed a disposition to help forward the work with alacrity. Those "steps" will involve great retributions in which the Jews themselves will take an active part. This is evident from such testimonies as the following:

"Turn you to the stronghold, ye prisoners of hope: even today do I declare that I will render double unto thee; when I have bent Judah for me, *filled the bow with Ephraim, and raised up thy sons O Zion, against thy sons, O Greece, and* **made thee as the sword of a mighty man**. And the LORD shall be seen over them, and his arrow shall go forth as lightning, and the Lord GOD shall blow the trumpet, and shall go as whirlwinds of the south. The LORD of Hosts shall defend them; and they shall devour, and subdue with sling-stones; and they shall drink, and make a noise as through wine; and they shall be filled like bowls, and as the corners of the altar. And the LORD their God shall save them in that day as the flock of his people: for they shall be as the stones of a crown, lifted up as an ensign upon his land." (Zechariah 9:12-16)

"Now also, many nations are gathered against thee, that say, let her be defiled, and let our eye look upon Zion. But they know not the thoughts of the LORD, neither understand they his counsel, *for he shall gather them as the sheaves into the floor*; **Arise and thresh, O daughter of Zion**: *for I will make thine horn iron, and I will make thy hoofs brass*. **And thou shalt beat in pieces many people**. I will consecrate their gain unto the

Lord, and their substance unto the Lord of the whole earth." (Micah 4:11-13)

From this, it is evident that God will make use of Israel in the work of subduing their enemies. This is perhaps still more specifically stated in the following verses from Micah 5:

"The remnant of Jacob shall be among the Gentiles in the midst of many people, *as a lion amongst the beasts of the forest, as a young lion among the flocks of sheep: who, if he go through, both treadeth down and teareth in pieces, and none can deliver.* **Thine hand shall be lifted upon all thine adversaries, and all thine enemies shall be cut off**." (verses 8,9)

To a similar purport is the following testimony from Isaiah chapter 11:

"In that day, there shall be a root of Jesse, which shall stand for an ensign of the people; to it shall the Gentiles seek, and his rest shall be glorious … The envy also of Ephraim shall depart, and the adversaries of Judah shall be cut off. Ephraim shall not envy Judah, and Judah shall not vex Ephraim: *but they shall fly upon the shoulders of the Philistines towards the west, and shall spoil them of the east together. They shall lay their hand upon Edom and Moab, and the children of Ammon shall obey them.*" (verses 10-14)

"Fear not, thou worm Jacob, and ye men of Israel; I will help thee, saith the Lord, and thy redeemer, the Holy One of Israel. **Behold, I will make thee a new sharp threshing instrument, having teeth**: *thou shalt thresh the mountains (kingdoms), and beat them small, and shalt make the hills (nations) as chaff. Thou shalt fan them, and carry them away, and the whirlwind shall scatter them*; and thou shalt rejoice in the Lord, and glory in the Holy One of Israel." (Isaiah 41:14-16)

Thus, as in the Egyptian deliverance, the miraculous interference which initiates the redemption of the Jews from universal bondage, will be followed up by military achievements on the part of the nation itself, which as of old, will strike terror into their enemies, and revive the fame of Israel's God as the foundation of the "glory to God in the highest", which will prevail in the age of Israelitish supremacy to follow. In view of this, the following statement will be intelligible:

> "**Thou art my battle axe and weapons of war**; *for with thee will I break in pieces the nations, and with thee will I destroy kingdoms.* And with thee will I break in pieces the horse and his rider; and with thee will I break in pieces the chariot and his rider; with thee will I break in pieces, man and woman … and with thee will I break in pieces, captains and rulers."
> (Jeremiah 51:20-23)

This judicial employment of Israel as a military instrument will precede the process by which they will themselves be prepared for settlement in the land of promise, even as Israel under Moses and Joshua were made the agent of punishment upon Egypt, Amalek, and other wicked nations in the east, before their own settlement in the land under the judges. "The nations shall see, and be confounded at all their might", even while perchance they may be in their present unsanctified condition. The object of the operations conducted by their agency, under the leadership of the saints, is to make God known among the nations of the Gentiles, as the indispensable preliminary to the establishment of His authority in peace over a rejoicing earth. This purpose carried out, and the Gentiles made willingly accessory to Israel's restoration, the next part of the divine programme will affect Israel themselves. The discipline of the nations will be succeeded by the discipline of Israel, who, as we have seen in a previous article, are not prepared for an immediate transfer to the jurisdiction of the Messiah. They have to be enlightened and purified and morally subdued, which will be accomplished by a second sojourn in the wilderness, where the corrupt elements of the nation will be expurgated, and the remnant brought into the bond of the covenant. They will likely be conveyed to some port in the Mediterranean, to the south of the land of promise, probably to Alexandria, whence they will be led to the scenes of the nation's birth, three thousand years ago, there to renew acquaintance with the God of their fathers under an administration which will rigorously convince them of the national crimes of which they have been guilty, and open their eyes to the glories of the new covenant which they have blindly despised, and whose messenger they put to death.

There is great reason for believing that Elijah the prophet, who like Enoch "was translated that he should not see death", will have something to do with this stage of affairs, and may, in fact, appear on the scene earlier than the point to which we have brought the development of events. The first testimony suggesting this supposition is as follows:

> "Behold, I will send you Elijah the prophet before the coming of the great and dreadful day of the LORD; and he shall turn the heart of the fathers to the children, and the heart of the children to their fathers, lest I come and smite the earth with a curse." (Malachi 4:5,6)

This promise has never been fulfilled in the specific sense that would be apprehended from the reading of the statement. It is true that Jesus said, "Elias has already come" (Matthew 17:12) in reference to the appearance and work of John the Baptist; but this statement does not preclude the coming of the real Elijah at a future time, for several reasons. In the first place, it was testified of John before his birth that he should "go forth *in the spirit and power of Elijah*" (Luke 1:17), which would warrant the saying of Christ – who often spoke in a representative sense – that Elijah *had* come. In the second place, Jesus while making the very statement in question, specifically said *"Elias truly* **shall first come** *and restore all things"* (Matthew 17:11) for which words there could be no meaning or application, if there was to be no other coming of Elijah than that which at the time Jesus spoke, was an accomplished fact, John having finished his testimony in martyrdom. In the third place, the coming of Elijah spoken of by Malachi was to occur *"before the coming of the great and dreadful day of the LORD"*. Now the mission of John related to "the acceptable year of the Lord" and not to the "day of vengeance of our God". He was the harbinger of Christ's appearance as "the Lamb of God to take away the sin of the world" and proclaimed his approach in these words (John 1:29). His mission was "to make ready a people prepared for the Lord" (Luke 1:17) by creating the expectation of Christ's approach and disposing the minds of the good and honest hearted of Israel to receive him when he should appear. Now, since Christ at his coming in weakness had a forerunner in the person of John the Baptist, who was invested with the "spirit and power of Elias", what more appropriate than that his coming in power and great glory, should also be preceded by the appearance of John's prototype, the stern judicial prophet of whom John was but the representative, viz. Elijah himself who must be presumed to have an engrossing interest in Christ's work seeing he appeared on the mount of transfiguration and "spake of the decease which he should accomplish at Jerusalem". The testimony of Malachi is that he will be sent as a forerunner of this great and dreadful day, and it specifies his mission in words which are significant enough, though at first they may not convey a very definite idea to Western minds, viz. "to turn the hearts of the fathers to the children and the hearts of the children to their fathers", that is, to induce such a moral change among the Jews that the fathers will have the humility and tractableness of children, and children the wisdom and understanding of their fathers, or in general, as paraphrased by the angel in his message to Elizabeth, the mother of John, "to turn the disobedient to the wisdom of the just" (Luke 1:17). John accomplished this to a limited extent at the first advent; and it is the mission of Elijah to realise it to the utmost at the second.

The testimony concerning Elijah does not require us to expect his appearance before Christ's actual presence in the earth, but simply that he shall precede Christ in his dealings with Israel. This is evident in the case of John, who was no less a forerunner than he, and yet Christ was in the midst of Israel before John commenced his proclamation. So in all probability, Christ will again arrive upon the scene of operations before Elijah commences those dealings with the nation which terminate in their introduction to the Messiah whom their fathers rejected. It is meet that this should be the case, because Elijah may be considered in the light simply of a lieutenant-general holding his commission from Jesus, as "King of kings and Lord of lords" whose prerogative it is to initiate the great drama of which Elijah's mission will form but a subordinate part. That he is to be sent "before the coming of the great and dreadful day of the LORD" may simply mean that his mission to Israel (while commencing actually after Christ's arrival from heaven) will be carried out before that final culminating outburst of divine judgment which, after the manner of the catastrophe at the Red Sea, will give the death-blow to the power of the enemy who till then will have been permitted to antagonise the divine operations. The nation's introduction to Jesus takes place at Jerusalem (Zechariah 12:10) and at this time they are in a subdued state. Softened with the "spirit of grace and supplication" poured abundantly upon them and enlightened by the great events of the period, they look upon him whom their fathers pierced, and mourn with the bitterness of genuine grief. But before this, the great forerunner, appointed "to make ready" on the national scale, "a people prepared for the Lord" will have completed the process which in the wilderness will put an end to "the blindness in part which hath happened unto Israel" and abolish the veil which for three thousand years has obstructed the spiritual vision of the nation.

It is mainly by reference to Jehovah's dealings in the past with His nation that we are enabled to lift the curtain which in the prophetic word conceals from our view the operations during the second sojourn of Israel in the wilderness. The fact that this sojourn will take place is apparent with its objects and effects; but the manner of it, and the shape of it, are not revealed. So much is said, however, as to give us the expectation that the miracles of the wilderness will be repeated. A nation of three or four millions led into the wastes of Arabia would be no less straitened for supplies under Elijah in the nineteenth century after Christ, than under Moses in the fifteenth century before

Christ. Accordingly, we have the following intimations which it is impossible to apply to any other crisis than that under consideration:

> "Remember ye not the former things neither consider the things of old. Behold I will do a new thing; now, it shall spring forth; shall ye not know it? *I will even make a way in the wilderness and rivers in the desert.* The beasts of the field shall honour me, the dragons and the owls; *because I give waters in the wilderness, and rivers in the desert, to give drink to my people, to my chosen.* This people have I formed for myself; they shall show forth all my praise." (Isaiah 43:18-21)

> "When the poor and needy seek water, and there is none, and their tongue faileth for thirst, I the LORD will hear them, I the God of Israel will not forsake them. *I will open rivers in high places and fountains in the midst of the valleys: I will make the wilderness a pool of water, and the dry land springs of water.* I will plant in the wilderness the cedar, the shittah tree, and the myrtle, and the oil tree: I will set in the desert the fir tree, and the pine and the box tree together: *that they may see and know and consider and understand together, that the hand of the LORD hath done this, and the Holy One of Israel hath created it.*" (Isaiah 41:17-20)

The completion of the subject must be reserved for a further article.

8 |

God's purpose with the Jews (7)

(June 1865)

IN previous articles on God's purpose to restore the Jews to national existence and power in the Holy Land under Christ, we have spoken of the nation as a whole without taking into account the political sections into which it is, or rather was divided, in relation to that event. Something must now be added about "both houses of Israel" (Isaiah 7:1) in order to complete the reader's apprehension of the events attending the 'restoration of the kingdom again to Israel.'

The division of the Jewish nation into "the house of Israel" and "the house of Judah" originated in the reign of Solomon's immediate successor, Rehoboam. Divinely considered, the event was consequent on the crimes of Solomon, in turning aside from the God of Abraham, and devoting himself, under feminine seduction, to the worship of the abominations of surrounding idolatry; from a human point of view, it was the result of Rehoboam's arrogant bearing towards the tribes who waited upon him on Solomon's death, to request a mitigation of the burdens which had prevailed during the reign of his father. The ten tribes revolted, and elected Jeroboam, one of Solomon's servants, as their king. Rehoboam summoned the hosts of faithful Judah and Benjamin, to bring back the refractory tribes to their allegiance; but while preparations for war were going forward, a message from God through the prophet Shemaiah deterred him from his purpose, and the ten tribes were allowed to go in peace. From that date (975 BC), the history of the Jews for a time ran in two separate channels – the history of Israel and the history of Judah – which are kept carefully distinct in the books of Kings and Chronicles. It was not long, however, before the former came to an abrupt termination. At the end of 270 years, after an unbroken career of idolatry and wickedness, the ten tribes were subjugated by Shalmaneser, king of Assyria, who from a desire to keep their territory effectually under his dominion, removed the inhabitants to a remote part of his empire, and replaced them by his own subjects. The testimony on the subject is as follows:

> "In the ninth year of Hoshea, the king of Assyria took Samaria, *and carried Israel away into Assyria*, and placed them in Halah and Habor by the river of Gozan, and in the cities of the Medes ... And the king of Assyria, brought men from Babylon and from Cuthah, and from Ava, and from Hamath, and from Sepharvaim, *and placed them in the cities of Samaria instead of the children of Israel*, and they possessed Samaria, and dwelt in the cities thereof." (2 Kings 17:6,24)

From this disaster, the ten tribes never recovered. Their captivity beyond the Euphrates so far as history informs us, proved final and hopeless, unrelieved by the smallest subsequent reversal of fortune. It is an impression with some that they shared in the favour subsequently manifested by Cyrus towards Judah and Benjamin, and returned with those two tribes in considerable bodies to settle in the land under Ezra and Nehemiah; but there does not appear to be any foundation for this supposition, which we may remark, is mainly put forward by those who, disbelieving in the future restoration of Israel, strive to find in the events of the Babylonish restoration, the fulfilments of certain predictions which include the ten tribes in the promise of restoration. The mention of "Israel" inhabiting "their cities when the restoration from Babylon was completed" (Ezra 2:70; 3:1; Nehemiah 7:1) does not necessarily suggest the participation of any part of the ten tribes in the return; because the word 'Israel' throughout the narrative is used in its national sense, and applied to the two tribes as integral parts of the nation. This is evident from verse 7 of Nehemiah 7, where introducing the pedigree of "the children of the province that went up out of the captivity, of those that had been carried away, *whom Nebuchadnezzar the King of Babylon had carried away*" it uses these words: "The number of *the men of the people of Israel* was this", etc., after which the families of Judah and Benjamin are enumerated, showing that Judah and Benjamin were regarded as "the people of Israel". The genealogical lists of those who returned furnish the best disproof of the supposition that the ten tribes took part in the return, since those lists are entirely restricted to Judah and Benjamin, and the orders connected with the temple service; and those lists, it must be remembered cover the entire number that came up from Babylon with the exception of 642, who could not prove their genealogies. The latter may have belonged to the ten tribes; but we may with equal reason presume that they were descendants of broken and isolated families of Judah and Benjamin, who had lost trace of their connection in the confusion of the captivity. Certainly no serious person would rest the theory of the restoration of the ten tribes on the circumstance of 642 unregistered people accompanying the attested descendants of Judah and Benjamin from Babylon. It is testified that when Nebuchadnezzar made Gedaliah governor of Judah, after completing the ruin of the country:

> "All the Jews that were in Moab, and among the Ammonites, and in Edom and in all the countries, returned out of all places whither they were driven, and came to the land of Judah."
>
> (Jeremiah 40:11,12)

Some construe this statement into evidence of the return of the ten tribes; but this is if possible a more untenable position than the other, for the natural supposition that the Jews spoken of were fugitive members of Judah and Benjamin, who, during the invasion of Nebuchadnezzar, had taken refuge in the adjacent mountain countries, is distinctly borne out by a statement in

Jeremiah 43:5, which describes them as "**the remnant of Judah** *that were returned from all nations whither they had been driven*". We find mention in the New Testament of least one person belonging to the ten tribes residing in Jerusalem, namely, Anna, of the tribe of Asher, who appeared in the temple on the occasion of Christ's circumcision. There may have been, and doubtless were, others of Israelitish stock residing in a settled manner in Judaea, but the fact is accounted for apart from the supposition that a restoration of the ten tribes had taken place. In the first place, when the ten tribes revolted from the house of David, they abandoned the Law of Moses, and the worship of God, and turned to idolatry; in consequence of which, all the devout-hearted among them separated from them and took up their stay in Judah. This fact is set forth in the following testimony:

> "And the priests and the Levites that were in all Israel resorted to him (Rehoboam) out of all their coasts ... and after them, *out of all the tribes of Israel* **such as set their hearts to seek the LORD God of Israel** *came to Jerusalem*, to sacrifice unto the LORD God of their fathers." (2 Chronicles 11:13-16)

This would account for such cases as that of Anna, of the tribe of Asher. On the day of Pentecost, there seems to have been representatives of the ten tribes present at Jerusalem: "Jews, devout men, out of every nation under heaven, Parthians, *Medes and Elamites, dwellers in Mesopotamia*" (Acts 2:5,9). We may presume that the Jewish exiles in these countries, comprising remnants of the ten tribes, had been in the habit within the previous hundred years at least, of coming up to the feasts from these remote parts, and not unlikely, some might settle in the land, and thus account for the presence of families belonging to the ten tribes in the land. But the idea that the tribes as such were restored is utterly untenable. It is entirely discountenanced by the fact that so late as the time of Jesus, the northern parts of Palestine, where the territories of the lost tribes principally lay, were still inhabited by "the Samaritans", that is, by the descendants of the alien race which Shalmanezer planted in the country when he deported the ten tribes; and so active was the sense of the national disgrace involved in this fact, that it was a notorious maxim of which the woman of Samaria reminded Jesus, that "the Jews had no dealings with the Samaritans".

As to where the ten tribes are, the question is one involved in considerable obscurity. Some eastern travellers who have extended their wanderings beyond the Euphrates in search of them, speak of coloured tribes to be found in Mesopotamia and the neighbouring regions, possessing copies of the law, and observing Mosaic practices. A satisfactory conclusion, however can scarcely be drawn from this circumstance, since other travellers allege that the Orientals in general have inherited Israelitish traditions and practices in a corrupted form. It is not improbable that some of these tribes may be the descendants of Israel; but it is still less improbable that the ten tribes are largely intermixed with the Jews now scattered throughout Europe and America. The military tornadoes that repeatedly swept over Assyria long after the Assyrian captors of Israel had disappeared commencing with the conquests of Alexander the Macedon whose invincible legions penetrated into Persia, could not fail to affect the captive tribes who lay in the path from Asia to Europe. Exposed to the constant depredations of military marauders, they would be prevented from consolidating into organised communities. Large numbers would be impelled to seek a safer asylum in other parts, while others would be impressed by the soldiery for menial services, and mayhap carried to other countries to be sold as slaves. In this way, they would come to be distributed as widely as their brethren of Jerusalem were, after the destruction of the city by the Romans. What changes of this sort might not take place in so many years in a country which for many centuries was the theatre of vast military operations? One thing is certain, that the ten tribes are not now to be found at the seat of their original captivity, in anything like the numbers that ought to be found if they continued in a body in the locality to which Shalmaneser removed them. On the other hand, if they have in great part been scattered throughout the world, and are now indiscriminately mixed with their brethren of Judah and Benjamin, how can they be spoken of or contemplated as the ten tribes? Genealogical reckoning has long ceased among the Jews. It was interrupted by the national catastrophe which broke up their commonwealth in the first century, and has never been resumed. The consequence is that the demarcation of the tribes is entirely obliterated, and the tribes themselves, even if existing in the unorganised multitude of modern Jews, are lost in hopeless confusion. Here is a difficulty in view of God's declared purpose to re-settle Israel in Palestine according to their tribes. All we can say is that God is equal to any difficulty. There may be ways out of it that are unknown to man. God may have preserved the lines of descent in spite of the adversity which to the human eye has entirely set them aside, and may be ready when the time arrives to reveal the tribes in their distinct genealogical divisions; or He may have hid the exiled tribes together in some of the countries contiguous to that to which they were originally removed by Shalmaneser, where, continuing, it may be, the practices of idolatry which distinguished them for so many years before their banishment from Jehovah's presence, they present to the traveller, after the lapse of 3,000 years, no evidences of their originality. However this may be, one thing is certain, and that is, that the ten tribes will *as such* participate in the great restoration under Christ which we have already seen to be God's declared purpose. This appears from a variety of testimony. Nothing more emphatic can be cited than the words which occur in Jeremiah 3:18:

> "In those days, the house of Judah shall walk **with the house of Israel**, and they shall come **together** out of the land of the north, to the land that I have given for an inheritance unto your fathers."

Following naturally upon these words, comes the declaration of the Spirit through Ezekiel in chapter 37 of that prophet's writings:

"I will make them **one nation** in the land upon the mountains of Israel, and one king shall be king to them all, *and they shall be no more* **two nations**, *neither shall they be divided into* **two kingdoms** *any more at all."* (verse 22)

The transaction in connection with which this statement was made, gives great point to the idea expressed. The prophet was commanded (verse 15) to take two sticks, and having written upon one, "for Judah and for the children of Israel his companions", and upon the other, "for Joseph the stick of Ephraim and for all the house of Israel his companions", he put them together and they became one, in his hand and then in answer to the natural question of the people, what was meant by such a strange procedure, he delivered the prediction that God would one day unite the two hostile sections of His people into one kingdom under a beloved one, even the Christ. The same purpose is apparent in other predictions. The new covenant for instance spoken of by Jeremiah is to be made *"with the house of Israel* **and** *with the house of Judah"* (31:31). In Ezekiel 16 the kingdom of Judah is addressed with reference to the greater magnitude of its sins as compared with those of Sodom and the ten tribes; and in allusion to God's ultimate purpose with the latter, it is stated that Samaria and her daughters (a comprehensive designation for the ten tribes) "**shall return to their former estate**". In Ezekiel 48, a re-apportionment of the territory of the holy land among the twelve tribes of Israel, is predicted. The words in which this is most specifically apparent are as follows: *"This is the land which ye shall divide by lot* **unto the tribes of Israel for inheritance**, and these are their portions saith the Lord GOD" (verse 29). There is another testimony in which the necessity for the restoration of the ten tribes is made apparent. We refer to Isaiah 8:1: "He (Christ as the manifestation of Jehovah) shall be ... for a stone of stumbling, and for a rock of offence to **both the houses of Israel**." This has only been fulfilled as regards one of the houses of Israel, viz., the house of Judah. The ten tribes have never been in contact with Christ, and have therefore never had an opportunity of stumbling at him from which it follows that they must be recovered from their present obscurity and ruin, and in some way brought into such a relationship with Jesus as that they will stumble at him like their brethren 1,800 years ago. We can only speculate as to the form which this relationship will take. It may be that when reclaimed from captivity, and nationally organised, they will refuse to believe in the prophet like unto Moses, who having returned to superintend the restitution of all things spoken of by the prophets, will claim their allegiance; following upon which disbelief, God's judgment may go forth against them as against their fathers, with whom he was grieved in the wilderness, and whose carcasses fell because of unbelief. Thus Christ would prove a rock of offence to them as he did to Judah, though with consequences of much less severity as regards duration, and this not without justice, since Judah with far greater privileges, was guilty of refusing the law of God, killing his prophets, and finally putting to death the Son of his love, in the guilt of which Israel had no part. Those consequences, however, though less severe than those which during a long night of 180 years has crushed out the life from the kingdom of Judah, will be effectual for the chastisement of Israel, and develop the same moral results as in the case of Judah, purging out from among them the rebels, subduing them to perfect submission to the God of their fathers, and generally prepare them for settling in the land of promise under the perfect government of their long promised Messiah.

9

God's purpose with the Jews (8)

(July 1865)

THE result of the chastisement to which the ten tribes will be subjected, is graphically set forth in the following testimony from Jeremiah, in which they are spoken of under the name of Ephraim:

> "*I have surely heard Ephraim bemoaning himself thus; Thou hast chastised me, and I was chastised, as a bullock unaccustomed to the yoke: turn thou me, and I shall be turned; for thou art the* LORD *my God.* Surely after that I was turned, I repented; and after that I was instructed, I smote upon my thigh: I was ashamed, yea, even confounded, because I did bear the reproach of my youth. Is Ephraim my dear son? Is he a pleasant child? For since I spake against him, I do earnestly remember him still; therefore my bowels are troubled for him; *I will surely have mercy upon him, saith the* LORD. Set thee up waymarks, make thee high heaps: set thine heart toward the highway, even the way which thou wentest: turn again, O virgin of Israel, turn again to these thy cities. How long wilt thou go about O thou backsliding daughter? For the LORD hath created a new thing in the earth, A woman shall compass a man. *Thus saith the* LORD *of hosts, the God of Israel; As yet they shall use this speech in the land of Judah and in the cities thereof, when I shall bring again their captivity; The* LORD *bless thee, O habitation of justice, and mountain of holiness. And there shall dwell in Judah itself, and in all the cities thereof together, husbandmen, and they that*

go forth with flocks. For I have satiated the weary soul, and I have replenished every sorrowful soul. Upon this I awaked, and beheld; and my sleep was sweet unto me. Behold the days come saith the LORD, *that I will sow the house of Israel and the house of Judah with the seed of man, and with the seed of beast. And it shall come to pass, that like as I have watched over them, to pluck up and break down, and to throw down, and to destroy and to afflict; so will I watch over them to build, and to plant, saith the* LORD." (31:18-28)

To the ten tribes in their present position, the following words are addressed:

"O Israel, thou hast destroyed thyself, but *in me is thine help*: I **will be thy king**. Where is any other that may save thee in all thy cities, and thy judges of whom thou saidst, Give me a king and princes?" (Hosea 13:9,10)

God has never been the help of the ten tribes since their self-destruction. He has never been their King since the day they were taken to Assyria by Shalmaneser. Their history in the dreary interval has been a blank desolation. They have had no national existence. Their very name has been struck off the roll of nations. We should know nothing about Ephraim but for the archives of the house of Judah which tell us of their missing tribes, and the cause of their downfall. But we are told in the testimonies quoted that God "will have mercy upon Ephraim"; that He "will sow the house of Israel with the seed of man, and the seed of beast", and that as He has broken down and destroyed them, "so will He watch over them to build and to plant them", and "will make a new covenant with them", under which they will have knowledge of Him to perfection, and obey Him to the full. We have also the following promise for them. God tells them they have reaped misfortune because of their iniquity, and exhorts them to repentance; and then says:

"I will heal their backsliding, I will love them freely, for mine anger is turned away; *I will be as the dew unto Israel: he shall grow as the lily, and cast forth his roots as Lebanon, his branches shall spread, and his beauty shall be as the olive tree, and his smell as Lebanon.* They that dwell under his shadow shall return (recover): they shall revive as the corn, and grow as the vine; the scent thereof shall be as the wine of Lebanon."

(Hosea 14:4-7)

A time of national prosperity and greatness is therefore in reserve for the ten tribes. The branches of Israel will spread till they cover the earth. "Israel shall blossom and bud and cover the face of the world with fruit" (Isaiah 27:6) and the nations dwelling under the cool shadow, and eating of the fruit of this wide-spreading tree of political life, will grow and prosper. "They shall revive as the corn, and grow as the vine." At present, the world in the figurative sense in which we speak is a parched and blighted wilderness. Wickedness prevails, and misery afflicts mankind: but the blessing of Abraham is promised for all nations, and will be realised when the seed of Abraham, individual and national, covers the earth as a garment of salvation in the days of the Branch of Righteousness.

According to the prophetic intimation of Hosea, "The children of Israel have abidden many days without a king and without a prince and without a sacrifice" but "**afterwards**", says the prophet, *"shall they return and seek the* LORD *their God and David* (Christ) *their king, and shall fear the* LORD *and his goodness in the latter days"* (Hosea 3:4,5).

When this occurs, when the ten tribes stand forth from their hiding place of centuries, and unite with the house of Judah in the formation of "one nation in the land upon the mountains of Israel", we may then look for the fulfilment of the following testimonies:

"Thus saith the LORD; Behold, I will bring again the captivity of Jacob's tents, and have mercy on his dwelling places; and the city shall be builded upon her own heap, and the palace shall remain after the manner thereof. And out of them shall proceed thanksgiving and the voice of them that make merry: and I will multiply them, and they shall not be few; I will also glorify them, and they shall not be small. Their children also shall be established before me, and I will punish all that oppress them. And their nobles shall be of themselves, and their governor shall proceed from the midst of them; *and I will cause him to draw near, and he shall approach unto me*: for who is this that engaged his heart to approach unto me? saith the LORD." (Jeremiah 30:18-21)

"I will cleanse them from all their iniquities whereby they have sinned against me: and I will pardon all their iniquities whereby they have sinned, and whereby they have transgressed against me. *And it shall be unto me a name of joy, a praise, and an honour before all the nations of the earth* **which shall hear all the good that I do unto them**; *and they shall fear and tremble* **for all the goodness and for all the prosperity that I procure unto it**." (Jeremiah 33:8,9)

"For in mine holy mountain, in the mountain of the height of Israel, saith the Lord GOD, *there shall all the house of Israel, all of them in the land, serve me*: there will I accept them, and there will I require your offerings and the firstfruits of your oblations with all your holy things. And I will accept you with your sweet savour, when I bring you out from the people, and gather you out of the countries wherein ye have been scattered, and I will be sanctified in you before the heathen." (Ezekiel 20:40,41)

"Thus saith the Lord GOD; when I shall have gathered the house of Israel from the people among whom they are scattered and shall be sanctified in them in the sight of the heathen, *then shall they dwell in the land that I have given to my servant Jacob. And they shall dwell safely therein and shall build houses and plant vineyards, yea, they shall dwell with confidence* **when I have executed judgments upon all them that despise them round about**; and they shall know that I am the LORD their God." (Ezekiel 28:25,26)

"I will make with them a covenant of peace, and will cause the evil beasts to cease out of the land: and they shall dwell safely in the wilderness and sleep in the woods. And I will make them and the places round about my hill a blessing: and I will cause the shower to come down in his season; there shall be showers of blessings. And the tree of the field shall yield her fruit, and the earth shall yield her increase and they shall be safe in their own land." (Ezekiel 34:25-27)

"Thus saith the Lord GOD; In the day that I shall have cleansed you from all your iniquities, I will also cause you to dwell in the cities, and the wastes shall be builded. And the desolate land shall be tilled, whereas it lay desolate in the sight of all that passed by; and they shall say, This land that was desolate is become like the garden of Eden, and the waste and desolate and ruined cities are become fenced, and are inhabited."

(Ezekiel 36:33-35)

"Violence shall no more be heard in thy land, wasting nor destruction within thy borders but thou shalt call thy walls salvation and thy gates praise. The sun shall be no more thy light by day; neither for brightness shall the moon give light unto thee: but the LORD shall be unto thee an everlasting light, and thy God thy glory. Thy sun shall no more go down; neither shall thy moon withdraw itself; for the LORD shall be thine everlasting light, and the days of thy mourning shall be ended. Thy people shall be all righteous; they shall inherit the land for ever, the branch of my planting, the work of my hands, that I may be glorified. A little one shall become a thousand, and a small one a strong nation, I the LORD will hasten it in his time." (Isaiah 60:18-23)

"For I will take away the names of Baalim out of her mouth, and they shall no more be remembered by their name. And in that day will I make a covenant for them with the beasts of the field, and with the fowls of heaven, and with the creeping things of the ground: and I will break the bow and the sword and the battle out of the earth, and will make them to lie down safely. And I will betroth thee unto me forever; yea, I will betroth thee unto me in righteousness, and in judgment, and in lovingkindness, and in mercies." (Hosea 2:17-19)

"And it shall come to pass in that day that the mountains shall drop down new wine, and the hills shall flow with milk, and all the rivers of Judah shall flow with waters, and a fountain shall come forth of the house of the Lord, and shall water the valley of Shittim. Egypt shall be a desolation, and Edom, shall be a desolate wilderness, for the violence against the children of Judah, because they have shed innocent blood in their land. But Judah shall dwell forever, and Jerusalem from generation to generation. For I will cleanse their blood that I have not cleansed: for the LORD dwelleth in Zion."

(Joel 3:18-21)

"Behold, the days come, saith the LORD, that the plowman shall overtake the reaper, and the treader of grapes him that soweth seed; and the mountains shall drop sweet wine, and all the hills shall melt. And I will bring again the captivity of my people of Israel, and they shall build the waste cities, and inhabit them; and they shall plant vineyards, and drink the wine thereof; they shall also make gardens, and eat the fruit of them. And I will plant them upon their own land, and they shall no more be pulled up out of their land which I have given them, saith the LORD thy God." (Amos 9:13-15)

We have quoted these testimonies, because they tell of Israel's coming glory more eloquently and impressively than any words of human dictation; they contain the essence of the subject undiluted with explanatory verbiage, and will strike home with the greater force upon every earnest mind convinced of the truth of the holy oracles. Taken as a whole, they present a picture of very definite outline and unmistakable tints: Palestine transformed from a wilderness to paradise; Jerusalem exalted from ruin and debasement to towering rank and importance over all nations; the Jews ingathered from universal exile, purified and made righteous, and settled in the land after their old estates; Christ returned and ruling them in righteousness on the throne of David; the curse removed, blessing outpoured, knowledge and wisdom abounding, righteousness overflowing, peace and unmolested happiness reigning over all, and all in the safe keeping of the Rock of Israel – the Eternal Power of the Universe who faints not neither is weary, who knows no change in His purpose nor limit to His power; this is the gorgeous vision which looms through the prophetic telescope, and sends the rays of coming light athwart the heavens of our present night. "Happy are the people that are in such a case: happy is that people whose God is Jehovah."

Israel's glory will eclipse that of the Gentiles: that is to say, the power and independence of Gentiledom as made up of European and other nationalities will cease to exist when the prosperity of the Jews has set in. The two could not co-exist; they are incompatible. The restoration of the Jews will be more than a restoration to national life. It will be more than a simple elevation to a place in "the family of nations" and a share in "the balance of power" after the style of the proposed Polish and Hungarian restoration. It will be the establishment of an overshadowing power in the earth – a power that will coerce the submission of every other. The times of the Gentiles will have run out in every sense, when "the year of recompenses for the controversy of Zion" arrives. Their kingdoms will fall when Zion uprises to the splendour portrayed in Isaiah 60; in other words, when the kingdom of God comes in, the kingdom of men must go out. The kingdoms of this world become the kingdoms of our Lord Jesus Christ, when Jesus descends to "build again the tabernacle of David that is fallen down". The kingdom of Israel will become the head. At present, it is "the tail", in accordance with the prediction of Moses who said:

> "If thou will not hearken unto the voice of the LORD thy God ... the stranger that is within thee shall get up above thee very high; and *thou shalt come down very low* ... he shall be the head and thou shalt be the tail."   (Deuteronomy 28:15,43,44)

But a change is coming. The divine decree is recorded:

> "The LORD shall make thee **the head**, and not the tail; and thou shalt be **above** only, and thou shalt not be beneath."
> (Deuteronomy 28:13)

> "To thee shall it come, even the **first dominion**; the kingdom shall come to the daughter of Jerusalem." (Micah 4:8)

> "The nation and kingdom **that will not serve thee** *shall perish*; yea those nations shall be utterly wasted."
> (Isaiah 60:12)

> "I will get them praise and fame in every land where they have been put to shame ... I will make you a name and a praise among all people of the earth when I turn back your captivity before your eyes, saith the LORD." (Zephaniah 3:19,20)

This position of political pre-eminence will be associated with moral influence of the most potent and salutary description. All that the Gentiles now possess in the shape of true civilization can be traced to the Jews. The high moral impulse which finds its expression in associative philanthropy and individual heroism, originated in Jerusalem. The stimulus which in the course of generations has quickened Gentile intellect and developed Gentile greatness, comes from the Bible; and the Bible is but the compiled archives of the Jews. "Beginning at Jerusalem": this is a principle illustrated in more ways than one. It has prevailed in the feeble past and it will triumph gloriously in the resplendent future. The Jews (nationally) will be the teachers of the world in the future age. From them, the Gentiles will learn the spirit and the institutions of the new order of things, for which they will first be prepared by a period of judgment that will take the pride from their arrogant hearts, and convince them of the entire folly of the order of things that now obtains, both political and religious:

> "The Gentiles shall come unto thee from the ends of the earth, and shall say, *Surely our fathers have inherited lies, vanity, and things wherein there is no profit.*" (Jeremiah 16:19)

> "Ten men shall take hold out of all the languages of the nations, even shall take hold of the skirt of him that is a Jew,

saying, *We will go with you, for we have heard that God is with you."* (Zechariah 8:23)

The Gentile nations will "go with" the Jews in that age for the purpose of learning the way of God. This appears from such testimonies as the following:

"Many people shall go and say, Come ye, and let us go up to the mountain of the LORD, to the house of the God of Jacob, *and he will teach us of his ways and we will walk in his paths*, for out of Zion shall go forth the law and the word of the LORD from Jerusalem." (Isaiah 2:3)

"The nations shall go up from year to year to worship the King the LORD of Hosts, and to keep the feast of tabernacles." (Zechariah 14:16)

"Yea, many people and strong nations shall come to seek the LORD of Hosts in Jerusalem, and to pray before the LORD." (Zechariah 8:22)

This agrees with Jeremiah 3:17:

"At that time they shall call Jerusalem **the throne of the LORD**: and all the nations shall be gathered unto it, to the name of the LORD, to Jerusalem: *neither shall they walk any more after the imagination of their evil heart."*

This will exalt Jerusalem to a position to which there is no parallel in all history. Rome and Mecca sink into contemptible insignificance before the splendour of a religious and political metropolis where Deity will be visibly manifested for the regulation of human turbulence, and the dissipation of human ignorance.

"In this mountain, I will make unto all people a feast of fat things, of fat things full of marrow, of wines on the lees well refined, *and in this mountain I will destroy the face of the covering cast over all people, and the vail that is spread over all nations."* (Isaiah 25:6-8)

The devotions and ceremonies connected with the shrines of popular superstition in various parts of the world, including even the "Holy places" themselves, which by the fooleries of fanatical "pilgrims" fostered by a corrupt and scheming priesthood, are made to stink as much in the divine nostrils as the brazen serpent of His own appointment when it was made an object of idolatry by Israel – have been fruitful of nothing but evil to men and nations; but the established ritual of the future age will develop the result upon which God has set His mind from the beginning – "Glory to God in the highest: peace upon earth and goodwill toward men". Jerusalem will then have obeyed the call to "Awake, and stand up, and put on her beautiful garments" (Isaiah 52:4); She will then have become "The city of righteousness, the faithful city" (Isaiah 1:26); "a crown of glory in the hand of the Lord; a royal diadem in the hand of thy God" (Isaiah 62:3); "a rejoicing and her people a joy" (Isaiah 65:18). "The Gentiles shall see her righteousness and all kings her glory" (Isaiah 62:2). In view of these things, we may understand the force of the divine injunctions:

> "Ye that make mention of the name of the Lord, keep not silence and give him no rest till he establish and till he make Jerusalem a praise in the earth."   (Isaiah 62:6,7)

> "Pray for the peace of Jerusalem; they shall prosper that love thee; peace be within thy walls and prosperity within thy palaces. Our feet shall stand within thy gates, O Jerusalem."   (Psalm 122:6,7)

Forcible also appears the exhortation of the prophet:

> "Rejoice ye with Jerusalem and be glad with her all ye that love her; rejoice for joy all ye that (now) mourn for her ... Behold I will extend peace to her like a river, and the glory of the Gentiles like a flowing stream. Then shall ye suck; ye shall be borne upon her sides, and be dandled upon her knees. As one whom his mother comforteth, so will I comfort you, *and ye shall be comforted in Jerusalem.*"   (Isaiah 66:10-13)

10 |

God's purpose with the Jews (9)

(August 1865)

WE have now arrived at that stage in the consideration of God's purpose with the Jews at which it becomes interesting and appropriate to enquire as to the relation of their restoration to the second advent, and as to the probabilities, in view of the proximate expiry of the prophetic periods, of an early development of that relation. Enough has been advanced to show that the two events are inseparably connected, and epochally considered must be simultaneous in their occurrence. The restoration of Israel cannot be accomplished in the absence of him who has been appointed "to raise up the tribes of Jacob, and restore the preserved of Israel" (Isaiah 49): and he will not assume the reins of government upon earth, and establish the "millennial" blessing of men until he have first "saved Israel out of all their distresses"; for "Jacob is the former (first) of all things". "To the Jew first and also to the Gentile." This is the divine order of events in everything. The Jew has been first in the offer of eternal life, and first in the infliction of judgment; and he will be the first to experience the blessing of the Messiah's glorified presence on earth, and the first in honourable position among the nations of the earth during the glorious era then to be established.

But the inquiry on this occasion relates to something more than these general and very obvious facts. It is, first, as to whether Christ will arrive on the scene before any step is taken in the restoration of Israel, or whether there will be a limited movement in that direction by human agency, as a preliminary to his appearance, to take the direction of affairs; and secondly, whether, on the latter supposition, there are such indications as to lead to the belief that such a movement is imminent, as the advance of the times would, if such a movement is to take place, require it to be.

Our attention has been specifically invited to the subject in a letter,[1] from which we make the following extract:

> "The brotherhood are not all of one mind as to the actual situation of affairs which will obtain when Christ comes. Our respected brother, Dr. Thomas, teaches a partial restoration of Israel before the advent, and I know that many of the friends hold the same opinion, but others of the brethren look for no restoration till the Lord comes. The prophet Ezekiel, in speaking of the discomfiture of Gogue, &c., points to a people newly collected, dwelling in unwalled villages, taken out of the nations, &c., which would seem to warrant the belief of a partial restoration before Christ comes, but on the other hand, we as yet see no signs of a partial restoration, and yet we are all looking for the appearance of our great master within a few – four or five – years. The Holy Land is just now less thought about and spoken of than was the case a few years ago. If the advent is to be on us within four or five years, would you not be looking for a commotion of some sort among the Jews?"

This fairly launches the subject of discussion. Is there, or is there not, to be a partial return of Israel to their land before that military conflux of nations at Jerusalem, which forms the occasion of Christ's thief-like return (Revelation 16)? In the state of the evidence, we are compelled to think there will; and a brief review of the evidence will probably work the same conviction in the minds of our readers.

The evidence naturally begins with the portion of scripture alluded to by our correspondent – Ezekiel 38 and 39. These

---

1   From Brother J. Grant, Carrbridge, Scotland.

chapters have to do with the exploits of a power described as "Gogue of the land of Magogue" dwelling "in the north parts", out of which he comes "against the mountains of Israel" "in the latter days". It is immaterial to the present enquiry who this power is. The main features to be noted are, the time at which the invasion of Palestine takes place ("in the latter years", Ezekiel 38:16) and the event in which that invasion terminates, viz. the total discomfiture of Gogue's numerous army by divine means (verses 18,22) and the consequent establishment of "God's glory among the heathen" in connection with the resettlement of Palestine by the Jews (39:23). These features of the prophecy enable us to decide with certainty that it has never been fulfilled; and the question therefore pressing for settlement is, to what special juncture of affairs in the future does it relate? This question seems to be directly answered in the prophecy itself, by the statements "In the latter years thou shalt come" and "It shall be in the latter days". The phrase "latter days" occurs in the scripture exactly ten times. The following are the passages in which it occurs: Numbers 24:14; Deuteronomy 4:30; 31:29; Jeremiah 23:20; 48:47; 49:39; Ezekiel 38:16; Daniel 2:28; 10:14; Hosea 3:5. From these it will be perceived that the phrase in question is used invariably to designate the closing days of the human dispensation. Accepting this, we are prepared to proceed with the investigation of the chapters. Before doing so, it would be well to enquire for a moment what weight is to be attached to the suggestion made on the subject by those who contend for no pre-adventual restoration of Israel, viz., that these chapters apply to the struggle at the end of the thousand years, described by John in Revelation 20. No doubt this view of them would at once account for the secure and prosperous condition in which Gogue finds Israel; but for this point of harmony secured, it would introduce many elements of confusion. For instance, in Ezekiel 38:16, it is said that God's purpose in bringing Gogue against the land, is "That **the heathen may know me**, *when I shall be sanctified in thee, O Gogue, before their eyes*". If the event referred to, does not transpire till the end of the thousand years, this passage would imply that the heathen do not know God *during the thousand years*, which it is unnecessary to say would be contrary to the truth. Again, if it occur at the close of the thousand years, when Christ will be royally manifested in the midst of Israel and the saints jointly administering the kingdom with him, it is a singular thing, that "Sheba, Dedan, and the merchants of Tarshish, with all the young lions thereof", a commercial and military power on the human basis, should be the first to stand up in defence of Israel against the marauding hosts of the invader. Another incongruity would be that a fire is to be sent among the careless dwellers in the isles "*that God's holy name may be known* **in the midst of Israel**" (39:6,7) as if the new covenant, creating the knowledge of God from the oldest to the youngest, had not been in force in the nation for a thousand years. Israel are to pollute his holy name *no more*, as if pollution had been the order of the day during the reign of Christ. God is, thereupon to bring again the captivity of Jacob, and have mercy upon *the whole house of Israel*, (39:26), as if He had not performed that "good thing" at the commencement of the thousand years. "Men of continual employment" are to be allotted to the work of burying the bones of the fallen army; as if menial labours would be practised when the world has passed the boundary of the sabbath age of a thousand years, and entered into the purely spiritual state; and the weapons and material of the routed army are to be used for domestic fuel, instead of wood from the forest, as if the immortalised residue of the human race, surviving the last ordeal of God's dispensations earthward, were to be beholden to the inferior processes of animal life in the spirit state. Finally, after the rout of Gogue, God is to set His glory among the heathen, as if it had not been set among them at the beginning of the thousand years; and Israel are to know for the first time that their captivity, a thousand years before, was attributable to their declensions from the divine law.

It must be evident that to make the chapters under consideration post-adventual, would entirely put them out of harmony with the whole of the facts of the case. There is no alternative but to accept the obvious application suggested by the declaration that the events described "shall be *in the latter days*". Adopting this course, a pre-adventual restoration of Israel at once appears to be a necessity. Gogue finds them in the land "brought back from the sword, gathered out of many people, and dwelling safely all of them" (verse 8). That this is before the advent is evident; they are possessed of much cattle and goods, and prosperously inhabit desolate places (verse 12) but are nevertheless ignorant of God, and unaware of their moral relations to him. They are evidently under the protection of another power, because they are without fortifications of their own, are dwelling in careless prosperity, and when attacked are immediately befriended by a power having political pre-eminence. Gogue is attracted by their wealth which has apparently come by trading, for "they **have gotten**" cattle and goods (verse 12). Gogue covers the land with the multitude of his army. He takes possession of Jerusalem (Zechariah 14:1,2). "He plants the tabernacle of his palaces between the seas in the glorious holy mountain" (Daniel 11:45); and may, without liberty, be imagined full of exultation and boast like Sennacherib or Nebuchadnezzar of old. He carries all opposition before him; he triumphs where popular superstition attaches a special omen to the triumph. He bears down the resistance of Sheba and Dedan, and the merchants of Tarshish and all the young lions thereof, and the Holy Places once again become the prize of the world's contests – Jerusalem a burdensome stone to all people (Zechariah 12:3). Standing on the prostrate body of the daughter of Zion, he looks around and surveys a world at his feet, and swells with the proud inflation of victory. This is the crisis when the most astounding event of history takes place. He shall come to his end, says Daniel How? Like Nebuchadnezzar, he has grown to the magnitude of a great tree giving shelter to all the beasts of the earth; and the decree has already gone forth, that like Nebuchadnezzar, the proud exuberance of his greatness will be shorn.

> "*The light of Israel shall be for a fire, and his* **holy one** *for a flame; and it shall burn and devour his thorns and his briers in one day,*

and shall consume the glory of his forest and of his fruitful field. The Lord, the LORD *of Hosts, shall lop the bough with terror: and the high ones of stature shall be hewn down, and the haughty shall be humbled."* (Isaiah 10:17-33)

"When Gog shall come against the land of Israel, saith the Lord GOD, my fury shall come up in my face. For in my jealousy and in the fire of my wrath have I spoken. Surely in that day there shall be a great shaking in the land of Israel; so that the fishes of the sea, and the fowls of heaven, and the beasts of the field, and all creeping things that creep upon the earth, and all the men that are upon the face of the earth, shall shake at my presence, and the mountains shall be thrown down, and the steep places shall fall, and every wall shall fall to the ground. And I will call for a sword against him, throughout all my mountains, saith the Lord GOD: every man's sword shall be against his brother. And I will plead against him with pestilence and with blood and I will rain upon him and upon his bands, and upon the many people that are with him, an overflowing rain, and great hailstones, fire, and brimstone. Thus will I magnify myself, and sanctify myself; and I will be known in the eyes of many nations, and they shall know that I am the LORD." (Ezekiel 38:18-23)

Zechariah's testimony is:

"Then shall the LORD go forth and fight against those nations, as when he fought in the day of battle. And his feet shall stand in that day on the mount of Olives, which is before Jerusalem on the east, and the mount of Olives shall cleave in the midst thereof toward the east and toward the west, and there shall be a very great valley; and half of the mountain shall remove toward the north and half of it toward the south. And ye shall flee to the valley of the mountains; for the valley of the mountains shall reach unto Azal: yea, ye, shall flee, like as ye fled from before the earthquake in the days of Uzziah king of Judah: and the LORD my God shall come, and all the saints with thee. And it shall come to pass in that day, that the light shall not be clear nor dark." (Zechariah 14:3-6)

The testimony of the Spirit in the Apocalypse is identical, when the symbolism is comprehended:

"Three unclean spirits like frogs come out of the mouth of the dragon, and out of the mouth of the beast, and out of the mouth of the false prophet. For they are the spirits of devils, working miracles, which go forth unto the kings of the earth and of the whole world, to gather them to the battle of that great day of God Almighty. (Behold, I come as a thief. Blessed is he that watcheth, and keepeth his garment, lest he walk naked, and they see his shame.) And he gathered them together into a place called in the Hebrew tongue Armageddon." (Revelation 16:13-16)

These combined testimonies conclusively show that the event which terminates Gogue's conquest of Palestine is the personal intervention of Jesus returned from heaven, revealed in the character portrayed in Revelation 19, "treading the winepress of the fierceness of the wrath of Almighty God". This being so, it follows that the restoration of which Ezekiel speaks in chapter 38:8-12, must take place before Christ's return, since it is an accomplished fact before Gogue enters the land.

It is not alone in Ezekiel 37 to 39 that we are forced to this conclusion. Every other portion of scripture that at all plainly deals with the incidents attending the closing scene of the human epoch, pictures Palestine as the habitation of Jews. It will not be lost time to look at one or two instances.

In Zechariah 12 where this epoch is the subject of prophetic discourse, we find the statement that the Lord shall save *the tents of Judah* and defend *the inhabitants of Jerusalem*, from the nations that come up against them, and that He will pour upon them the spirit of grace and supplication, causing them to receive their crucified Messiah. These words could not be applied to the present inhabitants of Jerusalem, who constitute for the most part, a motley aggregation of Gentile barbarism in its worst forms, and of whom the descendants of Judah form an insignificant and uninfluential part. It is obvious that before the situation of affairs at Jerusalem described in Zechariah's testimony can be realised, the partial restoration affirmed by Ezekiel must take place. The same inference arises on Zechariah 14 where the operations of the latter-day besiegers of Jerusalem are directed against the city *inhabited*, and also from Joel 3, where the recovery of Judah's captivity is marked as the time when God will gather all nations into the valley of Jehoshaphat, and when speaking of the judgment destructively inflicted on those nations at Jerusalem, the following language is used: "The LORD will be the hope of his people, and the strength of the children of Israel" (verse 16), showing that there is a nucleus of the nation assembled at the time spoken of. This also appears from Isaiah 59:

> "When the enemy shall come in like a flood, the Spirit of the LORD shall lift up a standard against him. And the Redeemer shall come to Zion, and *unto them that turn from transgression in Jacob*." (verses 19,20)

And also from Isaiah 29 in which the enemy is styled "the multitude of the nations that fight against *Ariel* (Jerusalem)" (verse 7). Isaiah 17:13,14, also tends in the same direction:

> "The nations shall rush like the rushing of many waters, but God shall rebuke them, and they shall flee far off, and shall be chased as the chaff of the mountains before the wind, and like a rolling thing before the whirlwind. Behold at evening-tide trouble, and before the morning he is not. *This is the portion of them that spoil* **us**, *and the lot of them that rob* **us**."

It is evident from the whole tenor of scriptural allusion to this period, that the proximate issue raised at Jerusalem is the old issued revived – God's people, the Jews, *versus* the heathen around them, and it is obvious that this issue could not be developed without a partial resettlement of Judaea by its original inhabitants. An army invading the country at present would only find wandering Bedouins, and the fanatical devotees of Greek and Latin superstition, outnumbered, it may be, by the worshippers of Islam, who hold their highest revel on the spot made sacred by the divine manifestation of former days. As has already been said, the Jews are few and uninfluential, and cannot be regarded as the inhabitants of the country. They are strangers in the land, and are mostly pilgrims from distant climes, returned to lay their bones in the dust of their ancestors. The country is possessed and inhabited by the heathen, and Jerusalem is the stronghold of their abominations. Under the circumstances, it must be obvious that the military situation which forms the occasion of the Lord's return cannot be created without a preliminary and partial return of the Jews to their ancient land and city. Reason and testimony combine strongly to establish this point. Hence the most notable sign of the Lord's approach is to be looked for in connection with Palestine and the Jews. There are other signs equally striking, and at present strongly manifested; but our attention must in the meantime be confined to that which has its centre at Jerusalem, and its radius in the scattered elements of the Jewish nation.

In our next, we shall say something about the indications that exist that this sign is about to come out in clear and strong light in the political heavens.

11 |

God's purpose with the Jews (10)

(September 1865)

SINCE it is evident there must be a partial restoration of Israel before the advent of the Messiah on the mountains of Israel to destroy human power as embodied in the armies of Gog, it becomes very interesting and important, at this late period of "the times of the Gentiles", when there ought to be some symptoms of the coming "situation", to enquire if there are any such changes in progress among the Jews as would lead to the anticipation of an early accomplishment of that restoration. The facts that meet such an enquiry are of the most encouraging character. Making every allowance for the undiscriminating enthusiasm that greedily catches every rumour and moulds it into the shape and colour suggested by its own ardent impulses, we think it must be admitted that there is something more in the present state of the Hebrew nation than the mere recurrence of the characteristic activities that may at any time have marked their history during the last eighteen centuries. We shall endeavour in a systematic form to place the facts of the case before our readers so that the features of the present crisis may appear in their true light.

In the first place, it cannot be doubted that a great change has taken place in the position of the Jews during the last twenty or thirty years throughout the world. Our own country has recently seen the last fetter of Jewish disability struck off, and we now see the sons of Abraham rising into positions of commercial, municipal, and even political influence. A Jew is the leader of one of the great political parties in this country. A Jew for a long time stood at the head of French finance, and the number of government officials and civic functionaries in France belonging to the Jewish communion, is greatly in excess of the Israelite population. In Austria, where not long ago the Jews were hunted like mad dogs, and had no security for life or property, they are now elevated to a position of almost complete citizenship; and two of their number are the leaders of the great liberal party in the Austrian Reichsrat, or Parliament.

The rise of the Jews in Prussia is even more marked than in Austria. In the political agitations of the past few years, Hebrew leaders have played a most conspicuous part, and according to the *Kreuz-Zeitung*, nearly one-fourth of the delegates chosen by the people of Prussia to elect the Deputies consisted of Jews, in consequence of which, the paper in question spoke of the chamber of deputies as the Jew Parliament. In the same country, statistics issued about four years ago by the government at the opening of the chambers, showed that the superior academies were attended by five times as many Jews as Christians in proportion to the population. The organ of the Ultramontane and feudal party published an article about the same time to show, first, that during the last fifty years the Jews had grown learned beyond measure for the express purpose of rising to the head of the government in all the states of Europe, and secondly, that they are getting to the top for the express purpose of upsetting all Christian rule and seeking their advantage in universal anarchy. The proof of this theory is found by the paper in question in the fact that "the educated Jews form part in all revolutionary movements, from the Ural to the Atlantic, and from Lapland to Sicily. They are as it were, the yeast in the European fermentation. It was in vain that the Czar Nicholas expelled every Hebrew soul from his capital on his accession to the throne. The yeast has returned under his successor stronger than ever, and is working now in full power wherever tyranny and oppression are rife. The Jew element is perceptible in the

Galician peasantry, in the Flemish malcontents, in the Servian progressists and in the surging masses of revolutionary Poland. The whole east of Europe, even more than the west, is in violent ferment, and everywhere the Jew is the living yeast".

In Russia, where, perhaps, more than in any other country, the Jew has for centuries been subject to the most remorseless tyranny, the same upward movement is manifest. Within the last three weeks, it has been announced that the Czar has the position of his Jewish subjects now under consideration. Up to the present time, they have been prohibited from settling in the eastern provinces of the empire, and are restricted by law from changing their places of abode. The practical consequence of this has been found to be that in eastern Russia, many branches of commerce which flourish in the western part of the empire, in the neighbourhood of the Jews, not only do not thrive, but can scarcely be said to exist. The proposal which the government is considering, will free the Jews from their social disabilities, and give them the privilege of migrating at pleasure from one part of the empire to another, and confer on them the right of settling anywhere.

It is evident that throughout the most important countries of Europe, in those countries where the bulk of the Jewish population is settled, a great change has taken place in their position within the last thirty years, and is now in full and active progress. Not the least important feature of that change is the elevation of the race as a whole to the position of the financiers of the world. The bulk of the wealth of Europe is in their hands. The Rothschilds, the celebrated family of Jewish bankers, could buy up the courts of Europe, and it is said, hold most of the crowns of Europe in bond for loans advanced. Their wealth, though something almost fabulous in extent, is too well known to require particular illustration; and they are but the head of a whole race of Jewish bankers, money lenders, stockbrokers and financiers of every description, scattered throughout the commercial communities of the world. These facts cannot but be regarded as eminently significant at a time when the era of Gentile dominion has nearly run to its close, and when there must of necessity be found some indications of that great revolution which, beginning with the slow process of natural development, and ending with the master strokes of miraculous intervention, raises the Jewish nation from a position of abject degradation to the proud eminence of universal glory and dominion.

These facts by themselves, however, would not afford that unmistakable degree of indication that would satisfy a thoughtful mind. Something more specific must be sought for to show that we are so near the event in question as the advance of the prophetic times would lead us to believe. And this is to be found in connection with the land of this ancient race, and the disposition of the Jews themselves towards the land.

We have first to note the general fact that within the last fifteen years, Palestine has come into a political prominence which it had not known since the days of the Crusades. It is never to be forgotten that the great war between Russia and Europe in 1853-1856 originated in a dispute about the holy places. Since that time, Jerusalem has been the subject of considerable attentions on the part of various powers in Europe. To begin with, the city itself was transferred to, and is still held in, the contingent possession of Baron Rothschild, as a deposit for the debt due to him by the Sultan of Turkey. This statement we make on the authority of Mr. Wiplech, an ex-Jewish Rabbi resident in Sheffield, who has been rejected by his Hebrew connections for believing in the Messiahship of Jesus of Nazareth. Concurrently with this singular fact, the city has during the last ten years been undergoing extensive improvements, slowly and unostentatiously, but yet on a scale which shows considerable result at the end of years. Building is progressing in and around Jerusalem. A detailed account of these operations appeared about three years ago in the *Times* newspaper, in the shape of a letter from an Oriental correspondent. These building operations are due to some extent to political intrigue. Russia and France watch each other's movements in that part of the world with a jealous eye, and have for several years been striving to overreach each other's influence by the consolidation of their respective political and ecclesiastical interests, but chiefly the latter. This has been attempted in connection with building in and around Jerusalem, in which Russia has more particularly excelled. The most notable achievement of the latter has been the erection of a species of Monastery, in the shape of a large institution for the accommodation of monks and pilgrims of the Greek Church. The Empress of the French, on the other hand, is said to have in contemplation, the erection of a new shrine at the Holy Places, in the interest of the Latin Church on behalf of which she has appealed to the Catholic Sovereigns. The rivalry between the Greeks and Latins on this spot is no new thing; but it has acquired fresh vigour from the direct manner in which the leading governments of the two superstitions have interfered. The prediction of the prophet is that the nations will burden themselves with Jerusalem till it becomes a burdensome stone that will cut them in pieces.

While politically, the city has risen to a position of notice, some remarkable physical changes are reported from various parts of the land. Ancient springs which have been dry for centuries are said to have reappeared; one in particular is said to have opened in the immediate neighbourhood of Jerusalem, and to have produced marked effects in freshening and fertilising the soil which has been arid and unproductive for ages. The early and latter rains peculiar in ancient times to Palestine, but which have been suspended since the destruction of Jerusalem by the Romans, are reported "both by converted and unconverted Jews" to have returned. The first symptoms of their reappearance occurred about twenty years ago, since which time, they have year by year become more steady, till at the present time, according to a correspondent whose letter is before us, they are becoming regular as in days of yore. The same correspondent states that "the consequence is that many localities once desolate and waste are now being cultivated, and signs of ancient fertility are returning". Whether these statements are to be relied on to their full extent, it is difficult to say. Doubtless, they have a basis in truth; and possibly they may not be much, if at all, ahead of the actual facts of the case. This and other matters will be authoritatively settled by the society which has just been formed for the purpose of making a critical survey of the Holy Land, in reference to which, we may observe that the formation of this society at the present time is in itself an indication among others of the growing interest which is arising in connection with the Jews and their land. The society is composed of "the first scholars, antiquaries and divines" of the present age. It is "supported by a goodly array of names from the ranks of dukes, bishops, and great Oriental travellers". The society was formed in the beginning of May of the present year, and a public meeting was held in London, in the middle of June, when the whole course of procedure was explained. Her Majesty has been invited to place herself at the head of the society, and it is hoped that the Prince of Wales will take an active part in the proceedings. The *Times* of April 22, 1865, has the following remarks on the subject:

> "What has immediately led to the project now in contemplation is the survey of Jerusalem under the direction of Captain Wilson, of the Royal Engineers. Few can be altogether ignorant of the controversies which have raged about the most important localities of the Holy City, such as Mount Zion and Calvary, and it will be more than we expect if this survey should finally set them at rest. 'Below the surface', however, as this paper reminds us, 'hardly anything has yet been discovered', and if it be true that modern Jerusalem is built on sixty feet of rubbish, coins and remains of all kinds may still be forthcoming. The fruits of excavation at Nimroud and on other Oriental sites have more than repaid its cost, but then they had remained undisturbed for many ages. It must not be taken for granted that Jerusalem, so often trodden down of the Gentiles, possesses crypts full of ancient monuments in a high state of preservation, or that the gorgeous ornaments

of Solomon's Temple will be found buried in the soil, if we do but dig deep enough. Short of this, we may look forward to the exhumation of many interesting relics in mounds and tombs hitherto inaccessible to the traveller. The promoters of the expedition attach great importance to the Prince of Wales's visit to the Sanctuary of Hebron, as throwing open Syria to Christian research. Here, again, we are disposed to be less sanguine, especially when we consider the scale on which it is proposed to institute the underground explorations. The same difficulty can hardly occur in verifying the course of old roads, tracing the boundaries of tribes, and stereotyping the vanishing customs and traditions of the East."

In addition to this influential movement, which cannot fail to bring the whole subject of the Holy Land into a prominence heretofore undreamt of, there are subordinate elements of activity the importance of which cannot be overestimated by those who are on the watch tower of the prophetic word. First among these are the rapid encroachments of Russia in central Asia, which, imperilling India, and creating a necessity for direct communication between this country and her Eastern dominions, has a tendency to invest the Holy Land and its neighbourhood with a political value which it never before possessed. The Euphrates Valley offers the shortest and most convenient route between England and India, and the British government is not insensible to this fact. Only three years ago, the *Daily News*, a semi-official organ, boldly advocated negotiations with the Porte for the purpose of neutralising a slice of Syrian territory to be used by the British as a basis of operations in the East in connection with India. In connection with this proposal, it recommended a settlement of the country by Jews on the ground that they are the only people who could be expected to find sufficient inducement to settle in such a barren part of the world. The only impediment at present in the way of this scheme (which no doubt will ultimately be carried into effect) is the ticklish condition of European politics; the balance of power is so even that the powers are nervously jealous of any movement which would have the effect of extending the influence of any of their number. Turkey, which holds Syria, is only permitted to exist. In herself she is powerless. She is propped and bolstered by the jealousies of the rival powers of Europe each of whom vies with the rest in efforts to keep her in political existence, not from any special liking for a Mahometan dynasty in Europe, but from a fear lest its fall would bring on territorial changes which might result in the undue aggrandizement of one or other of the powers. Thus the fears of Europe are the sick man's safety; but such an abnormal situation cannot long be maintained. European civilization and Mahometan institutions are incompatible; and the attempt of the former to maintain the latter is a kind of political patching of very old and rotten cloth which must eventually end in the hopeless rending of the whole Ottoman fabric. The sick man is dying: the great Euphrates is fast evaporating; and among the questions that must arise when the catastrophe is complete, is the disposal of Syria, at present one of Turkey's meanest dependencies. How this will be settled cannot of course be accurately determined; but in view of British and Jewish interests, it is most probable that England will step in, and taking the Jews under her wing, establish herself in the land as "the merchants of Tarshish and all the young lions thereof". In that position, she would evoke the certain antagonism of Russia, whose schemes are known to comprehend the subjugation of India, to accomplish which, she must sever England's communication with the East by seizing Syria. In this attempt, Russia, as Gog of the land of Magog, succeeds, and comes to a disastrous end, just as she gains the prize. The advent of Jesus changes the entire aspect of affairs, plunges the world in blood, and afterwards inaugurates the era of righteousness and peace.

Returning from this digression, we have to note the continued agitation for many years of a project for the formation of a line of railway through the valley of the Euphrates for the purpose of connecting Europe and the East, by the Persian Gulf. The project is gaining favour, and will doubtless in the end be accomplished. Within the last six months, M. Chas. F. Zimpel, an Austrian engineer of professional eminence, has issued a pamphlet advocating the formation of a railway from Jaffa to Jerusalem, and thence to the Dead Sea and Damascus. The scheme is "based on actual survey", and is illustrated with a large folding map. We have the pamphlet in our possession. One of Mr. Zimpel's arguments is, that the indications are favourable to a speedy return of the Jews to their land, in connection with which, he anticipates a remunerative traffic for the line! The latter-day colonization of Palestine by the Jews, may, of course, be accomplished independently of such projects, which of themselves afford no indication of the change we are looking for; but the existence of these projects constitute remarkable elements in the activity which has developed itself during the last thirty years in connection with the Jews and their land, and doubtless if carried out, they would greatly aid the development of the state of things which evidently must exist before Gog invades the country.

But the most remarkable feature of the situation is to be found in the schemes which are in agitation among the Jews themselves. We have the testimony of the editor of the *Jewish Chronicle*, who is privy to all Jewish movements, that –

> "There exists in Germany an association for the establishment of *Jewish agricultural colonies* in Palestine, the committee of which has its seat at Frankfort on the Oder, Prussia. Its secretary's name is Dr. Loge. The committee published its appeals about a year since in the German Jewish papers, and also advertised once or twice in this country in the *Times* newspaper. Nothing, however, has transpired of its proceedings within the last five or six months. The *Jewish Chronicle* has noticed this movement several times, and also had some controversy about it. The greatest obstacle to any general movement on the part of the Jews is, in the opinion of the editor (*Jewish Chronicle*), the intermeddling of the existing conversion societies in England and Scotland. These

so mix up the expected conversion of the Jews with their restoration, and evince such a readiness to avail themselves of any gathering of Jews to sow religious dissension among them, that their leaders deem it prudent not to encourage any such movement."

These sentences we extract from a letter addressed to the Editor by the editor of the *Jewish Chronicle*, March 27, 1865. They reveal the existence of an agitation which is assuredly in harmony with the advance of the "times" and which cannot fail to make the Jews thoroughly responsive to any authorised and well-ordered movement for their settlement in Palestine, such as it is evident is likely to take place. Such a movement for the present seems in its official form to be suspended, but we are informed that private immigration is going forward rapidly; and this may meet all the pre-adventual necessities of the case. The letter to which we have already referred (addressed to the editor by the authority of Mr. Wiplech, ex-rabbi), contains the following statement:

> "Many localities once desolate and waste are now being cultivated and signs of ancient fertility are returning. *Inhabitants are gathering in great numbers*: populous towns are rising where but a few years ago were only desert places. *The emigration of Jewish families from all nations is steadily and sometimes rapidly going on. It frequently happens that fifty and even one hundred families are landed on the shores of Palestine in a single day.*"

If this is the fact, it indicates a ripeness of events which may at any moment bloom into a full and organised return of the Jews on that preliminary natural basis considered in our last article.

In view of all these facts, it is evident that our correspondent (Brother J. Grant, Carrbridge, Scotland) is a little under a mistake in saying, "there are no signs of a partial restoration" and that "the Holy Land is just now less thought about and spoken of than was the case a few years ago". He rightly enquires, "If the advent is to be on us within four or five years, would you not be looking for a commotion of some sort among the Jews?" and we answer by pointing to the facts set forth in the present article, which may be summarised as follows:

1. Great change in the social and political condition of the Jews opening the way for their national organisation when the moment arrives for that event.
2. The concentration of the world's wealth in their hands.
3. The political resuscitation of Palestine in connection with Greek and Latin fanaticism and Russian encroachments in central Asia.
4. Mortgage of Jerusalem to Baron Rothschild, a Jew.
5. The improvement and growth of the city in connection with French and Russian intervention.
6. Increased fertility of the soil in connection with the reappearance of ancient springs and the return of the early and latter rains.
7. The formation of an influential society in England for the express purpose of making an exhaustive survey of the whole country.
8. Critical and helpless condition of Turkey, rendering an early consideration of the position of Syria by the British government, certain.
9. Projects for the construction of railways in and around the country.
10. The existence of schemes among the Jews for the agricultural colonization of Palestine.
11. The actual emigration of Jewish families in considerable numbers to Palestine.

These facts constitute a sign of the first magnitude – an eleven-starred constellation standing out in almost blinding brilliance in the East against the black firmament of Gentile dominion, and telling of the near approach of that glorious dispensation when God's purpose with the Jews will be consummated in the restoration of the chosen race, the magnification of Jehovah's name, and the blessing of mankind.

Part 2: The hope of Israel – still the Christadelphian hope

It was the work of Brother Thomas to delineate once more the first principles of the Hope of Israel, and that of Brother Roberts to establish and strengthen the Brotherhood in that hope as a worldwide body. In this section we see that the Israelitish nature of the Gospel has consistently been recognised among us, as is represented by the life and writings of the consecutive editors of *The Christadelphian*.

1 |

Share certificate for the Jewish Colonial Trust

(C.C. Walker, 1903)

As part of his manifesto for political Zionism outlined in *The Jewish State*, Theodor Herzl outlined a proposal in 1896 for 'The Jewish Company': *"The Jewish Company will see to the realisation of the business interests of departing Jews, and will organise commerce and trade in the new country."* On March 20, 1899, the company was incorporated as a limited company under the name of The Jewish Colonial Trust (*Jüdische Colonialbank*).

The Trust's authorised capital was £2,000,000 in shares of £1 each. An early supporter of the Trust was Brother C. C. Walker and his share certificate is reproduced below. Throughout his long editorship Brother Walker collected funds from the readers of *The Christadelphian* to pass on to the Trust. For transparency each month he reproduced his monthly deposit letter in *The Christadelphian*, along with the acknowledgement of receipt from the Trust. The repeated instruction he gave was that the money be used *"for the relief of Jewish refugees, and to help their resettlement in Palestine"*.

The resettlement of poorer Jews in the Land was itself usually an act of charity. The majority, coming from Russia, were escaping lives of persecution and hardship. The Trust gave them good quality housing alongside working hours and conditions designed ultimately to help, rather than hinder, family life. In this the Trust aimed to be world leaders. For many years this was done at the expense of profit, and thus the kindness of Brother Walker and his readers was vital.

1 – Share certificate for the Jewish Colonial Trust

2 |

The State of Israel

(John Carter, 1948)

The following article is taken from *The Christadelphian* of July 1948, the first issue printed after the Israeli Declaration of Independence. In reflective mood, Brother Carter notes that, although the broad sweep of the traditional Christadelphian understanding of prophecy had been brilliantly vindicated by recent events, the finer details had gone unforeseen by expositors. He therefore exhorts readers to remember that "*our hope rests not on the details of such interpretations, but on salvation in the Lamb of God*".

> "*In that day will I raise up the tabernacle of David that is fallen, and close up the breaches thereof; and I will raise up his ruins, and will build it as in the days of old; that they may possess the remnant of Edom ...*"

THE words from Amos 9:7-15 were the prophetical reading in the synagogues on Sabbath, the sixth of Iyar, 5708 – May 15, 1948. A few hours earlier the rebirth of the State of Israel had been proclaimed in Palestine where the Jews were fighting for their existence against "the remnant of Edom" and the children of Ishmael. And though the "Tabernacle" will be raised by a greater "David" than David Ben-Gurion (the new State's Prime Minister), the emergence of the people as a nation once more is a sign of the Messiah's approach, for it is one stage more in the reintegration of the "dry bones" of Israel. Though the throne of David was "overturned" in the reign of Zedekiah, and shall "be no more, until he come whose right it is", the Jews are now in a position which may be compared with that under the Hasmonean rulers (135-63 BC).

The Pentateuchal reading for the same day was Leviticus 19 and 20, which included the words: "I have said unto you, Ye shall inherit their land ... I am the LORD your God, which have separated you from the peoples." Once again they come unto a land already occupied by those who by human standards have a right to it, and conflict inevitably results. But the State of Israel exists as a historic fact, and apart from total conquest – which America and Russia, at any rate, are unlikely to permit – it is a fact which the Arabs cannot wipe off the slate. The United States President gave the new State instant recognition, apparently determined to be ahead of Russia, who with her satellites promptly followed suit.

The hope of restoration

In words which recalled the age-long fulfilment of prophecy – marred though they were by an unhappy touch of arrogance and forgetting of God – the proclamation said:

> "The Land of Israel was the birthplace of the Jewish people. Here their spiritual, religious and national identity was formed; here they achieved independence and created a culture of national and universal significance. Here they wrote and gave the Bible to the world. Exiled from Palestine, the Jewish people remained faithful to it in all the countries of their dispersion, never ceasing to pray and hope for their return and the restoration of their national freedom impelled by this historic association ... By virtue of the natural and historic right of the Jewish people and of the resolution of the General Assembly of the United Nations we hereby proclaim the establishment of the Jewish State in Palestine to be called

Israel ... The State of Israel will be open to the immigration of Jews from all the countries of their dispersions and will promote the development of the country for the benefit of all its inhabitants; will be based on the precepts of liberty, justice and peace taught by the Hebrew prophets ..."

So Theodore Herzl's dream of *A Jewish State* has come true – but in what strange conditions! For thirty years we have watched the undoubted fulfilment of Dr. Thomas' exposition in *Elpis Israel*; we have seen the Jews regathering in and rebuilding the Land in a way only made possible by the shadowing wing of Britain. But we have seen also the conflict with the Arabs, the machinations of Powers outside, and the growing breach between Jews and Mandatory Power, until the relationship has ended in one of the most pitiable failures in the Empire's history. The collapse of administration has been at once tragic and ludicrous; by the rigid application of the phrase, "Nothing must be done to implement partition", all that had been accomplished in thirty years was deliberately allowed to resolve into chaos.

Too confident interpretations

This is the most grievous of the many blows to too confident interpretations of the details of prophecy which have been experienced in the last half century; and it is time for us all to learn our lesson without abating one jot of our assurance in the fulfilment of the purpose of God. As recently as July 1945, it seemed likely that the political party which was pledged up to the hilt to the support of Zionism had come into power for the very purpose of promoting the Jewish restoration which other governments had frustrated. It has accomplished that end – not by fulfilling its pledges but by breaking them shamelessly. Being wise after the event, we can see easily enough that once the White Paper of 1939 was issued, Britain must go if the Jews were to return. And now that has been brought about in a way to humble the pride of Britain and advance the purpose of God; it has come because the man brought into the seat of authority has a powerful but ignorant mind subject to emotional prejudices, and his prejudices in this case coincided with those of his officials. The extraordinary position which results is that the Arabs are fighting with British weapons supplied under treaty; their protagonist is King Abdullah of the Transjordan, who owes his throne to Britain; and the one efficient force is the British-trained Arab Legion. Its British officers were withdrawn only when their presence had become plainly intolerable to world – and particularly American – opinion. The shells which have fallen on Jerusalem – where Jews in the Old City have been compelled to surrender – were British-made.

Our understanding of prophecy

Where do we now stand in prophecy? What is essential, and what merely incidental or speculative? To us, at any rate, it seems that Dr. Thomas was basically right in his understanding that a community of returned immigrants must be in the land, in relative prosperity and security, to provide the occasion for the invasion from the north described in Ezekiel 38 and (we believe) Daniel 11. If the nations are to be gathered against Jerusalem to battle, the city besieged and ravaged and ultimately delivered by divine intervention in which the Messiah is recognised by those who pierced him (Zechariah 12-14), then the Jews must be in the land at the time. With all due reserve, therefore – recognising the limits of interpretation, and recognizing also that our hope rests not on the details of such interpretations but on salvation in the Lamb of God – we would honestly express our view that we look for the survival of the remnant in the Land, and for some arrangement which allows an increase of immigration and for a recovery of the sadly damaged prosperity. If our understanding of Ezekiel 38 is in any way correct, we cannot separate the invasion from the prosperity which is given as an occasion for it. That Britain should be on the spot in the Land at the time of the invasion may no longer seem essential in view of the emergence of a modern "Sheba and Dedan"; but however broadly we can now construe Ezekiel 38:13, Britain must doubtless somehow "muddle her way back into the Middle East" to enable her to say to the invader, "Art thou *come*?"

The Arabs' fear

The hands of the Arab leaders have largely been forced by popular feeling. The resistance of the Palestine Arabs with the aid of volunteers was inflated with a great deal of bombast, and collapsed so utterly as to compel the Arab States to intervene openly sooner than they had intended. Having once taken up arms they were reluctant to yield what seemed a position of advantage; but the UN mediator, Count Folke Bernadotte, has obtained a four-week "cease fire" to give a chance of negotiation. That he has succeeded thus far is largely due to the fact that the wiser heads among Arab statesmen are reluctantly compelled to draw towards the Western Powers for fear of Communism and Russian aims. Egypt has surprisingly thrown her weight on the side of moderation. In spite of the fact that Palestine is the one subject on which America and Russia have found common ground, the shadow of the Bear and the fear it causes dominates all Middle Eastern policies.

Shadow over South Africa

General Smuts, faithful to the policy in the making of which he shared in 1917, was the only Commonwealth statesman to welcome the emergence of Israel; and his defeat at the polls almost immediately after was a blow to world Jewry. To the Jews of South Africa it was something more, for Dr. Malan's party are no friends of theirs. The *Zionist Review* had a significant comment: "At the beginning Dr. Malan may be cautious. But we have learned from bitter experience that those who preach intolerance do not possess the habit of stopping halfway. The time has arrived for a South African Aliyah. The sooner this is appreciated the better for all concerned. Let us for once learn from history." Is every door to be shut to the Jews but the door of Eretz Israel?

3 |

Israel and the purpose of God

(L. G. Sargent, 1946)

Once it is understood, the Hope of Israel is something to be communicated to others. Storytelling is one of the most ancient ways of passing on information, and is one of the most effective. In this article Bro. Sargent tells the story of Israel from Abraham through to the kingdom age. The article was originally published in 1946 as a pamphlet, and underwent numerous revisions throughout the next two decades as the State of Israel was born and grew in prosperity.

IN the valleys of the Nile and Euphrates arose the earliest great civilizations. Their growth was prompted by the need to control the river waters which flowed through canals and dykes to irrigate the land. By the time Khammurabi, in Babylon, was dictating his code of laws, somewhere near 2,000 BC, there was regular contact between these peoples by way of the narrow bridge of country bounded by the desert and the sea.

The rocky hills which cover most of this bridge-land's area are severed into two masses by a great rift from north to south, in which lie the Lake of Galilee, the river Jordan, and the Dead Sea. From east to west the hills are broken through by the Plain of Esdraelon; and towards the Mediterranean Judaea slopes down into lowlands and the fertile plain of Sharon. Through this coastal plain on the west, or along the edge of the desert plateau east of the Jordan Valley, were the two highways to Damascus; from there travellers went by way of the wells of Palmyra to Babylonia. These were the two channels for trade and for war; through these the two great streams of culture met and clashed or mingled. Between these highways was a fastness aloof among the hills of Canaan: a stronghold which was to become Jerusalem.

The widening world

In time the seat of political power passed northwards from the Euphrates Valley to the Iranian uplands; then west to the isles and coasts of the Aegean; and further west to the Central Mediterranean. Persians and Greeks alike pushed out the bounds of their empires to India; and the Romans who followed them held all the lands far up the Nile and nearly to the Persian Gulf. The lines of communication north and south were therefore now crossed by lines east and west, passing through the channels of the Red Sea and the Euphrates Valley. Judaea became an island surrounded by the crossing current of human ambition.

Israel still the centre

Passing time has not lessened that land's importance, because it rests on the broad facts of the world's shape. Though the great river civilizations have long declined Syria still links Africa with the main seat of the human race in Europe and Asia. Moreover, the use of the Suez Canal and the developments of air routes by the way of the Euphrates Valley has given greater significance than ever to the lands that lie in the path between Orient and Occident. The expansion of the inhabited world, the extension of European political and commercial power to every part of the globe, and now the development of the Asiatic and African nations as a political force, have only made more evident that by the facts of geography Jerusalem is the world's true strategic centre.[1]

---

1   Cf. Sir Holford Mackinder's *Democratic Ideals and Reality* (page 71, "Pelican" edition).

The setting for God's promise

To this land came the Semite Abram from Ur on the Euphrates. In this land he was commanded to look north, south, east and west: for, said the Lord, "to thee will I give it, and to thy seed for ever".[2] And this material promise was the foundation for a loftier blessing, for God declared He would join Abram and his descendants to Himself in an everlasting covenant, "to be a God unto thee, and to thy seed after thee" (Genesis 17:7,8). Further, not only was Abraham to be the father of many nations, but he was promised a "Seed" who should "possess the gate of his enemies", and in whom "all the nations of the earth" should be blessed (Genesis 22:17,18; cf. Galatians 3:16). Abraham, his descendants, and the land to which they were brought, were therefore joined together to form the starting point of a divine purpose which is in the end to embrace all mankind.

The nation enters the land

The metaphor of a bridge is only partly accurate, for Palestine has been subject to influxes from the desert. In their wanderings in the wilderness the descendants of Abraham through Jacob were forged into a nation after their bondage in Egypt; and from the desert they poured across Jordan to occupy the land where their forefathers had been strangers. For nearly a thousand years their history was moulded by this land, so singularly placed at the meeting point of world forces, so remarkable in its mingling of mountain, plain and abyss: a land which through these peculiarities not only possessed a great variety in climate and scene, but combined seclusion at its centre with a constant traffic with the outside world. Their geographical position gave Israel the opportunity to be a witness for God to all the peoples of the earth (Deuteronomy 4:5-8); but it also exposed them to the temptation of imbibing the degraded religions of the

---

2   Genesis 13:14-17; the land which he viewed is now divided between the States of Israel and Jordan.

nations around them – for the danger and the opportunity were inseparable.

The promise of the King

Centuries after the entry into Canaan, David captured the stronghold of Zion, and made it the political and spiritual centre of the kingdom over which he reigned as a viceregent of God. For him, as for other psalmists and prophets, Zion was the chosen point from which God's rule would extend in the earth.[3] It was when he planned to build a "House of the Lord" on this hill that he received the promise, "the LORD will make thee an house":

> "I have sworn unto David my servant, Thy seed will I establish for ever, and build up thy throne to all generations."
>
> (Psalm 89:3,4)

David himself found in this covenant of God the assurance of an ideal King to come – "a righteous one" (RV margin) who should be "as the light of the morning, when the sun riseth, a morning without clouds" (2 Samuel 23:3,4). This hope of the "Son of David" – "the fruit of his body" – is not a poetic dream: for this people it becomes a force working like a ferment in their history; and for the devout reader of the Bible in all ages it is part of the substance of faith (Psalm 89:3,4).

Faith in conflict with the world

The later history of the two kingdoms into which Israel split shows the conflict between faith in God, who had made them a nation in the wilderness, and the influence of the world around them. That influence was both religious and political, and the catastrophe which overwhelmed both these minor states was partly due to their efforts at worldly wisdom in playing off one against the other the great powers of the river valleys north and south. From his exile the prophet Ezekiel pronounced doom on the throne of David; but it was a doom which kept inviolate

---

[3] 1 Chronicles 28:5; Psalm 68:16; 102:13-16; 110:2; 132:13; Isaiah 2:3, etc.

the hope of God's promise: "Thus saith the Lord GOD; Remove the diadem, and take off the crown ... I will overturn, overturn, overturn, it: and it shall be no more, until he come whose right it is; and I will give it him" (Ezekiel 21:26,27).

The scene prepared for Christ

Judah's return from captivity prepared the scene for the greatest events, not only in their history, but in all history. Could it be chance that in this land at this time – on the stage of the Roman Empire, and at the meeting point of Europe, Asia and Africa, and of east and west – Jesus Christ lived, died, and rose from the dead? He had said: "And I, if I be lifted up from the earth, will draw all men unto me" (John 12:32). He was "lifted up" on the Cross, not in some mysterious Tibetan mountain, but here, at the meeting point of the world, where men of all lands and all times could see. "This thing was not done in a corner" (Acts 26:26). And from Jerusalem the message in his name could be carried throughout the known world in the First Century.

The sequel to these events for the Jews was the destruction of Jerusalem, their dispersion among every people under heaven, and the long desolation of the land.

The scattered flock of God

Ezekiel, who had spoken the doom of the Davidic kingdom, saw in a vision the sheep which fed on the hills around Jerusalem to provide the daily offerings required by the Law of Moses. Under the guidance of the spirit of God, they became to him a parable of the people of Israel; for he saw them neglected by hirelings, and wandering lost and leaderless. As he watched, a call came in a voice they knew; they ran together to follow One who searched for the lost and climbed down rocks to rescue the injured. He poured oil on their hurts, and bound up broken limbs. He led them to good pasture, where they could feed and lie down content. So said God, "I will both search my sheep, and seek them out ... And I will set up one shepherd over them, and he shall feed them, even my servant David ... And ye my flock, the flock of my pasture, are men, and I am your God, saith the Lord GOD" (Ezekiel 34:11,23,31).

Long afterwards the Son of David, when he saw much people on the shore of Galilee, "was moved with compassion towards them, because they were as sheep not having a shepherd"; and there in the open country he both taught the multitude, and fed them with the five loaves and two fishes (Mark 6:34,38-42). In that act he revealed himself as the true shepherd of Israel foretold by the prophets. The miracle was a type of a greater work he was to do for the salvation of Israel and of all men.

The hope of regathering

Ezekiel saw other visions which pictured the destiny of Israel. He saw a valley full of bones, very many and very dry. When he prophesied, as he was commanded, there was a shaking among them and they came together, bone to bone. Then they were clothed with sinews, flesh and skin; and breath entered into the bodies, and they stood up living, an exceeding great army. And the Lord says: "Behold, O my people, I will open your graves, and cause you to come up out of your graves; and I will bring you into the land of Israel ... And I will put my spirit in you, and ye shall live" (Ezekiel 37:1-14). The reunion of the Northern and Southern Kingdoms into one is represented by the joining of two sticks. "I will make them one nation in the land, upon the mountains of Israel", says God; "and one king shall be king to them all ... My tabernacle also shall be with them: yea, I will be their God, and they shall be my people" (Ezekiel 37:22,28).

This theme of the regathering of the dispersion, and their reunion with God and with the Land, pervades all Bible prophecy. Jeremiah says: "He that scattered Israel will gather him, and will keep him, as a shepherd doth his flock" (Jeremiah 31:10). Isaiah says: "The ransomed of the LORD shall return, and come with singing unto Zion and everlasting joy shall be upon their heads" (Isaiah 35:10; 51:11). Through Micah the Lord says:

"I will make her that halted a remnant, and her that was cast far off a strong nation: and the LORD shall reign over them in Mount Zion from henceforth even for ever" (Micah 4:7). The "reign" of the Lord is no mere figure of speech, but in the prophet's thought it implies a dominion as real as that of David or Solomon; their citadel will be its centre of rule: "And thou, O tower of the flock, the hill of the daughter of Zion, unto thee shall it come; yea, the former dominion shall come, the kingdom of the daughter of Jerusalem" (Micah 4:8, RV). The disciples looked to Jesus to "restore again the kingdom to Israel", and after his ascension he left them with the firm belief that he would return to accomplish the work (Acts 1:6). It became an essential part of the Gospel which they preached that his coming again would mark the time of the "restitution of all things, which God hath spoken by the mouth of all his holy prophets since the world began" (Acts 3:21).

God's purpose with the world

Such a national hope could only become part of the universal Gospel because it was a part of the whole purpose of God with man; and Micah's prophecy shows that this Israelitish dominion is to be the nucleus of a new world. He has spoken of the desolation to come even on the Temple of God, as a punishment for the nation's sin. And from that, without a break, he goes on to look into a more distant future, and there he sees a restoration no less real than the overthrow. "But in the last days it shall come to pass that the mountain of the house of the LORD shall be established in the top of the mountains, and it shall be exalted above the hills; and people shall flow unto it" (Micah 3:12; 4:1).

In those words there is a beautiful blending of the literal and the figurative. There is to be a real House of the Lord on the hill of Zion. Yet the mountain becomes a poetic type, a figure of something more than a geographical fact; and the hills over which it is exalted are nations and empires. It is the peoples of all the lands who come to seek light and understanding at the world's centre of worship: "And many nations shall come, and say, Come and let us go up to the mountain of the LORD, and to the house of the God of Jacob: and he will teach us of his ways, and we will walk in his paths." Nations who resist "the word of the LORD" which goes forth from Jerusalem will be subjected to a "rebuke" whose power is not diminished by distance, and will be compelled to turn their weapons of war to implements of peace: "And he shall judge among many people, and rebuke strong nations afar off; and they shall beat their swords into plowshares, and their spears into pruning hooks; nation shall not lift up sword against nation, neither shall they learn war any more." And, peace being assured, freedom from fear and want follows: "They shall sit every man under his vine and under his fig tree: and none shall make them afraid" (Micah 4:2-4).

The message of the prophets

Nor is this an isolated prophecy. It is of the very substance of the message of the prophets. Ezekiel has a detailed vision of the glorious temple which is to be. Zechariah describes the nations going up from year to year "to worship the King, the LORD of Hosts, and to keep the feast of tabernacles"; for, he declares, "the LORD shall be king over all the earth: in that day there shall be one LORD, and his name one" (Zechariah 14:9,16). Prophet after prophet looks forward to this universal rule of God in an age of universal peace and universal worship. And all the prophets see at its very heart the restored realm of Israel ruled directly by the King in Zion – that King of whom it was said at his birth: "The Lord God shall give unto him the throne of his father David: and he shall reign over the house of Jacob for ever; and of his kingdom there shall be no end" (Luke 1:33).

What sort of people?

What sort of people will they be who will form the central nation of this worldwide empire? Here is a vision of a new world order – a political fact, yet much more, because it will rest on spiritual foundations. And the nucleus from which this order is to extend over the globe is this people of Israel restored to their land. We know them as a people "stiffnecked" from their beginnings, in earlier ages turning again and again to idolatry. In later times we see them substituting for idols a barren self-righteousness, a self-worship disguised as piety, a religious perversion which made possible that depth of infamy in which they handed over their Shepherd and Messiah to be crucified. We know them today as a people of infinite suffering, often great in mind and character, yet also marred by the effects of centuries of persecution. How could they be otherwise? Homeless and scattered, yet separated from the very nations among whom they lived: marked out for contumely and shame, herded into ghettos, driven from the soil and forced by Gentile law into soul-deadening occupations – it is little wonder if they have sometimes become warped.

Today we see them recolonizing their homeland, working prodigies as pioneers in restoring its fertility, gaining a new confidence and poise as they work. We see them bringing all their vigour and strength of character to its service, and setting new standards in social experiments as they join in living communities wedded to the soil. We see them knit together as a people as they develop learning, sciences and arts. Since 1948 we see them a nation once more in the State of Israel, and leading other new nations in the development of their resources.

Jewish revival foreseen

In all this revival in Palestine students of the Bible see a wonderful fulfilment of prophecy. The recolonisation was clearly foreseen solely on Biblical grounds as long ago as the middle of the last century, when there seemed no practical possibility of it being realised.[4] Even the fact that this colonizing would grow up under British protection was exactly anticipated in the light of the prophecies in Ezekiel and Isaiah. When, therefore, the Balfour Declaration in November, 1917, announced the British policy that Palestine should be a national home for the Jews,

---

4   See *Elpis Israel* (John Thomas), Part 3, chapter 6, written in 1849.

believers in prophecy throughout the English-speaking world rejoiced with an overwhelming conviction that the age-long purpose of God was being fulfilled before their eyes. And in the developments in the years that have followed – the return of the wanderers in their thousands, the material achievements in tilling the land, and the growth of the mind and spirit of this people – in all this Bible readers see bone coming to bone, and sinews and flesh growing upon them.

Yet they have been under no illusion about the secular form which the Jewish movement would take. Splendid as the Zionists' achievements have been, for many their faith is in themselves and their national future rather than in God. The movement has been so far mainly a triumph for the spirit of man. Are these, then, the people who are to form the nucleus of a spiritual world order?

The reconciling of Israel

To find the answer we must look deeper in the prophets. Zechariah gives a picture of the people, regathered in their own land, once more suffering siege in that dreadfully besieged city, their capital. Once more they fight with the valour of fanaticism which has marked them from the days of Titus in AD 70 to the battle of the Warsaw Ghetto in 1943 and the Israel-Arab war of 1948-49. "He that is feeble among them at that day shall be as David." But it is not in their own strength that they defeat their enemies: it is the Lord Himself who will "seek to destroy all the nations that come against Jerusalem". It is He who determines that those who "burden" themselves with Jerusalem "shall be cut in pieces, though all the people of the earth be gathered together against it". For, says the Lord, "I will smite every horse with astonishment, and his rider with madness".

In their joy in the hour of victory the Jews turn to look upon their Deliverer, who is representative of the Lord of hosts: and (says the Voice through the prophet) "they shall look upon me whom they have pierced, and they shall mourn for him, as one mourneth for his only son, and shall be in bitterness for him, as one that is in bitterness for his firstborn". With their grief is mingled shame which robs them even of companionship in sorrow; for they mourn "every family apart, and their wives apart" (cf. Zechariah 12:1-14).

The spiritual climax

That moment is the spiritual climax of their history. They are a people "terrible from their beginning hitherto" (Isaiah 18:2). Brought by the power of God out of the bondage in Egypt, they were confronted at the start of their national history with the choice of "life and death, blessing and cursing" (Deuteronomy 30:15,19). They went the way of departure from God that brought upon them that awful catalogue of punishment which is given in Deuteronomy 28 and Leviticus 26:

> "The LORD shall smite thee with madness, and blindness, and astonishment of heart: and thou shalt grope at noonday, as the blind gropeth in darkness, and thou shalt not prosper in thy ways: and thou shalt be only oppressed and spoiled evermore, and no man shall save thee ... And thou shalt become an astonishment, a proverb, and a byword, among all nations whither the LORD shall lead thee ... Because thou servedst not the LORD thy God with joyfulness, and with gladness of heart, for the abundance of all things; therefore shalt thou serve thine enemies which the LORD shall send against thee, in hunger, and in thirst, and in nakedness, and in want of all things: and he shall put a yoke of iron upon thy neck, until he have destroyed thee ..."
>
> (Deuteronomy 28:28,29,37,47,48)

The story of their suffering

The centuries have unfolded the fulfilment of these prophecies in all their horror. From exile in Babylon the Jews returned to suffer the persecution by Antiochus Epiphanes which brought the revolt of the Maccabees. The Hasmonean kingdom which followed became first an ally, then a client, and finally a subject of the Roman power; and the Jews' national life ended with the destruction of Jerusalem after the terrors of the siege of AD 70. Scattered throughout the Roman Empire, the Jews suffered bitterly under those emperors from Constantine onwards who in name were Christian. Turned from the Mohammedan East, they found refuge in Arab Spain. Here they made Cordova a centre of learning until with the expulsion of the Moors they were given over to the tortures of the Inquisition. In Europe and in Asia they were massacred by the Crusaders, who thought that they honoured the greatest of the Jews by inflicting torment on his race. Throughout the Middle Ages they were pursued all over Europe by foul legends which accused them of using the blood of Christian children for their rites. They became a kind of devil-myth to whom superstition could attribute every calamity; and with every new suggestion of evil they fell victims to the violence of the bloodthirsty mob.

The nineteenth century found them still suffering pogroms in Tsarist Russia, and made subjects of deliberately nurtured anti-Semitism in Bismarck's Germany. The twentieth has seen the great belt between the Baltic and the Black Sea which contained half the Jewish population of the world caught in the fires of two wars between Teuton and Slav. Crowded into a few years from the coming of Hitler to supreme power in Germany, all the afflictions of their past were enacted over again. Deprived of means of livelihood – hunted and held in fear by day and by night – torn husband from wife and mother from child – driven as refugees from Central Europe to every land from Iceland to Shanghai – overtaken by the floods of war and persecution in almost every country where they sought refuge – their story found its last depth of horror in the gas chambers of Poland where in their thousands they were exterminated as though they were vermin.

The love that pursued them

Yet through all that history of sorrow a divine love has followed them – a love that would not give them up:

"When Israel was a child, then I loved him, and called my son out of Egypt ... How shall I give thee up, Ephraim? How shall I deliver thee, Israel? ... I will not execute the fierceness of mine anger, I will not return to destroy Ephraim: for I am God, and not man; the Holy One in the midst of thee."

(Hosea 11:1,8,9)

As the heavens are high above the earth so are God's thoughts high above man's. Man may cry in his suffering:

"Ah! Must –
Designer infinite –
Ah! must Thou char the wood ere
Thou cans't limn with it?"

But their suffering – drawn out through age on age, racking to body and soul though it be – is the cost to God of that redemption by which He brings them to Himself. It is His means of breaking down the hardness of their hearts so that they may be made one with Him: for He has said, "I have loved thee with an everlasting love; therefore with loving kindness have I drawn thee" (Jeremiah 31:3).

In the final crisis in which it seems that after all their return and rebuilding of the Land their hopes are even then to be swept away, the divine love that has followed overtakes them and delivers them. In the moment of victory that love stands before them, embodied, personified in one who can say, "He that hath seen me hath seen the Father"; and he has wounds in his hands with which he was wounded in the house of his friends (John 14:9). Through those "cruel nails' impress" they recognise with an overwhelming anguish the Jesus of Nazareth of whom their forefathers had said, "His blood be upon us, and upon our children".

The humbled in heart

In that last heart-rending recognition they know their utter helplessness before God. They have no righteousness of their own with which to stand before Him; they have nothing but shame. And with that burning knowledge their hardness of heart is melted away, and their redemption comes; for "the sacrifices of God are a broken spirit: a broken and contrite heart, O God, thou wilt not despise" (Psalm 51:17). When they know that they have no refuge but in His infinite forgiveness, "the spirit of grace and supplications" is poured out upon them, and "there shall be a fountain opened to the house of David and to the inhabitants of Jerusalem for sin and for uncleanness" (Zechariah 12:10; 13:1). Like Gentiles, they are saved only through the Cross, by baptism for the remission of sins.

And of the remaining Jews scattered throughout the world, the Lord says: "They will come with weeping, and with supplications will I lead them: I will cause them to walk by the rivers of waters in a straight way wherein they shall not stumble: for I am a father to Israel, and Ephraim is my firstborn" (Jeremiah 31:9).

Teachers for the world

In their ancient land, "ransomed, healed, restored, forgiven", "their soul shall be as a watered garden; and they shall not sorrow any more at all" (Jeremiah 31:12). All the beauty of imagery which language can command is used by the prophets to paint the joy and blessing of that day, when "the wilderness and the solitary place shall be glad for them; and the desert shall rejoice, and blossom as the rose"; or when it is said to the Land, "As a young man marrieth a virgin, so shall thy sons marry thee; and as the bridegroom rejoiceth over the bride, so shall thy God rejoice over thee" (Isaiah 35:1; 62:5).

Yet all the material blessing, and all the glory of their status as God's chosen dominion at the heart of His worldwide kingdom, are the expression and the result of a spiritual change. All these come because that long and awful pursuit of love has at last brought them as a people to know themselves and God, and in that knowledge their destiny is fulfilled; for then they are God's people, and He is their God. That end being reached, they become a source of light to the world, for in those days men out of all languages of the nations "shall take hold of the skirt of him that is a Jew, saying, We will go with you; for we have heard that God is with you" (Zechariah 8:23).

God's work for His name's sake

"Thus saith the Lord GOD: I do not this for your sakes, O house of Israel, but for mine holy name's sake" (Ezekiel 36:22). But if it is not for any virtue of theirs that they are saved, neither is it because they are worse than the rest of mankind that they have been so punished. God has taken them as a sample of the human race to show forth in them the wonder of His ways with men. "Ye are my witnesses, saith the LORD, and my servant whom I have chosen" (Isaiah 43:10).

They are living witnesses to the knowledge and power of God, who has so fully foretold their future. They are witnesses to His faithfulness, for He has said, "I will not make a full end of thee", and so they remain when ancient empires have passed like a dream (Jeremiah 30:11). But more than all, they are witnesses to the cost to God of bringing mankind back to oneness with Himself without destroying man's freewill. It is not easy for the Father in Heaven to use the dreadful instruments of affliction to purge and chasten this people beloved for their fathers' sakes. And they, like all men, can only ultimately be saved through God's supreme gift of His beloved Son, that through him men might not perish.

The burden of the Gentiles

Nor was it Jews alone who crucified Christ: nor even Jews and Romans together: it was all humanity. It was the human nature we all bear that conspired to kill the Prince of Life; and it was because of human nature that he needed to die so that the purpose of God might be fulfilled. We all bear the stain of his death until we wash it away in the very baptism that identifies us with him and his Cross.

We are one with the Jews. We share with them in human nature in all its darkness, whether we will it or no. But we can, if we will, share with them in a place in God's purpose. It was Jesus who said that "Salvation is of the Jews" because through them comes the knowledge of God; God Himself designed that they should be the instrument through whom His revelation was given to men (John 4:22; Romans 9:4,5). Making them the custodians of His word, God made them at the same time the bearers of His promise that through Abraham and his Seed blessing should come to all nations. Even the hope of eternal life is involved in the promise to Abraham, because he must be raised from the dead to inherit the land which he never possessed in life; and those who would share in the hope must share in the promise by baptism into Abraham's Seed.[5]

"All Israel shall be saved"

The way for Gentiles to be associated with that hope was, it is true, opened up by Jewish rejection of their Messiah and by their being cast aside by God in consequence: but Paul says "if the casting away of them be the reconciling of the world, what shall the receiving of them be, but life from the dead?" (Romans 11:15). He compares the people of Israel to an olive-tree from which branches have been broken off, and wild olive branches grafted into their place. But the grafted branches do not bear the root; the root bears them. They owe their position now to a humbling faith in God; and that faith carries with it the conviction that the rejected branches will be restored, so that "all Israel shall be saved" (Romans 11:25,26).

The divine drama

The Greeks said that the purpose of tragedy is to purge our emotions with pity and terror. Here unfolded age by age is a story of pity and terror beyond any imagining of their poets. But it is

---

5   Acts 7:5; Hebrews 11:19,39,40; Galatians 3:26-29.

a story that ends not with death, but life; not in the gloom of tragedy but in supernal beauty and imperishable joy. And it is a story which if we will search it out and ponder it deeply, leads us to the core of the problem of human suffering and to the heart of God's purpose for the redemption of the world.

4

For the Hope of Israel

(Alfred Nicholls, July 1977)

Throughout 1977 Brother Nicholls dedicated his Editorials in *The Christadelphian* to a series entitled *Remember the Days of Old* (later published in book format). In this first part of the series he gave his rationale for writing it. He gave thanks for both the progress the Brotherhood was making worldwide and the facets of the modern world that aided such growth. At the same time he wished the reader not to forget the solid foundations put down by previous generations, and thus wrote:

> "We intend, therefore, if the Lord will, to pass under review in subsequent Editorials some of the abiding values in the heritage committed to us, with a view to strengthening the things that remain. We shall endeavour to put into perspective some of those practical things which a younger generation feels ought to be changed and remind ourselves of those fundamental truths which collectively distinguish the Christadelphian community and which are in danger of being overlaid, either by controversy or a trend towards an ecumenism which blurs our identity." (page 1)

The seventh article considered the continuing importance of the Hope of Israel and quoted extensively from *Elpis Israel*. He concludes by looking beyond the material hope to the hope of spiritual reconciliation through the blood of the Lord Jesus.

4 – For the Hope of Israel

THE first page of every issue of *The Christadelphian* still bears the words "Dedicated wholly to the Hope of Israel". This dedication first appeared on the front cover of the magazine in January 1888, when it was fashionable to fill covers with texts and quotations. It remained there until the 1940s, when wartime restrictions forced us to dispense with a cover altogether. The redesigned cover of 1950 was greatly simplified, but the dedication has always appeared somewhere in the magazine, either on the title-page for bound volumes, or latterly where it now appears each month.

Why adopt such a device at all? And why keep it throughout the periods when the format changed and the interior was rearranged? The answer is, simply, that Christadelphians and the Hope of Israel have been inseparably linked for over 130 years, and it is right that *The Christadelphian* magazine should proclaim that fact. The first major work of Dr. Thomas, a standard Christadelphian work since 1848, he called by the title of *Elpis Israel*, The Hope of Israel, for in that hope lies the key to the understanding of the Gospel of the kingdom. For our early brethren this understanding was truly a key of knowledge, which not only opened up the whole scriptures, linking the two Testaments together, but stimulated their desire for personal study and gave them a well-defined personal hope in the promises of God.

Having already considered in previous Editorials "the things concerning the name of Jesus Christ", we turn now to these "things concerning the kingdom of God", since the apostolic preaching of the Gospel comprised these two aspects which we shall see are in fact a unity (Acts 8:12). Dr. Thomas wrote:

> "Whatever ignorance may be overlooked, ignorance of the things pertaining to this kingdom *alienates men from the life of God* (these italics ours) ... '*Gospel*' is a word which signifies *good news*, or glad tidings; and *the* gospel some particular good news. 'Blessed', say the scriptures, 'are they who know the *joyful sound*', or the gospel; and the reason is, because

it makes known the 'blessedness' which is to come upon the nations, and will give everyone an interest in it who believes and accepts it. The gospel of God is the good news of blessedness promised in the scriptures of the prophets; and *summarily* expressed in the saying, 'In thee, Abraham, shall all nations of the earth be blessed'. The making of this promise to Abraham is termed by Paul, the preaching of the gospel to Abraham; for, says he, 'the scriptures, foreseeing that God would justify the heathen through faith preached before the gospel to Abraham, saying, In thee shall all nations of the earth be blessed' (Galatians 3:8). This he styles, 'the blessing of Abraham', which is to come upon the nations through Jesus Christ.

"Abraham holds a conspicuous place in relation to the blessedness of the gospel. He is named by Paul six times in the third chapter of the Galatians, which he concludes by saying, 'If ye be Christ's, then are ye *Abraham's seed*, and heirs according to the promise'. Hence men are required to be Christ's that they may be Abraham's seed. But why is it so important to be of the seed of Abraham? For the very obvious reason that, as the promise was made to Abraham, it is only by being *constitutionally* 'in him' that any Son of Adam can obtain a participation in what belongs to Abraham."

(*Elpis Israel*, pages 203-205, fifteenth edition)

The messenger and the message

To this question of being "in Christ" and therefore "Abraham's seed and heirs according to the promises" we shall return in the next Editorial. For the present we examine further the importance of "the Hope of Israel" in relation to the Gospel which is so distinctive of Christadelphian teaching. Again we allow Dr. Thomas to speak for us:

"The gospel is not preached when the things of the kingdom are omitted. *And this is one grand defect in modern preaching* (italics ours) … Simply to believe in Jesus is to believe no more than in '**The Messenger**', but, he was sent to preach the gospel to the poor; to show the glad tidings of the kingdom of God: this was his **Message**, the message of God to the Jew first, and afterwards to the Greek. Let it be remembered then, that salvation is predicated upon *belief in the* **Messenger** *and in the message he brings from God*." (pages 207,209)

Here is a profound statement, to which we would do well to take heed in our own day, when the influence of the "Jesus movements" and "Jesus cults" is abroad. It can so easily be forgotten that to "believe in Jesus", or simply to believe that "Jesus is alive", is only part of the Gospel message. For the Apostles the important thing about Jesus was that he is "the Christ, the Son of the living God", and that in his sufferings, death and resurrection the believer has present comfort in the forgiveness of sins, a motive, or even a "motivation" for living, and a hope of personal resurrection and a part in the coming kingdom. For early Christadelphians it was through the proclamation of the kingdom as a *literal* kingdom that substance was added to their hope. They had, in the words of a teenager looking in vain for a message in the religious teaching in his school, "something to look forward to, something to come". The connection between the Gospel of the kingdom and the national hope of the people of God comes out clearly in our early writings and was the basis for all their preaching of the Gospel.

Reviewing the passages in Acts where Paul links his preaching with the hope of "the twelve tribes" and the hope of the resurrection, Dr. Thomas said:

> "But, we will let the apostle state his case in his own words. When he stood before Ananias, the high priest, and the council of the Jews, he cried out, 'on account of *the hope* and resurrection of dead persons I am called in question' (Acts 23:6). But, it may be asked here, 'Concerning what hope was the question between Paul and his persecutors about?' He tells us in his defence before Agrippa; 'I stand and am judged', says he, 'for the *hope of the promise* made of God unto our fathers;

unto which promise our twelve tribes, instantly serving God day and night, hope to come. *For which hope's sake*, king Agrippa, I am accused of the Jews' (Acts 26:6). Now, from this statement, it appears:

1. That God had made a certain promise to the fathers of Israel;
2. That this promise became *the hope of the nation*, and was therefore a national question;
3. That this promise had been the hope of the twelve tribes in all their generations; was the ground of their worship; and that they hoped to attain it by rising from the dead.

"But we have a still plainer avowal, if possible, of the identity of this national hope with the hope for which the Apostle suffered so much ... He told them of the assembled 'Chief of the Jews' who visited the imprisoned Paul in Rome: '*On account of* **the Hope of Israel** ... am I bound with this chain.' This is conclusive. *The hope of the promise made to the fathers*, was, and, indeed, is to this day, the *Hope of Israel*; and for preaching this hope and inviting the Gentiles to a participation in it without other circumcision than that of the heart, he was denounced as a pestilent fellow, and unfit to live." (pages 240-241)

The promise of the kingdom

In the broad sweep of the book through the whole purpose of God, we see how the Gospel as the Apostles preached it was partly a matter of promise, partly a matter of history and partly doctrinal. The promise to Abraham was of a land to inherit, of a seed in whom all nations would be blessed, and of a great nation in whom the promise would be fulfilled. This developed into the promise of the kingdom when the seed was declared to be also the Son of David, who would sit upon the throne in Jerusalem (also called "the throne of the LORD"), and "reign for God and dwell with men". In these promises, everlasting as they were, there was the promise of eternal life for the men who participated in them. These things God confirmed in an everlasting covenant centred in Jesus Christ, "the Son of David, the son of Abraham" – appropriately the opening words of the New Testament – who was "a minister of the circumcision for the truth of God, to confirm the promises made unto the fathers" (Romans 15:8).

The historical aspect of the kingdom was those promises which had been fulfilled already in the things concerning Jesus; the things concerning the kingdom of God looked forward to promises yet to be fulfilled, and the third aspect, the things concerning the name of Jesus, were the doctrinal importance of the fulfilled promises and their significance in the life of the believer.

Of the "doctrinal aspect" we hope to write more later. For an everlasting covenant has important implications about forgiveness of sins and redemption before a mortal man can participate in it, and is therefore closely identified with "the new testament in my blood", to which Christ referred. Or as Dr. Thomas put it, commenting on 1 Peter 1:10:

> "The mystery of the kingdom, then, has been made known and we find it had relation to *the sufferings of the Christ, and repentance, remission of sins, and eternal life in his name, to the Jews first and afterwards to the Gentiles.*" (page 212)

A hope with solid foundations

So satisfying was the sense of having a hope so solidly based on historical foundations, connected with a real land, a real city, and a future life on earth, all of which made sense of the world and current events, that as a result of Dr. Thomas' work the Brotherhood has always paid great attention to the affairs of the nation of Israel, as an indication of the stages reached in the divine plan of the ages. This provided a witness to the sureness of God's promises. Sometimes, however, preaching has been directed exclusively to the political aspect of the kingdom and the prophecies surrounding it – the "signs of the times".

At times of crisis in the Middle East great excitement has been kindled, almost to the point where brethren have forgotten that the divine purpose with Israel does not depend upon the skill of her politicians nor the cunning of her commanders – "not by might, nor by power, but by my spirit, saith the LORD of hosts" (Zechariah 4:6) – and that if we were citizens of the modern Israeli state our very profession as Christadelphians would demand that we be conscientious objectors to the bearing of arms in her defence!

Reaction to this attitude has tended to swing towards the opposite extreme. Abraham is rarely mentioned, the literal aspect of the kingdom excluded, and the concepts of Christ as the Messiah of Israel, "of the seed of David according to my gospel" (2 Timothy 2:8), and of salvation being "of the Jews", have been lost sight of.

There is need for a balance to be struck in all this. Although Dr. Thomas devoted a major section of his work to the prophetic and political aspects of the kingdom, centred on the land of Israel, he himself recognised, and indeed *Elpis Israel* itself assumes, that these were parts of a greater whole; and that the purely *nationalistic* hope of Israel, against which Paul himself had to contend, was the essence neither of the Gospel nor of the promises themselves.

For the promise of God to Abraham was a promise of reconciliation and of fellowship with Him. "Fear not Abraham, *I am* thy shield, and *thy exceeding great reward*" (Genesis 15:1). In using the phrase "the hope of Israel" (uniquely in that form in the New Testament), Paul no doubt has Jeremiah in mind, for he, like Jeremiah, was reminding Israel of the true nature of their national hope, of which the throne of David and their possession of the land was an important part but still only a part:

> "O LORD, though our iniquities testify against us, do thou it for thy name's sake; for our backslidings are many; we have sinned against thee. O *the hope of Israel*, the saviour thereof in time of trouble, why shouldest thou be as a stranger in the

land, and as a wayfaring man that turneth aside to tarry for a night? Why shouldest thou be as a man astonied, as a mighty man that cannot save? Yet thou, O LORD, art in the midst of us, and we are called by thy name; leave us not."
(Jeremiah 14:7-9)

"A glorious high throne from the beginning is the place of our sanctuary. O LORD, *the hope of Israel*, all that forsake thee shall be ashamed, and they that depart from me shall be written in the earth, because they have forsaken the LORD, the fountain of living waters. Heal me, O LORD, and I shall be healed: save me, and I shall be saved; for thou art my praise."
(Jeremiah 17:12-14)

Waiting for the Lord

The word used here for "hope" is a rare one in the Old Testament, apparently used elsewhere with this meaning only by Ezra when he says that "there is *hope in Israel* concerning this thing", that is, concerning their great transgression against the Lord who was righteous, if only they would make a covenant with their God according to "the counsel of those who trembled at His commandment" (Ezra 9:15–10:3). It is, however, related to the idea of *waiting for the Lord* in numerous Psalms and chapters in Isaiah. "Therefore turn now to thy God" says Hosea, "Keep mercy and judgment and *wait on thy God* continually", and Jeremiah 14 already quoted, concludes "Remember, break not thy covenant with us … Art not thou he, O LORD our God, therefore we will *wait upon thee*, for thou hast made all those things".

That Dr. Thomas would have agreed with the above is beyond question:

> "This kingdom is that which is to be restored again to Israel (Acts 1:6), at the restitution of all things (Acts 3:21), spoken of by Moses (Deuteronomy 30:1-10), and all the prophets; and is therefore the Hope of Israel. Now the Christ is also the Hope of Israel (Jeremiah 14:8), and he is such because he will save Israel from their present dispersion, raising up

the tribes, and restoring the desolations of their land and commonwealth; for He is 'The Repairer of the breach, The Restorer of the paths to dwell in' (Isaiah 49:5,6,8; 57:12). The idea of the Christ and the kingdom are inseparable. The Christ, or the Anointed, is Israel's Hope, because through him 'the Hope of the promise made of God to their fathers', Abraham, Isaac and Jacob, will become an accomplished fact. Jesus, whom we believe to be that Christ, is our hope and formed in us the hope of glory, the hope of honour, the hope of the kingdom, the hope of life and incorruptibility, because without his appearing in his kingdom, we can have none of those things which constitute our salvation. The kingdom was Israel's Hope, as well as the gospel hope; for without the kingdom there would be, they well knew, neither king, nor saviour, nor redemption ... To omit one of these is to mutilate the gospel. No man can be saved by the belief of a mutilated or perverted gospel (Galatians 1:6-9)."

(*The Christadelphian*, 1888, pages 258-259)

Striving to maintain a balance

In remaining wholly dedicated to all that is implied by the Hope of Israel, Editors of *The Christadelphian* have always striven to maintain a proper balance in these things, which we believe is the balance of both prophets and apostles, to expound, exhort, comfort, preach and make relevant comment on contemporary events with the object of making ready a people for the Lord. Let Brother John Carter (Editor, 1937-1962), sum it all up for us:

"Abraham was told that he must leave where he was dwelling and go to a land that God would show him; that God would make of him a great nation; that God would bless him and he would be a blessing; that God would have regard to how others treated him; and lastly that in him all families of the earth should be blessed. This promise fixes the land of Palestine as the centre of God's operations with men and puts the natural descendants of Abraham in a place of privilege as God's nation.

"The last item of all is the one of outstanding importance to us in this study. In the past three generations when the gospel has been preached there has been great emphasis on the material benefits of the millennial age when blessings of security, freedom from want, freedom from oppression and freedom from ill-health would fulfil the terms of the covenant. These things are included beyond question. No further proof is necessary than the seventy-second Psalm which, after setting out the glories of Messiah's reign in the wise judgment, the consideration for the needy, the abundance of food, concludes with the reference to the covenant with Abraham, 'Men shall be blessed in him; all nations shall call him blessed'.

An even deeper need

"Nevertheless, the blessings of the Abrahamic covenant touch an even deeper need. Material benefits without the right mind to appreciate the gifts would be harmful in the final results. Men need a changed mind and a changed relationship to the Creator. As interpreted by scripture the foremost feature of the blessing of Abraham is reconciliation with God. The Psalmist describes the 'blessed man' as 'he whose transgression is forgiven' (32:1,2). The word 'blessed' is the link with the Abrahamic covenant, forged beyond breaking by Paul's words, 'What saith the scripture? Abraham believed God, and it was counted to him for righteousness ... Even as David describeth the *blessedness* of the man, unto whom God imputeth righteousness without works, saying, *Blessed* are they whose iniquities are forgiven, and whose sins are covered'. This use of the word 'blessed' as a link between Genesis 12:1-3 and Psalm 32:1,2 suggests that an examination of other passages in the Psalms where the word blessed occurs might be a profitable exercise. But Paul's application of the 'blessing' to the forgiveness of sins shows that the blessing of

all nations involves reconciliation to God."
(*The Christadelphian*, 1953, page 200)

5 |

What hope now for Israel?

(Michael Ashton, 1988)

The year 1988 was the fortieth anniversary of the formation of the State of Israel, a milestone celebrated by many in the Christadelphian community. As well as looking back over the momentous events that had occurred in the intervening years, some prophecy students looked forward, predicting that 1988 would be the year of Christ's return. This was based upon Matthew 24:

> "Now learn a parable of the fig tree; when his branch is yet tender and putteth forth leaves, ye know that summer is nigh: so likewise ye, when ye shall see all these things, know that it is near, even at the doors. Verily I say unto you, this generation shall not pass till all these things be fulfilled."
> (verses 32-34)

If the fig tree's leafing was 1948 and a generation is forty years (Numbers 32:13), then it was reasoned that 1988 would see the fulfilment of all things.

Although the predictions were premature, they served to add energy to the community's witness efforts for the year. In this Editorial for the January edition of *The Christadelphian*, Brother Ashton recommended that enthusiasm for God's nation should be tempered by a degree of circumspection.

THROUGHOUT all ages the people of God who have considered His purpose, and prayed earnestly for its fulfilment, have eagerly examined those prophecies which detail the events which will herald its completion. By so doing they have reminded themselves of the need to redeem the time and of the fact that those things around them which appear so settled and secure are merely transient and ephemeral. None of these considerations would be complete without an examination of the events which concern the land and nation of Israel. There is nothing more distinctive in these days, and nothing which has so marked out the faithful remnant in all ages than an absorbing interest in the people of God's possession.

In the history of our own community, in common with "Protesters" of other times, concern with the things of Israel has been to the fore. Our early brethren, against all natural reason so to do, confidently expected and anticipated the regathering of the nation and its re-establishment in the land of Palestine. It is highly significant that the publication which above all others is the statement of what Christadelphians believe to be true scriptural teaching is called *Elpis Israel*, the Hope of Israel. What in hindsight seems equally significant is that it was in that book's centenary year that the hope it expressed began openly to flourish for the nation of which it treated. It is well-nigh impossible to insist that this was just a chance coincidence.

As we now read words penned 140 years ago, they have a greater effect than the writer can possibly have imagined. The preface opens with the words: "The year 1848 has been well and truly styled the 'Annus Mirabilis', or Wonderful Year." That it presaged an even more wonderful year exactly one century later can hardly have been perceived. As far as the author was concerned, of course, he had expected events to move more quickly, but this expectation does not affect one whit the validity of the message about which he wrote:

"It is a book, not for these times only, but for all the years which constitute 'the time of the end', and thenceforward to the restoration of the kingdom and throne of David. It is named ELPIS ISRAEL, or *Israel's Hope*; for the kingdom of which it treats is that which is longed for by all intelligent Israelites, and for which, said Paul, 'I am bound with this chain'."

It is this same hope which binds all Christadelphians in fellowship, for it is centred on the redeeming work of the Lord Jesus Christ, which will be fulfilled at the time when the kingdom will be restored to Israel. But it must not be confused with some sort of blind patriotism supporting everything which happens under the name of Israel. Our hope is the hope *of* Israel, it is a sharing of the hope which was given to them, but which cannot yet be equated with the hope of Jews presently living in Israel, nor yet with that of many Jews in other countries who express the strong desire to live there, but who are restrained by the governments of the countries where they live.

A true perspective

In the desire this year to show forth a belief in the promises which are still to be fulfilled through this people, it is important that a true perspective is kept of the current situation in Israel. We rightly glory and rejoice that God's purpose of regathering His people to their homeland has occurred in our lifetime, but we must recognise that as yet, their hearts have not changed. An increasing proportion denies even the existence of God. By far the majority falls into this category. Of the rest, there is a strong hard-core fundamentalist group maintaining traditions constructed from the laws of men, not those of God. Though they originally grew out of the Law given through Moses, and still bear many of the hallmarks of the worship of their ancestors, they stand condemned by Jesus' words that they "bind heavy burdens and grievous to be borne, and lay them on men's shoulders" (Matthew 23:4).

The extent to which by their energies they are involved in the realisation of the prophecy that "the desert shall blossom as the rose" can equally blind us to the blasphemy of their pride in what they see as their own achievements. Little do they realise that unless it was in accord with God's great master plan, their skills would be useless. In earlier centuries the same land from which Jacob and his family had to flee because of the famine, flourished and was prepared in their absence for their return under Joshua. If God has chosen on this occasion to prepare it by their own hand, no real credit can accrue to them.

No political support

In what ways therefore are we to proclaim our interest in the affairs of the Jewish peoples, and particularly to speak about the fortieth anniversary of the establishment of the State of Israel?

Firstly it must be made clear that Christadelphians do not support in any form the political government of Israel. For this reason, financial support has always been directed towards the assistance of child refugees. The situation is now different from the times before there was a national home when brethren rightly channelled their endeavours in ways which could assist the colonisation of the land by Jews. That can no longer be done without associating ourselves with the present government of Israel. In just the same way as we recognise the command to "be subject to the higher powers" of the countries in which we sojourn, we also understand that it is not for us to attempt by protest (or any involvement other than witnessing to the truth) to frame the policies even of the countries in which we live, let alone the governments of another country.

Our hope is that we shall be citizens of a kingdom centred upon Israel, and indeed that in a very special sense we are so now. But that is very different from saying, or inferring, that we believe we are citizens of the present State of Israel.

If there is no support for the Israeli government, a corollary must be that we also do not display partisanship in our treatment of, and references to, their Arab enemies. It is a very different thing to point out how the Arab and Palestinian antipathy to the Jews is fulfilling ancient words of prophecy, from actively launching invective against their every move. This is much harder to practise than to preach. Who, during the momentous events of the six-day war in 1967, did not thrill to the exploits of the Israeli forces and, in words of imprecation similar to those found in the Psalms, say 'Happy shall he be that taketh and dasheth thy little ones against the stones' (137:9)?

Israel must recognise Christ

But the promise to Abraham does not read, as we sometimes give the impression it does, "I will bless them that bless thee, and curse him that does not also curse thy enemies" (see Genesis 12:3). No, our treatment of the current tense situation in the Middle East must be even-handed concerning the governments involved even though it is vital that every opportunity is taken to point out the teaching about the nations which is contained in scripture. What better way to show our lack of partisanship than to concentrate on the things written within our community long before the days of Theodor Herzl and David Ben-Gurion, and which were unaffected by the presence in the land of a nation bearing the ancient name?

The only answer to the question posed in our title is for the nation to recognise their king. Some of them have a hope that Messiah will come, but like many of their forebears almost two thousand years ago, their expectations are very different from the reality of the Lord Jesus Christ. The presence of Messianic Jews in the land is not the indication that there is hope for Israel, nor is the cause furthered if we determine only to buy Israeli produce, understandable though it is that we should wish to benefit from the production of the Land. No, the Jews need to realise that the "blessing of Abraham (has) come on the Gentiles through Jesus Christ" (Galatians 3:14); they must recognise him as their Saviour too, and they must learn to depend on their God, who alone is able to save them.

6 |

The God of Israel

(Andrew Bramhill, 2015)

March 2015 saw the elections for the twentieth Knesset (or parliament) in Israel. The election had been held early, partly as a result of the 'Jewish State' proposal being pushed by the incumbent Prime Minister Benjamin Netanyahu. This proposal had the driving principle that *'Israel is the homeland of the Jewish people in which the Jewish people fulfil their ambition to self-determination according to their cultural and historical legacy'*. With the Muslim population of Israel still rising as a proportion of the whole, the principle was controversial, at home and abroad. This meant that when the election saw Netanyahu's Likud party again win the most seats, there was an upturn in anti-Semitic sentiment around the world. By contrast, *The Christadelphian* for the month saw Brother Bramhill restate the Christadelphian position that God is, in a special sense, the God of Israel.

TO the casual onlooker, Christian groups all look the same. Our appreciation of Bible truths tells us the differences are great, not least concerning God's people Israel. Few Christian churches and groups place emphasis on the Jews being God's people today. Theirs is a religion which regards the Old Testament as something of an irrelevance, useful perhaps for its moral lessons and teachings, but not for its great covenants and prophecies. The promises made to the Fathers concerning the land and the seed are to be viewed (they say) only in type and shadow with the substance brought about through the work of Christ in the New Testament.

This particular view is based on the behaviour of the Jewish people years ago. Having rejected and crucified the Son of God, the Jews have forfeited any claim or right to the inheritance promised. For its adherents this particular theology goes under different names. Sometimes it is called 'Replacement Theology' because the Christian Church is said to be the new Israel, replacing the Jewish people, and has become the rightful heir to the inheritance. Elsewhere the theology is known as 'supersessionism', the idea that the new covenant has superseded the covenant made with Israel through Moses.

As is usual with subjects of this kind, a range of views is to be found. Some evangelicals regard the nation of Israel as having a significant part to play in God's plan, a view which developed after the Holocaust. Even the Catholic Church, which for centuries blamed the Jews for crucifying Christ, softened its supersessionist position at the Second Vatican Council (1962-1965).

A distinguishing doctrine

There are few groups, however, who embrace the promises to the fathers and the hope of Israel in quite the same way as Christadelphians. Putting it rather simply, most other Christian groups limit the Bible to its introduction of a Creator God and His desire to recover man who fell at the beginning. As the work of redemption only reaches its fulfilment in Christ, the scripture narrative (in their view) leaps from the early chapters of Genesis to the Gospel of Matthew, the birth of Messiah and his redeeming sacrifice. The whole history of Israel can be glossed over. We know differently. Starting with the promise of the woman's seed in Genesis 3:15, this hopeful promise is repeated in varying forms to Noah, Abraham, Isaac, Jacob, David and others. God's work of redemption, we know, cannot be separated from His work with Israel. This is an important distinguishing doctrine for us, and one that we do well to remember so that boundaries which others may blur remain clearly defined.

There are several well-founded reasons for holding this view. For example many Christians declare a belief in the gospel, but which gospel is it? On seven occasions Paul and Peter refer to the Gospel of God (Romans 1:1; 15:16; 2 Corinthians 11:7; 1 Thessalonians 2:2,8,9; 1 Peter 4:17). And the God that is revealed to us in scripture is the God of Israel, a God we know as Yahweh, the God of Abraham, Isaac and Jacob. This is the God who rules and made promises concerning His people. This is the God who sent His Son "unto the lost sheep of the house of Israel". He is not a distant or abstract God, but one who cares and shows mercy, not least in the covenant relationship that He formed with Abraham and his family. The God of the Lord Jesus and of the New Testament is still the God of Israel.

The New Testament could not do more to emphasise the importance of the Gospel's connection to Israel. As the Bible develops its Old Testament theme regarding Israel's history, the start of the New Testament brings over-brimming hope to the reader as the long-promised seed finally appears. Before the New Testament narrative tells us about Messiah's arrival, however, it concentrates on his heritage. Matthew, under inspiration, wants us to know that Jesus Christ, God's own Son, is a descendant of Abraham and David, and gives the detailed genealogy to prove it. This might not make for exciting reading or great literary drama, but it is the most important point as far as the inspired writer is concerned. God's Son is in the same line as the fathers, and ultimately he will sit on the throne of his father David, ruling over the house of Israel.

To the Jew first

All this is further illustrated through the work of Christ and his apostles. Preaching was undertaken initially to Israel, and even when carried abroad, it was usual for a synagogue to be found as the first place for preaching. Paul himself, the great Apostle to the Gentiles was to declare, "God has not cast away His people whom He foreknew" (Romans 11:2).

This understanding of the unbreakable link between the Gospel of salvation and the hope of Israel has been the fabric of our faith for over 160 years. As all doctrines should, this has guided our thinking and influenced our behaviour. As a community we position ourselves as friends of the Jews, expressing full confidence in the promise made to Abraham:

> "I will bless those who bless you, and I will curse him who curses you; and in you all the families of the earth shall be blessed." (Genesis 12:3)

In the last century we played our part in the efforts to rescue Jewish children from Nazi control in continental Europe. Today through the work of various Christadelphian organisations and charities we endeavour to support the Jews in practical ways, believing all the time that they are still God's people and that a mighty work is still to be done in Israel.

This position is not always an easy one to hold. As a sentiment of anti-Semitism spreads across Europe, declaring oneself to be a friend of Israel may become a challenging experience for many of us. Similarly the actions of Israel's secular government are not always moral, and like many other governments today are not ones that demonstrate good standards of honesty. But we are not the supporters of political parties or of human governments; we are believers who understand the role Israel is still to play in God's great plan of filling the earth with His glory.

A modern miracle

There is strong evidence that Israel are still God's people. We often reflect on the miraculous regathering of a people, 1,900 years after they were scattered to all corners of the earth. This was remarkable indeed and brethren who remember May 14, 1948 still recall the excitement of that time. For those of us who have never known a time when Israel have not occupied their land, events since 1948 have been just as stirring. Israel was already fighting a civil war with the Arab Liberation Army in Palestine when its nationhood was declared. The following day (May 15, 1948) four Arab nations (Transjordan, Egypt, Syria and Iraq) joined forces against Israel. The nascent country should have been strangled at birth, yet under God's good hand not only were the Jews victorious, but they extended their borders, taking sixty per cent of the land earmarked for the Arabs. Successive wars in 1967, 1973 and later have seen borders secured and the nation become firmly established. Even today prophecies regarding Israel are being fulfilled before our eyes, not least in the growth of anti-Semitism and the return of European Jews to their homeland.

A time of testing lies ahead, we know, for the nation will be brought to its knees one final time before the Almighty intervenes. Only then will they come to recognize that it has been God's will and not their own ingenuity that has brought all this to pass. Until that day let us be the ones who proclaim the hope of Israel, with all its attendant promises, as our hope, and let us do this with clarity and without fear. It is doctrines such as these which make us different from other Christians, a difference we do well to preserve.

Part 3: Zionism – an autobiography (1791-1948)

The return to the Land had a variety of causes – social, political and religious. Some of the people involved were Jewish, some were Christians sympathetic to the plight of the Jewish people. Others, however, contributed by their anti-Semitism, either by looking to remove the Jews from their countries, or by persecuting them to a degree that aroused sympathy in others. People of all different tongues and nationalities aided the process in one way or another. This being true, we wonder at the level of angelic involvement in reuniting the Israelites to their ancestral territory.

To give a flavour of this complexity, what follows is a selection of historical documents – speeches, laws, diary entries and more – that contributed to the Zionist cause. It begins in 1791 with the great earthquake of Revelation 11, the French Revolution, and leads up until the declaration of Israeli independence in 1948.

1 |

Loi relative aux Juifs

(Louis XVI of France, 1791)

Although the idea of restoring the Jews to their homeland had been mooted in Gentile governments since the times of the English Lord Protector, Oliver Cromwell (protectorate 1653-58), the French Revolution brought about a sudden and radical metamorphosis in the form these notions took.

The Revolution swiftly led to the beginning of the establishment of political rights for European Jewry. Jewish emancipation was grudgingly granted in Europe over a period of at least a hundred years, beginning in Revolutionary France with the decree reproduced below. In combination with the spirit of the nationalism spread across the world by the same Revolution, these rights (although fragile) were a necessary prelude to political Zionism. They also functioned as one of its causes, the emancipation leading to an unprecedented degree of assimilation that threatened the Jewish way of life that had developed through the centuries of mediaeval persecution.

Napoleon Bonaparte continued the promotion of Jewish rights (although his decrees had intentionally mixed results). As French General at the Siege of Acre (1799) he was reported to have called for Levantine Jews to return to Palestine to recreate ancient Jerusalem,[1] and in 1806, as Emperor, he created a 'Great

---

1   'Bonaparte has published a proclamation in which he invites all the Jews of Asia and Africa to gather under his flag to re-establish the ancient Jerusalem. He has

Sanhedrin' of European Jews as an advisory body on religious affairs.

LOUIS, by the grace of God, and by the constitutional law of the State, King of the French. To all present and all to come: greetings. The National Assembly has decreed, and we desire and command, the following:

DECREE OF THE NATIONAL ASSEMBLY

September 27, 1791

The National Assembly, considering that the necessary conditions for being a French citizen, and to become an active citizen, are fixed by the constitution and that any man who meets said conditions, swears a civic oath, and commits to carry out all the duties that the constitution imposes, has a right to all the benefits it ensures;

Revokes all adjournments, reservations and exceptions inserted into past decrees relating to Jews who take the civic oath, the doing of which shall be taken as a renunciation of all privileges and exceptions previously inserted in their favour.

We demand and command all administrative bodies and tribunals to enter this in their registers; read, publish and post it in their respective departments and areas of responsibility, and execute it as the law of the kingdom. In faith of which We have signed the present, to which We have fixed the seal of state, in Paris, the thirteenth day of the month of November, the year of grace one thousand seven hundred and ninety-one, and the eighteenth of our reign.

Signed,

LOUIS.

---

already given arms to a great number, and their battalions threaten Aleppo' (*Le Moniteur Universal*, May 22, 1799). Although unconfirmed by other sources, it is likely that a proclamation of some kind was published, the effect of which may have been exaggerated by *Le Moniteur*.

2 |

Promoting Christianity amongst the Jews

(Joseph Frey, 1810)

The early Christian movements for the return of the Jews to the Land tended to be part of wider efforts to convert the Jews to Christianity. The belief that the majority of Jews would convert were in contrast to the ideas of Brother Thomas, who outlined in *Elpis Israel* his scriptural reasons for believing that the Jews would return to the Land on *"purely political principles ... in unbelief of the messiahship of Jesus, and of the truth as it is in him"*.

In 1809 a group broke away from the general London Missionary Society to form the London Society for Promoting Christianity amongst the Jews. Many members were converts themselves including the leader, Reverend Joseph Frey. Gentiles were influential in the group too, most notably the anti-slavery campaigner William Wilberforce.

The first extract below is from the second biannual report of the society (1810). In it the society seeks to separate the effort toward the conversion of the Jews from the keen anticipation of their restoration to the Land. The second extract is from Reverend W. T. Gidney's *The History of the London Society for Promoting Christianity amongst the Jews: From 1809 to 1908* and explains the general trend in Evangelical prophetic interpretation between the formation of the society in 1809 and the 1840s when *Elpis Israel* was written.

a. A charge of enthusiasm has been made by some persons concerning the views of the society; and it has been asserted that your Committee are influenced by foolish and Utopian expectations. Your committee have already expressed their sentiments in respect of the present circumstances and events of the world. They certainly consider the occurrences of a few years past as peculiarly awful and surprising, and are roused to exertion by the signs of the times. Nevertheless they are not determined to any measures which they adopt by visionary and uncertain calculations. They wish to distinguish between the restoration of Israel to their own country, and the conversion of Israel to Christianity. If nothing peculiar appeared in the aspect of the times, if neither Jews nor Christians believed the future restoration of Israel, if no exposition of prophecy had awakened attention or excited expectation in men's minds, if it were possible to place things as they stood many centuries ago, still your Committee would urge the importance and propriety of establishing a Jewish Mission. They cannot conceive any just reason why the Jews should be wholly neglected, and no means employed for their conversion.

b. The sermon of the late Patron, Bishop Longley, who had become Bishop of Durham in 1841, on Romans 11:12, was a model of brevity, for those days at all events, and is notable for his prophetic interpretation of that passage. He said, speaking of the 'fulness' of the Jews:

> *"By this term is to be understood the restoration of the Jewish nation to their ancient privileges, by their admission into the Christian Church."*

In fact, up to about this time most of the advocates of the Society believed in the gradual conversion of the Jews and their complete incorporation into the Church, just as the gradual conversion of the whole world to Christ was the popular belief. The rise of 'Plymouth Brethrenism' with its 'Futurist' views of unfulfilled prophecy, and the publication of E. B. Elliott's *Horae Apocalypticae*, advocating 'Presentist' views, gradually introduced into Evangelical circles the idea of the 'Pre-Millennarian Advent', as it is called, common to both schools of interpretation, but opposed to the general Church teaching of that day – and probably of this day also – a teaching grounded on the Prayer Book interpretation of Holy scripture. These new views were resisted by Edward Bickersteth, for a time, and by Scott, Simeon, Bishop Waldegrave and others, as crude speculations injuring the missionary cause. Again, it was held, in the early part of last century, that the Jews would return to Palestine as a converted nation; but later, when 'Pre-Millennarian' views began to spread, that they would return in an unconverted state; and now, once again, the opinion seems to be gaining ground that the Jews will not be settled in Palestine except as a Christian nation. We ought to repeat, however, that the Society, as such, has never held any particular or special prophetical views, its platform being solely a missionary one.

3 |

Memorandum to Protestant Powers

(Lord Shaftesbury, 1839)

In 1831 Muhammad Ali Pasha, Wali of Egypt launched an invasion of Syria, at that time held by his nominal overlord, Mahmud II, the Ottoman Emperor. Ali's victory opened up the potential for British influence in Palestine, and as a result the minds of the British political elite turned toward the Holy Land.

Foremost among the Christian Zionists was Lord Ashley, later the seventh Earl of Shaftesbury. In 1839 he sent the memorandum below to the leaders of the Protestant world. Two years later it was printed in *The Colonial Times* on February 23, 1841 and provoked continuing discussion within British society upon the restoration of the Jews.

The text below contains the memorandum and an accompanying letter sent to the Editor of *The Times*.

TO *the Protestant Powers of the North of Europe and America – Victoria by the grace of God, Queen of Great Britain and Ireland, Frederick, (William) III, King of Prussia; William (Frederick) (Frederich), King of the Netherlands; Charles (John) XIV, King of Sweden and Norway: Frederick VI., King of Denmark; Ernest Augustus, King of Hanover; William, King of Württemberg; the Sovereign Princes and Electors of Germany; the Cantons of the Swiss Confederation professing the Reformed Religion; and the States of*

North America, zealous for the glory of God; grace, mercy, and peace from God the Father, and the Lord Jesus Christ,

HIGH AND MIGHTY ONES,

The Most High God, who reigns in the kingdoms of men (Daniel 4:32), by whom kings reign and princes decree justice (Proverbs 8:15), having in these days granted a season of repose to his witnessing church (Acts 9:31, Revelation 12:16), planted in the lands whereof ye are kings and governors (Isaiah 49:23); the vine of his planting among the Gentiles (Acts 28:28) hath extended her boughs unto the seas and her branches unto the rivers (Isaiah 49:6), that now in nearly all the world the gospel of the kingdom is being lifted up as a witness unto all nations (Matthew 24:14), and in the isles afar off. The days are drawing near (Revelation 22:20) when the dominion, and the glory, and the kingdom, with all people, nations and languages, shall serve him who cometh in the clouds of heaven (Daniel 7:14, Revelation 1:7), whose dominion is an everlasting dominion, and kingdom that which shall not be destroyed (Psalm 45:6). Blessed be he! He hath given him waiting people to hear the sound of his approaching footsteps, and to mark the signs of his drawing near (1 Thessalonians 5:4). The fig-tree putteth forth her leaves again (Matthew 26:32). Israel's sons are asking the way to Zion, by which we know that the summer is at hand. Blessed are all they that wait (2 Thessalonians 3:5) and hold fast (Revelation 3:11), for quickly He cometh. Amen.

In the prospect of the Christian church, of the speedy appearing of her glorified head, the zeal of the Lord's servants hath been stirred up (Revelation 3:2) to a multiplied diligence in those labours of faith and love which were devolved upon her (Matthew 28:19), when the Son of God, as a man taking a journey into a far country, bade his servants occupy, until he returned again (Luke 19:13). With other responsibilities, the circumstances of one peculiar people, whom the Most High hath separated (Genesis 12:1) and taken into covenant with him (Genesis 17:7; Exodus 34:7), and which covenant no act of theirs, however iniquitous and rebellious, can repeal or destroy (Malachi 3:6), whom he hath scattered in all lands as witnesses of his unity and power (Isaiah 43:19), connected with whom the welfare of mankind is bound up, and in the lifting up of whose head the most stupendous consequences are made to depend (Romans 11:15), are presented at this eleventh hour for the repentance and faith of Christendom, that the blood of our brethren of the circumcision which has been unjustly shed, may be atoned for in the blood of the Lamb (Isaiah 1:18), and the fruits of forgiveness be manifested (Matthew 3:8) in presenting the children of this people continually at the throne of grace (1 Peter 2:5; Psalm 122:6) for the atoning sacrifice of Christ to cover them (Joel 2:16); and as the Almighty, in his providential appointments, shall make the way plain to present the children of Israel who may be willing to go up (Psalm 110:3) as an offering to the Lord of Hosts in Mount Zion (Isaiah 18:7).

For three hundred years the testimony of the churches, planted in the lands over which Almighty God hath made you rulers, hath been lifted up against that apostasy which usurped the authority of the Lord Jesus Christ in the earth (Revelation 17:5; 18:5) daring presumptuously to assert power over nations (Revelation 18:7) and over kingdoms, to root up and to pull down, to build, to plant, and to destroy (Daniel 7:20; Revelation 13:2,7). The millstone which shall sink the Great Babylon in the abyss of an unfathomable perdition (Revelation 18:21) when her hour arrives (and it may be soon!), with the judgment under which she hath long lain, for being drunken with the blood of the saints and of the martyrs of Jesus (Revelation 17:6) shall include the avenging of the wrongs of God's ancient people (Isaiah 51:22,23) and a terrible account it is; and the issue shall be joy and gladness to the whole earth, for it is written, "Rejoice, O ye nations, with his people: for he avengeth the blood of his servant, and shall render vengeance unto his adversaries, and will be merciful to his land, and his people" (Deuteronomy 32:43). "Happy art thou, O Israel; who is like unto thee, O people saved by the Lord, the shield of thy help and the sword of thy excellence; and thine enemies shall be found liars unto thee, and thou shalt tread on their high places" (Deuteronomy 33:29).

In the events, on which the eyes of nations are fixed, taking place around, whilst the continuance and stability of your thrones and sway, O kings, is the earnest prayer of the Christian church (1 Timothy 2:2), she cannot but uphold the witness that the days draw nigh, when, under the hallowed sway of Messiah the Prince, the now despised nation of the Jews shall possess the kingdom (Daniel 7:27) and she directs, with reverential awe, your eye to that mighty empire in the east which is crumbling to the dust, and drying up in all her streams (Revelation 16:12) to make way for the event. Palestine hath been a burdensome stone (Zechariah 12:2) unto the followers of the false Prophet (Revelation 16:13) as it was to the ancestors of many of you, O Princes, when, under the banners of the Popish Antichrist, their mistaken zeal sought to recover the Holy City from the Saracen's grasp. But the fulness of the Gentiles is at hand (Romans 11:21) and unto Israel the dominion shall return (Micah 4:8).

The apostate Julian sought to plant the children of this people in the seats of their fathers, in despite of that holy faith, one of the external evidences of whose truth was, that their house was left unto them desolate, until they should say, "Blessed is he that cometh in the name of the Lord" (Matthew 23:38,39). But is it anywhere declared in the word of our God, that the children of Israel, scattered and pealed, humbled and dispirited, impoverished and broken down, should not be presented as an offering in faith to Jehovah of Hosts in Mount Zion? that there they may be pleaded with face to face by the God of their fathers (Ezekiel 20:13), that there the veil may be rent (Isaiah 25:7) which is over their hearts (2 Corinthians 3:15), that there they may look on him whom they have pierced (Zechariah 12:10). Your attention, high and mighty ones, is directed to the recorded fact that such an offering is expected. And before that full and final gathering which follows the judgments poured out on all the earth (Isaiah 63:15,16,20), a power, and that power a northern one (Jeremiah 3:12; 31:6,9; 23:7,8; Isaiah 43:6; 49:12), shall be employed to lead a people wonderful from her beginning hitherto – a nation expecting and trampled under foot – whose land rivers have spoiled, unto the name of the Lord of Hosts in Mount Zion (Isaiah 18). These designs and purposes of the Lord God of Israel, King of Kings and Lord of Lords, are declared unto you, high and mighty ones, his servants (Daniel 5:23) that you may ponder them, and know his will, from the voice with which he is about to speak unto nations and unto men (Haggai 2:6; Isaiah 1:10) for the time is at hand (Revelation 1:3).

Your wisdom hath been exercised to mark the boundaries of kingdoms and to define the limits of empires; and has not the aggressor overleaped all barriers, and the strength of treaties snapped asunder as tow? And why! Because when the Almighty awarded to the nations their inheritance, when he separated the sons of Adam, he set the bounds of the people according to number of the children of Israel (Deuteronomy 32:7,8). By an unrepealed covenant, the Lord God declared unto Abraham, concerning the land of Palestine, "Unto they seed have I given this land, from the river of Egypt to the great river, the river Euphrates" (Genesis 15:18). This gift was ratified unto him for an everlasting possession, and to his seed after him, when the Almighty gave him His covenant, and changed his name to Abraham (Genesis 17:4,8). For the purposes of infinite wisdom fast hastening to maturity, the Lord God hath scattered his inheritance to the four winds of heaven. But hear the word of the Lord, O ye nations, and declare it in the isles afar off. He that scatted Israel will gather him, and keep him as a shepherd doth his flock (Jeremiah 31:10).

As the spirit of Cyrus, King of Persia, was stirred up to build the Lord a temple, which was in Jerusalem (2 Chronicles 36:22,23), who is there among you, high and mighty ones of all the nations, to fulfil the good pleasure of the holy will of the Lord of heaven, saying to Jerusalem, "Thou shalt be built", and to the temple "Thy foundations shall be laid" (Isaiah 44:28)? The Lord

God of Israel be with such. Great grace, mercy, and peace shall descend upon the people who offer themselves willingly; and the free offerings of their hearts and hands shall be those of a sweet-smelling savour unto him who hath said, "I will bless them that bless thee (Genesis 12:3), and contend with him who contendeth with thee" (Isaiah 49:25).

The grace of our Lord Jesus Christ, and the love of God, and the communion of the Holy Ghost, be with you all. Amen.

Signed and sealed in London, 8th of January, in the year of our Lord 1839, in the name of the God of Abraham, of Isaac, and of Jacob, on behalf of many who wait for the redemption of Israel.

TO THE EDITOR OF THE TIMES.

Sir, – Every right-minded person must feel gratified at the general expression of interest in the Jewish nation which has been elicited by the recent sufferings of their brethren at Damascus. It is to be hoped that the public feeling will not be allowed to evaporate in the mere expression of sympathy, but that some effectual measures may be adopted to prevent a recurrence of these atrocities, not merely in our own times, but in generations yet to come. We must not forget, when giving utterance to our indignation at the late transactions in the east, that but few centuries have passed since our country was the scene of similar enormities on a far larger scale. What reader of English history does not recall with shame and sorrow the wholesale tortures, executions, and massacres of the Jews who had sought shelter here, or who can estimate the amount of property seized and confiscated, or the number of hearts wrung by the endless repetition of cruelty and injustice? If in England they have till lately been thus treated, how can they look for more security elsewhere? Instead of wondering that they should become sordid and debased, the only cause for surprise is that any should rise to intelligence and respectability. Subject to the caprice and cruelty of any nation among whom they may dwell, fleeing from persecutions of one only to meet with like treatment from another, having no city of refuge where they can be in safeguard, no single spot to call their own, they are in a more pitiable condition than the Indian of the forest, or the Arab of the desert.

"The wild bird hath her nest, the fox his cave, Mankind their country, Israel but the grave."

Is this state of things always to continue? They think not. Though many hundreds of years of hope deferred might have been enough to quench the anticipations of most sanguine, they still hope on, and turn with constant and earnest longing to the land of their forefathers. Their little children are taught to expect that they shall one day see Jerusalem. They purchase no landed property and hold themselves in readiness at a few hours' notice to revisit what they and we tacitly agree to call "their own land". It is theirs by a right which no other nation can boast, for God gave it to them, and though dispossessed of it for so many ages, it is still but partially peopled, and held with a loose hand and a disputed title by a hostile power, as if in readiness for their return.

There are political reasons arising from the present aspect of affairs in Russia, Turkey, and Egypt, which would make it to the interest not only of England but of other European nations, either by purchase or by treaty, to procure the restoration of Judaea to its rightful claimants. About a year since, I heard it said by a German Jew, that a proposal had some time before been made by our (then) Government to the late Baron Rothschild, that he should enter into a negotiation for this purpose, and that he declined, assigning as a reason, "Judaea is our own; we will not buy it, we wait till God shall restore it to us". The desirableness as well as the possibility of such a step seems daily to become more evident, but England has lately proved that she needs no selfish motives to induce her to discharge a debt of national honour and justice, or to perform an act of pure benevolence. The one now suggested would not, judging from appearances, cost 20,000,000 of money, or be unaccomplished after fifty years of exertion, or be so vast and so laborious an undertaking as the extinction of slavery throughout the world. It would be a noble thing for a Christian nation to restore these wanderers to their homes again. It would be a crowning point in the glory of England to bring about such an event. The special blessings promised in the scriptures to those who befriend the Jews would rest upon her, and her sons and daughters would sit down with purer enjoyment to their domestic comforts when they thought that the persecuted outcasts of so many ages had, through their agency, been replaced in homes as happy and secure as theirs.

Hoping that some master mind may be led to take up this subject in all its bearings, and to form some tangible plan for its accomplishment, and that some Wilberforce may be raised up to plead for it by all the powerful and heart-stirring arguments of which it is capable,

I am, Sir, your obedient servant,
AN ENGLISH CHRISTIAN.

4 |

A mission of Inquiry ...

(A. Bonar and R. M. M'Cheyne, 1842)

This chapter contains an extract from *Narrative of a Mission of Inquiry to the Jews from the Church of Scotland in 1839*. This mission was a survey of the Land made by prominent members of the Church of Scotland, including Dr. Alexander Keith (author of *Sketch of the Evidence from Prophecy* and *Evidence of the Truth of the Christian Religion*). The trip was designed to establish the state of the Jewish people with an eye to later mission work. The report of the journey became a bestseller, increasing awareness of the Jewish presence in the Land. The Church of Scotland, and later the Free Church of Scotland, was actively involved with Jewish affairs throughout the nineteenth century. The Church has now shifted position. A 2013 report (later revised under political pressure) spiritualised the promises to Abraham saying: *"They are a way of speaking about how to live under God so that justice and peace reign, the weak and poor are protected, the stranger is included, and all have a share in the community and contribution to make to it. The 'promised land' in the Bible is not a place, so much as a metaphor of how things ought to be among the people of God. This 'promised land' can be found – or built – anywhere."*

"Thus saith the Lord of Hosts, I am jealous for Jerusalem and for Zion with a great jealousy, and I am very sore displeased with the heathen that are at ease." (Zechariah 1:11,15)

THE subject of the Jews had but recently begun to awaken attention among the faithful servants of God in the Church of Scotland. The plan of sending a Deputation to Palestine and other countries, to visit and inquire after the scattered Jews, was suggested by a series of striking providences in the case of some of the individuals concerned. The Reverend Robert S. Candlish, D. D., Minister of St. George's, Edinburgh, saw these providences, and seized on the idea. On the part of our Church, "the thing was done suddenly;" but it soon became evident that "God had prepared the people" (2 Chronicles 29:36).

The Committee of our General Assembly, appointed to consider what might be done in the way of setting on foot Missionary operations among the Jews, were led unanimously to adopt this plan after prayerful and anxious deliberation. Our own anticipations of the result of our inquiries might be described by a reference to Nehemiah (Nehemiah 1:2,4). We thought we could see that, if the Lord brought us home in safety, many people would ask us "concerning the Jews that had escaped and were left of the captivity, and concerning Jerusalem"; and that our Report might lead not a few to "weep, and mourn, and fast, and pray, before the God of heaven", for Israel. We have good reason to believe that this has been the effect. In Scotland, at least, many more "watchmen have been set upon the walls of Jerusalem" (Isaiah 62:6,7), men of Nehemiah's spirit, who keep their eye upon its ruins, favouring its very dust, and who "will never hold their peace, day nor night, till the Lord make Jerusalem a praise in the earth".

It was a token for good at the very outset, that Dr. Black, Professor of Divinity in the Marischal College, Aberdeen, and Dr. Keith, Minister of St. Cyrus, whose writings on the evidence from fulfilled prophecy have been so extensively read and blessed, were willing to give themselves to this work, along with two younger brethren. Reverend R. M. M'Cheyne, Minister of St. Peter's, Dundee, and Reverend Andrew A. Bonar, Assistant Minister of Collace, Perthshire. Mr. Robert Wodrow, an Elder of our Church, whose whole heart had yearned over Israel for many a year, was also appointed by the Committee, but ill health compelled him reluctantly to decline. Being all of one mind in regard to Israel, and eager to seek their good, a few weeks sufficed to have every preparation completed. Those of us who had Parishes to leave behind, felt that, in a case like this, we might act as did the shepherds at Bethlehem, leaving our flocks for a season under the care of the Shepherd of Israel, whose long lost sheep we were now going to seek. Nor have we had any cause to regret our confidence, and one at least of our number found this anticipation of the Good Shepherd's care more than realized on his return.

As we went on our way through Glasgow, Greenock, and Liverpool, the members of our Church commended us to the Lord. On our arrival in London, the office-bearers and members of the London Jewish Society, and many other Christian friends in the city, showed us no small kindness. The Religious Tract Society furnished us with their publications in various languages. What we saw of the Jews there, and of the operations of the London Society among them, was very useful to us. Provided with Lord Palmerston's passport, and letters to her Majesty's foreign Consuls, through the kindness of Sir George Grey and Lord Ashley, as well as with letters to friends and merchants in the various countries we expected to visit, we were commended to the Lord in Regent Square Church the night before we set out. Many prayers also followed us, and the prayers of our brethren have not been in vain …

5 |

An extract from the twelfth letter of *Romans und Jerusalem*

(Moses Hess, 1862)

Hess' *Romans und Jerusalem*, although not particularly influential upon publication, gradually grew to become a key Zionist text, inspiring the efforts and ideologies of no lesser figures than Herzl and Ben-Gurion. An often prescient book, it was written as a series of letters to a grieving woman and was the first major work to present the Zionist case within the prevailing European discourses of nationalism, Marxism, Hegelianism and the like. Hess saw the Jews as a nation and not merely a religious group. He did, however, see Judaism as a unique religion which the Jews, if they returned to their Land, could use, within a broadly socialist framework, to spread its values to the rest of the world.

Although Hess' exact meaning is at points disputed, some of the ideas in *Romans und Jerusalem* made their way into Herzl's *Der Judenstaat*. A Franco-German, Hess is now seen as one of the forefathers of the socialist Labour Zionism that was a driving force leading up to 1948, and remains a part of Israeli politics to this day.

IF the Jewish nationality is a living one, it will not allow any reservations to deter it from getting down to the job of its political rebirth. Even if the time is not yet come when the lamb will graze peacefully with the wolf, still the ruling majority have lost their wolf's appetite, and the suppressed minority have lost their lamb's patience. Religious tolerance has become a much more common article of faith than any other. Besides, I think, as I said, that the future religious culture[1] of all reborn nations will be so different from today's religious culture, which has come to us from a time when a people's individuality was suppressed. Therefore, I cannot perceive that this religious culture, which cannot exist for much longer anyway, will cause any difficulty for our future national religious culture. Ultimately, I must emphasize once again, our future religious culture, like that of all other people, will not precede the rebirth, but rather follow it. The first thing to be done is to awaken a patriotic sense in the hearts of the educated Jews and to release the mass of the Jewish people from a soul-destroying formalism by this newly rejuvenated patriotism. If we are successful in initiating this process, the many difficulties which it causes will be resolved through the implementation itself. Only if all Jewish hearts were dead, only if the Jews were no longer capable of patriotic enthusiasm, would we have to give up a work, which like every great work of history cannot be carried out without great struggles.

Despite misunderstood reform and orthodoxy, the Jews have too much good sense to endorse religious effusion, which has no foundation in the present. But this sense of realism which our race possesses to such a high degree, will finally win over our brothers, who still have a Jewish heart, whether Reformed or Orthodox, for national endeavours, which are based only on reality.

The objections of Reformed Jews against the re-establishment of the Jewish state do not have their fundamental motivation in this attitude of heart and mind, which would never recoil from the difficulties of a great work, would never calculate in advance the cost of the sacrifices which might be necessary to

---

1 The German *Cultus* (now *Kultus*) could refer to religion and religious practice as well as culture (in the case of the Jewish people the two are closely related). We have generally translated it as "religious culture" (G. B. + C. B.).

its implementation; but these objections originated rather from a moral and intellectual narrow-mindedness, which is incapable of elevating itself to a higher moral point of view from which one can view the magnitude of the misfortune which should be alleviated, as well as the precise means of remedial action. For the last two thousand years, as Heine and all his educated Jewish contemporaries rightly felt, the Jewish religion has really been more a misfortune than a religion. One cannot however, as the educated would like to persuade themselves, escape from this misfortune, through reform or baptism. Whether he likes it or not, each Jew is bound in solidarity with his whole nation. Not until the Jewish people is freed from the burden which it has carried with heroic willingness for self-sacrifice on its bowed neck for thousands of years, will the burden also be lifted from the shoulders of those Reformed Jews, of whom there will only ever be an insignificant number. We all must carry the "Yoke of the Kingdom of Heaven" until the end.

In the initial euphoria of the modern reform endeavours one could be deluded into thinking that the whole Jewish people was alienating itself from its national religious culture through universal humanistic tendencies, in which Judaism and its special life, as one would like to persuade oneself, was bound to disappear. Today not even the most superficial nationalist can harbour this philanthropic illusion. Despite the lack of a deep look at nature and history, the historical movement in contemporary Judaism has already ensured that the rationalists open their eyes; even in the West, where the Jews are in the closest contact with the general civilisation through thousands of connections, reform could not harm the old Jewish religious culture. The majority of Western Jews still embrace the old Jewish religious culture. Neither emancipation nor Christian proselytizing, which plays upon material advantages and religious indifference, could move the majority to apostasy. On the contrary, it has become evident recently that, even among those who earlier pursued rebellion against Judaism as a humanist ideal, sympathies with the old Jewish life are increasing daily. The levelling tendencies have

5 – An extract from the twelfth letter of Romans und Jerusalem

not had any influence on those Jews who make up the masses of the Jewish people, and will continue to have no influence on these people. The masses are never moved to progress by abstract ideas. The motivating forces for progress always lie much deeper than even the socialist revolutionaries thought. In the case of the Jews, national independence must precede any sociopolitical advance, much more so in the case of the Jews than in the case of nations who are oppressed in their own lands. For the Jews, a common homeland is the first requirement for healthier working conditions. People are convivial, and like plants and animals, they need space to flourish and develop, without which they become parasites, only able to nourish themselves through the efforts of others. The parasitical way of making a living through the exploitation of people has however played a great role in man's developmental history up to now, and is in no way only typical of the Jews. As long as science and industry were in their infancy, the land which a nation had once taken into possession was never sufficient to nourish its inhabitants; the peoples had to fight each other and make each other into slaves, or allow the emergence of ruling and serving classes in their own midst. But this social "animal kingdom", which lived from the reciprocal exploitation of people, is coming to an end, since modern science and industry have begun to dominate the world. The civilised nations are preparing themselves for a collective exploitation of nature, through work based on the achievements of science. This no longer requires the involvement of parasites, and therefore they are not permitted to emerge. The civilised nations are preparing themselves for this new era (not to be confused with the Prussian one) by securing a national terrain, by the destruction of every race and class dominion from within and without, and by a free association of all productive forces. In this, the hostile opposition between capitalist speculation and productive work will dwindle simultaneously with that between all philosophical speculations and scientific work. I know very well that the need for healthy working conditions, which have the exploitation of nature by man as their foundation, is felt deeply among the Jews. I am aware of the great efforts which are made among us, to bring up our younger Jewish generation as useful workers. But I know too, that at least the majority of Jews in exile could never devote themselves to such work, because they do not have their own ancestral land, which is a basic requirement for such work, and because they cannot mix with the people among whom they are scattered, without being disloyal to their own national religious culture. Such laudable efforts for healthy Jewish working conditions contribute indirectly to the destruction of Jewish religious culture and will therefore be just as fruitless ultimately as efforts at reform, which contribute directly to its destruction. Judaism cannot be rejuvenated in exile. The most that can happen is that reform and philanthropic endeavours can bring it to rebellion. No reformer or tyrant will be able to achieve this. The Jewish people will not take part in the great historical movement of modern humanity until the Jews have a fatherland. As long as the majority of the Jews persist in their exceptional situation, then even the relatively few individual Jews who give up everything in vain, in order to escape the wrong position of the Jewish people, will be touched much more painfully by the situation than the majority, who consider themselves to be unhappy, but not dishonoured. Therefore the Jew, whether Orthodox or not, cannot withdraw from the task of elevating the whole of Jewry. Each Jew, even those who are baptized, is responsible (through their solidarity) for the rebirth of Israel.

If one comprehends the endlessly tragic role which the Jewish people have played in history until the present day, then one recognises as well the only means to remedy our misery. Today, this means is no longer as impracticable as it may appear at first glance. It is in accordance with the sympathies of the French people, as well as in the interests of French politicians, for France to extend her redemptive work to include the Jewish nation, after her victorious army has toppled the modern Nebuchadnezzars from the heights, from which they were able to impose arrogant decrees and edicts on the repressed peoples.

5 – An extract from the twelfth letter of Romans und Jerusalem

It must be important to France, to see the road to India and China occupied by peoples who will be loyal to the end; in order to fulfil the historical task, which has fallen to her since her great revolution. But which people could be more suitable to such a task than the Jewish, which has been intended for the same mission since the beginning of history?

6 |

Disraeli's purchase of a stake in the Suez Canal

(November 1875)

Throughout history it has often been the case that a power wishing to control the Holy Land must also have control over Egypt. During the Crusades, for example, Richard I of England held back from taking Jerusalem, knowing that unless he took Egypt first his efforts would ultimately prove futile.

From his exposition of the prophecies given through Isaiah, Brother Thomas concluded that Britain would take Egypt before it became the facilitator of the Jewish Return. This they eventually did in 1882. As a preliminary to this, they gained control of the Suez Canal, the key strategic waterway that links the Mediterranean to the Red Sea (thus allowing ships to avoid a long trip around Africa). This was done in 1875 by the then Prime Minister, Benjamin Disraeli (the UK's only leader of Jewish origin), also known as Lord Beaconsfield. His bold move is described below by Sir Henry Lucy, in an extract from his book *Sixty Years in the Wilderness*, published in 1909.

ON a certain Sunday night in the spring of 1875 he chanced to be dining in Bruton Street with Henry Oppenheim, one of the original proprietors of the *Daily News*. During a residence in Paris and Egypt that gentleman, just settling down in London, was brought into close connection with Egyptian financial affairs. On the previous day he heard of the intention of the impecunious Khedive to sell *en bloc* his holding in the capital of the Suez Canal. Greenwood instantly saw the opportunity for a great stroke of State. On leaving Bruton Street he went direct to the private residence of the Foreign Secretary (Lord Derby) and told him of the rare chance. Lord Derby informed the Prime Minister, whose Oriental mind glowed at the prospect of so stupendous a deal. Inquiry secretly made at Cairo disclosed the fact that the Khedive would 'part' for a sum of four millions sterling. But it must be money down.

It was Greenwood told me, on Lord Beaconsfield's personal suggestion that the difficulty, at the moment apparently insuperable, was overcome. The consent of Parliament was necessary to confirmation of the deal. That involved both delay and publicity, either fatal to success. Late on the Thursday night following the Bruton Street dinner, the Premier sent his private secretary, Monty Corry, to call upon Baron Rothschild, the Sidonia of 'Coningsby', at the time head of the great financial house. Even a Rothschild did not happen to have about him at the moment a trifle of four million sterling. Nor was it possible, in accordance with the traditions of the house, that such a transaction should be entered upon without having been considered in family council. Corry accordingly returned to the Premier without definite reply. It came promptly on the following morning, the terms being that the money would be advanced on the commission of 2.5%.

These terms were pretty stiff, involving a payment of £100,000. The City heard of them with envy, and they were discussed with much severity when the matter came before the House of Commons. The Rothschilds and their friends defended them on the ground that the colossal transaction involved a certain measure of risk. There was absolutely no security beyond the influence of the Premier, still master of a majority in the House of Commons, and pledged to invoke its aid in order to obtain Parliamentary sanction. The whole thing happened between two Sundays. On the first Greenwood dined at Bruton

Street; on the second, calling on Lord Derby, he learned that the transaction had been successfully carried through, and was invited to say what form his personal recompense should take. He declined to specify a request, protesting he had done nothing but his duty, and was content that its accomplishment should be his reward.

7 |

The Basel Programme

(August 30, 1897)

The First Zionist Congress was held from August 29-31, 1897, and was called by Theodore Herzl as a symbolic Parliament for those sympathetic to the Zionist cause. Herzl sought to put forward the plans he articulated a year previously in his book *Der Judenstaat* (in English, *The Jewish State*). The Congress resulted in the formation of the World Zionist Organisation (WZO). Membership of the WZO was open to all Jews worldwide, and the right to vote for Congressional delegates to any who purchased a Zionist Shekel. The formation of the WZO was accompanied by the declaration of the 'Basel Programme', a list of the four initials goals of the Zionist movement.

ZIONISM is striving for the creation of a publicly and legally secured homeland in Palestine for the Jewish people.

In order to achieve this aim, the congress is seeking to implement the following measures:

1. The promotion of the purposeful settlement of Palestine with Jewish farmers, craftsmen and tradesmen.
2. The organisation and uniting of the whole Jewish community through suitable local and general functions, according to the laws of the land.

3. The strengthening of Jewish national feeling and consciousness.
4. Preparatory steps towards the attainment of government agreement which will be necessary, in order to achieve the aim of Zionism.

8 |

Diary entry for January 26, 1904

(Theodore Herzl, 1904)

On January 25, 1904 Theodore Herzl met with Pope Pius X in the Vatican to seek his support for a Jewish state in Palestine. He gained access to the Pope through the Papal portrait artist, Count Berthold Lippay, who Herzl had met in Venice. The Pope outlined his position, namely that Rome could not support the Jewish claim until they accepted Christ as their Messiah. This was the Vatican's position until 1993, when diplomatic relations with Israel were finally established by the signing of the 'Fundamental Accord'. The change was influenced by:

- The unbroken Israeli control of the whole of Jerusalem since 1967.
- The Palestinians talking openly with the Israelis at the Madrid conference of 1991.
- The outworking of *Nostra aetate*, the declaration on the Relation of the Church with Non-Christian Religions of the Second Vatican Council (1965) which called for interfaith dialogue.
- The personal commitments of Pope John Paul II and Cardinal Ratzinger (later Pope Benedict XVI) to better relations with the Jews.

YESTERDAY I was with the Pope. The route was already familiar since I had traversed it with Lippay several times.

We passed Swiss footmen, who looked like clerics, and clerics who looked like footmen, the Papal officers and chamberlains.

I arrived 10 minutes ahead of time and didn't have to wait at all.

I was conducted through numerous small reception rooms to the Pope.

He received me standing and held out his hand, which I did not kiss.

Lippay had told me I should do so, but I didn't.

I believe that I incurred his displeasure by this, for everyone who visits him kneels down and kisses his hand at least.

The hand-kissing had caused me a lot of anxiety. I was quite glad when the moment was past.

He seated himself in an armchair, a kind of throne for minor occasions. Then he invited me to sit down close beside him and smiled in friendly anticipation.

I began:

"*Ringrazio Vostra Santità per il favore di m'aver accordato quest'udienza* [I thank Your Holiness for granting me the favour of this audience]."

"*È un piacere* [It is a pleasure]", he said with kindly deprecation.

I apologized for my wretched Italian, but he said:

"*No, parla molto bene, signor Commendatore* [No, Commander, you speak very well]."

For on Lippay's advice I had put on for the first time my Mejidiye ribbon. Consequently the Pope always addressed me as Commendatore.

He is a kindly, unrefined village priest, to whom Christianity has remained a living thing even in the Vatican.

8 – Diary entry for January 26, 1904

I briefly explained to him my request. He, however, possibly annoyed by my refusal to kiss his hand, answered sternly and resolutely:

"*Noi non possiamo favorire questo movimento. Non potremo impedire gli Ebrei di andare a Gerusalemme – ma favorire non possiamo mai. La terra di Gerusalemme se non era sempre santa, è santificata per la vita di Jesu Christo* (he did not pronounce it Gesu, but Yesu, in the Venetian fashion) *Io come capo della chiesa non posso dirle altra cosa. Gli Ebrei non hanno riconosciuto nostro Signore, perciò non possiamo riconoscere il popolo ebreo* [We cannot support this movement. We cannot prevent the Jews from going to Jerusalem – but we could never support it. The soil of Jerusalem, if it was not already sacred, has been sanctified by the life of Jesus Christ. As the head of the Church I cannot tell you anything different. The Jews have not recognised our Lord, therefore we cannot recognise the Jewish people]."

With these words the conflict between Rome, represented by him, and Jerusalem, represented by me, was once again opened up.

At first, however, I tried a conciliatory approach. I recited my little piece about extraterritorialization, *res sacrae extra commercium* [holy places excluded from the national territory]. It didn't make much of an impression. *Gerusalemme*, he said, must not fall into the hands of the Jews.

"And the present situation, Holy Father?"

"I know, it is not pleasant to see the Turks in possession of our Holy Places. We simply have to put up with that. But supporting the Jews in obtaining control of the Holy Places, that we cannot do".

I said that our point of departure had been solely the distress of the Jews and that we desired to avoid the religious issues.

"Yes, but we, and I as the head of the Church, cannot do that. There are two possibilities. Either the Jews will cling to their faith and continue to await the Messiah who, for us, has already appeared. In that case they will be denying the divinity of Jesus and we cannot help them. Or else they will go there without any religion, and then we will be even less able to give them our support.

"The Jewish religion was the foundation of our own; but it was superseded by the teachings of Christ, and we cannot concede it any further validity. The Jews, who ought to have been the first to acknowledge Jesus Christ, have not done so to this day."

It was on the tip of my tongue to say, "That's what happens in every family. No one believes in his own relatives". But I said instead: "Terror and persecution may not have been the right means for enlightening the Jews."

But he rejoined, magnificent this time in his simplicity:

"Our Lord came without power. *Era povero* [He was poor]. He came *in pace* [in peace]. He persecuted no one. He was persecuted.

He was *abbandonato* [forsaken] even by his apostles. Only later did he grow in stature. It took three centuries for the Church to develop. So the Jews therefore had time to acknowledge his divinity without any pressure. But they haven't done so to this day."

"But, Holy Father, the Jews are in terrible straits. I don't know if Your Holiness is acquainted with the full extent of this sad situation. We need a land for these persecuted people."

"Does it have to be *Gerusalemme*?"

"We are not asking for Jerusalem, but for Palestine – only the secular land."

"We cannot support it."

"Does Your Holiness know the situation of the Jews?"

8 – Diary entry for January 26, 1904

"Yes, from my Mantua days. There are Jews there. And I have always had good relations with Jews. Only the other evening two Jews were here to see me. After all, there are other relationships than those of religion: those of courtesy and philanthropy. These we do not deny to the Jews. Indeed, we also pray for them: that their minds be enlightened. This very day the Church is celebrating the feast of an unbeliever who, on the road to Damascus, became miraculously converted to the true faith. And so, if you get to Palestine and settle your people there, we shall have churches and priests ready to baptize all of you."

Count Lippay had had himself announced. The Pope permitted him to enter. The Count kneeled, kissed his hand and then joined in the conversation by telling of our "miraculous" meeting in Bauer's Beer Hall in Venice. The miracle was that he had originally planned to spend the night in Padua. And, he said, I had expressed the wish to be allowed to kiss the Holy Father's feet.

At this the Pope made *une tête* [pulled a face], for I hadn't even kissed his hand. Lippay went on to say that I had spoken of Jesus Christ, acknowledging his noble qualities. The Pope listened, taking a pinch of snuff now and then, and blowing his nose on a big red cotton handkerchief. Actually, these peasant touches are what I like best about him and what compels my respect.

By speaking this way Lippay was trying to account for his introducing me, perhaps to excuse it. But the Pope said: "On the contrary, I am glad you brought Signor Commendatore to me."

But as far as the subject of our meeting was concerned, he repeated what he had told me: *Non possumus* [We cannot]!

Finally, he dismissed us. Lippay knelt before him for quite some time and couldn't seem to get enough of kissing his hand. Then I realised that the Pope liked that. But on leaving I again simply shook his hand warmly and made a low bow.

Duration of the audience: about 25 minutes.

In the Raphael *stanze* [rooms], where I spent the next hour, I saw a picture of the Emperor kneeling to be crowned by a seated Pope.

That's the way Rome wants it.

9 |

The Balfour Declaration

(November 1917)

The Balfour Declaration was a short letter written by the British Foreign Secretary, Arthur Balfour, to the influential Zionist Walter Rothschild. It was the first official charter from a major power sanctioning action toward "*the establishment of a national home for the Jewish people*".

As such it acted as an immense spur to the activities of the Zionist cause, but also faced instant opposition from both Arab and European powers. This controversy was particularly complex as the declaration followed quickly on from the McMahon-Hussein Correspondence and the Sykes-Picot Agreement.

The McMahon-Hussein Correspondence was an exchange of letters between Sir Henry McMahon, the British High Commissioner in Egypt, and Hussein bin Ali, the Sharif of Mecca. Arab readings of the letters saw Palestine as being part of the area promised to them upon independence after World War One, whilst the British took the opposite view.

The Sykes-Picot Agreement was made between British and French diplomats, and defined the areas that each nation would control after the War. It is seen as a reneging of the promise by the British Colonel, T. E. Lawrence, for a national Arab homeland in return for military help during the War.

Periods of historical turmoil are full of such diplomatic toing and froing, with governments desperately seeking to cover all contingencies. Often these hastily compiled agreements can have long-lasting effects. In November 2016, in a meeting in the House of Lords in London, a British Baroness started a petition seeking a national apology for the writing of the Declaration. The event was tinged with anti-Semitism, one speaker reportedly blaming the Jews for antagonizing Hitler. Such is the level of feeling that the Balfour Declaration still generates one hundred years on.

Foreign Office,

November 2nd, 1917.

Dear Lord Rothschild,

I have much pleasure in conveying to you, on behalf of His Majesty's Government, the following declaration of sympathy with Jewish Zionist aspirations which has been submitted to, and approved by, the Cabinet.

"His Majesty's Government view with favour the establishment in Palestine of a national home for the Jewish people, and will use their best endeavours to facilitate the achievement of this object, it being clearly understood that nothing shall be done which may prejudice the civil and religious rights of the existing non-Jewish communities in Palestine or the rights and political status enjoyed by Jews in any other country."

I should be grateful if you would bring this declaration to the knowledge of the Zionist Federation.

Yours sincerely,

Arthur James Balfour.

10 |

British policy in Palestine

(Winston Churchill, 1922)

The extract below is from *Correspondence with the Palestine Arab Delegation and the Zionist Organisation*, a document commonly known as 'the Churchill White Paper'. In May 1921 Jewish communists in Palestine had distributed leaflets in Jaffa calling for the overthrow of the British administration, and at the same time organized a May Day parade. Another Jewish group had already planned an officially sanctioned parade. Predictably the two parades collided and physical fighting ensued. The Arabs, aware of the commotion, assumed the Jews were attacking Arabs, and so went on a rampage of revenge. This campaign of violence continued for a number of days, and dozens were left dead (both Jews and Arabs among them). The whole affair came to be known as the Jaffa Riots.

Winston Churchill, then Secretary of State for the Colonies, arranged for a white paper to investigate the causes of the trouble, and to recommend corrective action. The paper highlighted as the major factor the Arab concern over British facilitated growth of the Jewish influence and population in Palestine. Other reasons for the riots, and the suggested remedies, can be found in the extract below.

THE Secretary of State for the Colonies has given renewed consideration to the existing political situation in Palestine, with a very earnest desire to arrive at a settlement of the outstanding questions which have given rise to uncertainty and unrest among certain sections of the population. After consultation with the High Commissioner for Palestine the following statement has been drawn up. It summarises the essential parts of the correspondence that has already taken place between the Secretary of State and a delegation from the Moslem Christian Society of Palestine, which has been for some time in England, and it states the further conclusions which have since been reached.

The tension which has prevailed from time to time in Palestine is mainly due to apprehensions, which are entertained both by sections of the Arab and by sections of the Jewish population. These apprehensions, so far as the Arabs are concerned, are partly based upon exaggerated interpretations of the meaning of the Declaration favouring the establishment of a Jewish National Home in Palestine, made on behalf of His Majesty's Government on 2nd November, 1917.

Unauthorized statements have been made to the effect that the purpose in view is to create a wholly Jewish Palestine. Phrases have been used such as that Palestine is to become "as Jewish as England is English". HMG regard any such expectation as impracticable and have no such aim in view. Nor have they at any time contemplated, as appears to be feared by the Arab Delegation, the disappearance or the subordination of the Arabic population, language or culture in Palestine. They would draw attention to the fact that the terms of the Declaration referred to do not contemplate that Palestine as a whole should be converted into a Jewish National Home, but that such a Home should be founded in Palestine. In this connection it has been observed with satisfaction that at the meeting of the Zionist Congress, the supreme governing body of the Zionist Organization, held at Carlsbad in September, 1921, a resolution was passed expressing as the official statement of Zionist aims "the determination of the Jewish people to live with the Arab people on terms of unity and mutual respect, and together with them to make the common home into a flourishing community, the upbuilding of which may assure to each of its peoples an undisturbed national development".

It is also necessary to point out that the Zionist Commission in Palestine, now termed the Zionist Executive, has not desired to possess, and does not possess, any share in the general administration of the country. Nor does the special position assigned to the Zionist Organization in Article IV of the Draft Mandate for Palestine imply any such functions. That special position relates to the measures to be taken in Palestine affecting the Jewish population, and contemplates that the Organization may assist in the general development of the country, but does not entitle it to share in any degree in its Government.

Further, it is contemplated that the status of all citizens of Palestine in the eyes of the law shall be Palestinian, and it has never been intended that they, or any section of them, should possess any other juridical status.

So far as the Jewish population of Palestine are concerned it appears that some among them are apprehensive that His Majesty's Government may depart from the policy embodied in the Declaration of 1917. It is necessary, therefore, once more to affirm that these fears are unfounded, and that that Declaration, re-affirmed by (the Conference of the Principal Allied Powers at San Reino and again in the Treaty of Sèvres, is not susceptible of change.

During the last two or three generations the Jews have recreated in Palestine a community now numbering 80,000, of whom about one-fourth are farmers or workers upon the land. This community has its own political organs; an elected assembly for the direction of its domestic concerns; elected councils in the towns; and an organization for the control of its schools. It has its elected Chief Rabbinate and Rabbinical Council for the direction of its religious affairs. Its business is conducted in Hebrew as a vernacular language, and a Hebrew press serves its needs. It has its distinctive intellectual life and displays considerable economic activity. This community, then, with its town and country population, its political, religious and social organizations, its own language, its own customs, its own life, has in fact "national" characteristics. When it is asked what is meant by the development of the Jewish National Home in Palestine, it may be answered that it is not the imposition of a Jewish nationality upon the inhabitants of Palestine as a whole, but the further development of the existing Jewish community, with the assistance of Jews in other parts of the world, in order that it may become a centre in which the Jewish people as a whole may take, on grounds of religion and race, an interest and a pride. But in order that this community should have the best prospect of free development and provide full opportunity for the Jewish people to display its capacities, it is essential that it should know that it is in Palestine as of right and not on sufferance. That is the reason why it is necessary that the existence of a Jewish National Home in Palestine should be internationally guaranteed, and that it should be formally recognized to rest upon ancient historic connection.

This, then, is the interpretation which His Majesty's Government place upon the Declaration of 1917, and, so understood, the Secretary of State is of opinion that it does not contain or imply anything which need cause either alarm to the Arab population of Palestine or disappointment to the Jews.

For the fulfilment of this policy it is necessary that the Jewish community in Palestine should be able to increase its numbers by immigration. This immigration cannot be so great in volume as to exceed whatever may be the economic capacity of the country at the time to absorb new arrivals. It is essential to ensure that the immigrants should not be a burden upon the people of Palestine as a whole, and that they should not deprive any section of the present population of their employment. Hitherto the immigration has fulfilled these conditions. The number of immigrants since the British occupation has been about 25,000.

It is necessary also to ensure that persons who are politically undesirable be excluded from Palestine, and every precaution has been and will be taken by the Administration to that end.

It is intended that a special committee should be established in Palestine, consisting entirely of members of the new Legislative Council elected by the people, to confer with the Administration upon matters relating to the regulation of immigration. Should any difference of opinion arise between this committee and the Administration, the matter will be referred to His Majesty's Government, who will give it special consideration. In addition, under Article 81 of the draft Palestine Order in Council, any religious community or considerable section of the population of Palestine will have a general right to appeal, through the High Commissioner and the Secretary of State, to the League of Nations on any matter on which they may consider that the terms of the Mandate are not being fulfilled by the Government of Palestine.

With reference to the Constitution which it is now intended to establish in Palestine, the draft of which has already been published, it is desirable to make certain points clear. In the first place, it is not the case, as has been represented by the Arab Delegation, that during the war His Majesty's Government gave an undertaking that an independent national government should be at once established in Palestine. This representation mainly rests upon a letter dated the 24th October, 1915, from Sir Henry McMahon, then His Majesty's High Commissioner in Egypt, to the Sharif of Mecca, now King Hussein of the Kingdom of the Hejaz. That letter is quoted as conveying the promise to the Sherif of Mecca to recognise and support the independence of the Arabs within the territories proposed by him. But this promise was given subject to a reservation made in the same letter, which excluded from its scope, among other territories, the portions of Syria lying to the west of the District of Damascus. This reservation has always been regarded by His Majesty's Government as covering the vilayet of Beirut and the independent Sanjak of Jerusalem. The whole of Palestine west of the Jordan was thus excluded from Sir Henry McMahon's pledge.

Nevertheless, it is the intention of His Majesty's government to foster the establishment of a full measure of self-government in Palestine. But they are of the opinion that, in the special circumstances of that country, this should be accomplished by gradual stages and not suddenly. The first step was taken when, on the institution of a Civil Administration, the nominated Advisory Council, which now exists, was established. It was stated at the time by the High Commissioner that this was the first step in the development of self-governing institutions, and it is now proposed to take a second step by the establishment of a Legislative Council containing a large proportion of members elected on a wide franchise. It was proposed in the published draft that three of the members of this Council should be non-official persons nominated by the High Commissioner, but representations having been made in opposition to this provision, based on cogent considerations, the Secretary of State is prepared to omit it. The legislative Council would then consist of the High Commissioner as President and twelve elected and ten official members. The Secretary of State is of the opinion that before a further measure of self-government is extended to Palestine and the Assembly placed in control over the Executive, it would be wise to allow some time to elapse. During this period the institutions of the country will have become well established; its financial credit will be based on firm foundations, and the Palestinian officials will have been enabled to gain experience of sound methods of government. After a few years the situation will be again reviewed, and if the experience of the working of the constitution now to be established so warranted, a larger share of authority would then be extended to the elected representatives of the people.

The Secretary of State would point out that already the present Administration has transferred to a Supreme Council elected by the Moslem community of Palestine the entire control of Moslem Religious endowments (Waqfs), and of the Moslem religious Courts. To this Council the Administration has also voluntarily restored considerable revenues derived from ancient endowments which have been sequestrated by the Turkish Government. The Education Department is also advised by a committee representative of all sections of the population, and the Department of Commerce and Industry has the benefit of the co-operation of the Chambers of Commerce which have been established in the principal centres. It is the intention of the Administration to associate in an increased degree similar representative committees with the various Departments of the Government.

The Secretary of State believes that a policy upon these lines, coupled with the maintenance of the fullest religious liberty in Palestine and with scrupulous regard for the rights of each community with reference to its Holy Places, cannot but commend itself to the various sections of the population, and that upon this basis may be built up that spirit of cooperation upon which the future progress and prosperity of the Holy Land must largely depend.

11 |

Buying the Emek

(Dr. Arthur Ruppin, May 1929)

Zionism is often thought of in political or military terms – its great heroes are often men like Menachem Begin who was both a unit commander and the founder of a political party. No less important, however, were those working from desks to buy up the Land commercially. Published in the *New Palestine* journal of New York, in the following article Arthur Ruppin (the chief Zionist land agent in the early twentieth century) highlights the struggle that such transactions entailed. The Emek Yizael is the fertile area known in the Bible as the Valley of Jezreel, meaning '*El* sows'.

THE acquisition of the Emek Yizael for Jewish colonization has been the object of Jewish efforts for many years. It was natural that this region, the largest fertile plain of Palestine, should have aroused the interest of the Jewish colonization societies at the very beginning. When the pogroms of 1890 caused large numbers of Jews to emigrate from Russia, some of them turned to Palestine. As a result there arose, in the larger Russian cities, Jewish societies whose aim was the acquisition of land in Palestine for purposes of colonization. These societies had connections with the Odessa Committee of the 'Hovevei Zion, which accordingly commissioned its Jaffa office to buy suitable land in Palestine for these societies. The

11 – Buying the Emek

directors of this office, Tiomkin, Pines and Bentovim, conceived the plan of purchasing a considerable part of the Emek Yizael and of the Plain of Acco. It was not only the fertility of these plains that attracted them, but also the fact that these were the only regions where it was possible to purchase a large stretch of land from a single owner, while the remainder of Palestine was broken up into small parcels belonging to many individuals, so that the acquisition of a considerable continuous expanse was exceedingly difficult.

In order to execute this plan the Jaffa office communicated with Messrs. Kalvariski and Joshua Hankin. The latter, then a young man of twenty-five had already demonstrated his skill in such negotiations in the acquisition of land for the colonies Rehoboth and Hederah. By energetic work he succeeded, in 1891, in reaching an agreement with large owners in the Emek Jezreel and the Plain of Acco for the purchase of 160,000 dunams at fifteen francs per dunam. These 160,000 dunams included the territory which came into the possession of the Haifa Bay Development Company a few years ago, and, lately, of the Jewish National Fund. Hankin had not found it easy to reach this agreement to a low price, for even then speculators of all kinds were surrounding the land owners and attempting to frustrate his efforts by offering a higher price. But Hankin enjoyed the confidence of the Arabs, so that he succeeded in overcoming the competition of the speculators. Before the consummation of the agreement, however the Turkish Government, alarmed by the increasing inflow of Russian Jews, prohibited Jewish immigration entirely. This blow proved disastrous for the negotiations. The Russian societies formed for the purposes of purchasing land were dissolved, failed to send in the money they had promised, and the entire magnificent project fell through.

Two decades passed before another attempt was made to acquire the Emek Yizrael (The Valley of Jezreel). It was only in 1910 that Hankin – who, in the meanwhile, had purchased land in Lower Galilee for the ICA – resumed his negotiations for land in the Emek. Authorized by a Russian Jew, Elias Blumenfeld, to arrange for the purchase of 1,000 dunams on which he, Blumenfeld, intended to establish a farm with his own means, Hankin concluded an agreement for a stretch of 9,500 dunams in Fule, later Merchavia [Al-Ful in Arabic]. He hoped that the ICA, in whose employ he was at that time, would buy the remainder of the land. When, however, the ICA refused to do so, he inquired of me, who was then the director of the Palestine Bureau of the Zionist Organization, whether the Zionists would be prepared to purchase this land. Even before that it had occurred to me, whenever, going from Haifa to Nazareth, I had viewed the broad expanse of the Emek Yizrael, that, because of its proximity to Haifa, its excellent railroad and highway connections, and the ease with which its soil could be cultivated, this land would be preeminently suited for Jewish colonization.

But it was no simple matter to obtain the money for this purchase. Only the fact that Franz Oppenheimer was just then seeking land for the co-operative colonization society he had recently organized, and the simultaneous appearance of some private purchasers made it possible to carry through this project. 3,500 dunams were taken over by the National Fund for the co-operative colonies, and the rest by the Palestine Land Development Company.

This, however, did not mean that the transaction was consummated, for the Turkish Government refused to authorize the sale, even though official permission was applied for not by the National Fund, nor by the Palestine Land Development Company, but by a Jew, Efraim Krause, who was a Turkish citizen. The Governor in Nazareth, a rabid anti-Zionist, declared that he would fight this purchase to the utmost; furthermore, he ignored the orders of his superior, the District Governor in Acco, who wished no difficulties put in the way of this transaction. We were forced, therefore, to appeal to the Vali, the Governor General in Beirut. Great haste was necessary, for the purchase was beginning to attract attention, and influential circles were doing their best to nullify it.

I still remember how, in February, 1910, Hankin and I rode on horseback (for the roads were unfit for carriages) from Haifa to Beirut, through a fearful rainstorm that prevented any ships from plying between the two cities; it was midnight when we reached Sidon, so that we arrived in Beirut only on the second day. But although we remained there for two weeks, and although official permission for the purchase was promised us from day to day, we were, finally, obliged to leave Beirut without accomplishing our purpose. Only through the efforts of Hankin and his friends in Constantinople did we at last succeed in obtaining from the ministry the necessary sanction. This meant the gaining of our first foothold in the Emek, and before long the Oppenheimer co-operative settlement and some private colonists commenced their agricultural work there.

About this time, too, the interest of the wealthier Russian Jews in the purchase of Palestinian land was revived. After the acquisition of Merhaviah, Hankin had gone over from the ICA to the Palestine Land Development Company, which offered him the opportunity to exercise his abilities to the fullest extent. He neglected no occasion for the increase of our land holdings in Palestine, and, in 1913, commenced negotiations for a stretch of 20,000 dunam in Meshach, adjoining Merhaviah, reaching a provisional agreement for a price of about forty francs per dunam.

On a visit to Russia, and by correspondence, I endeavoured to find buyers for this land; the Odessa Committee, too, made efforts in this direction. With the assistance of the late engineer Nachum Syrkin of Kiev the interest of the wealthy sugar manufacturer Brodski was aroused in this land, where he expected to attempt the cultivation of sugar beets. Accordingly Brodski commissioned us to buy the land. But he had hardly declared himself willing to purchase it when Baron Rothschild also decided that he wanted it. There was no doubt that Brodski would have to cede to the Baron. I therefore telegraphed to Brodski – it was late in July, 1914, asking him to let Baron Rothschild purchase the land; he immediately telegraphed his assent from a German bathing resort. This was approximately the time of the outbreak of the war, so that Brodski manifestly was no longer in a position to forward the purchase money. Baron Rothschild, on the other hand, sent half a million francs to Palestine for the land. As the war had already broken out it was, of course, impossible to use this money for the purchase of the land; but it was the last contribution received by the ICA during the war, and proved of inestimable value for the continuation of its work.

During the war, and for two years after, land purchases were prohibited by law. It was only after the establishment of the civilian government under Herbert Samuel, in 1920, that they were permitted again. Hankin immediately grasped the opportunity to conclude a provisional agreement for 70,000 dunam. Half of this land (Nahalal, Djindjar and Nasra) was not irrigated, and cost £3 per dunam, while the other half (Nuris) was partly irrigated, and therefore sold at the higher price of six and a half pounds sterling. The entire amount was about £300,000, which was to be paid upon transfer of the deed. But when Hankin submitted this agreement to me I was forced to point out that the financial situation of the Zionist Organization and its institution precluded any purchase of this sort. Hankin, however, repeatedly emphasized the importance of the transaction, and I realized that this represented our first opportunity to commence extensive colonization on a stretch of land larger than any which had ever been placed at our disposal.

But I saw no way of raising the huge sum required. We discussed the matter at length, and apparently without result, until I finally told Hankin that I would try to persuade the Jewish National Fund to buy the land, provided it would be possible to pay the purchase price in ten annual instalments. This suggestion appeared almost Utopian at that time, for the

Arabs were willing to sell their land only because they wanted to have the cash immediately, and had never agreed to accept payment on an instalment basis. Hankin, too, seriously doubted the possibility of carrying through this plan; nonetheless he did attempt it, and actually succeeded in obtaining from the owners an option according to which they were to be paid not in ten, but in six yearly instalments.

The Committee which then represented the Jewish National Fund in Palestine, consisting of Messrs. Ussishkin and Ettinger and myself, ratified this agreement in principle, and submitted it to the European governing board of the National Fund for approval. Here, however, the purchase met with keen opposition. The Reorganization Commission, which came to Palestine just then, declared itself against it; and the Director of the National Fund vetoed it. The Purchase would probably have fallen through had not the Zionist Executive intervened and, with the deciding vote of Dr. Weizmann, declared itself in favour of it. Thus, and despite many other difficulties, the purchase was finally made, rendering possible the establishment of a considerable number of new colonies in the Emek (Nahalal, Djindjar, Kfar Yeheskel, Geva, Ein 'Harod, Tel Yosef, Beth Alpha).

In the next few years Hankin succeeded in acquiring further large expanses in the Emek Yizrael for the National Fund, the Palestine Land Development Company, and the American Zion Commonwealth. In addition he bought, in 1924, 60,000 dunams in the Plain of Acco, of which 46,000 dunams lay on the coast between Haifa and Acco. One fourth of this was taken over by the National Fund, and the remaining three-fourths by the Palestine Land Development Company, which later sold this land to the Haifa Bay Development Company, founded by the American Zion Commonwealth together with and at the initiative of Joseph Löwy. Then, in 1928, the major portion of the Haifa Bay Development Company's land came into the possession of the Jewish National Fund. The acquisition of this land is, therefore, of unusually great importance, for it assures the Jewish National Fund of a lasting influence upon the development of Haifa.

Thus there have been acquired, since 1910, approximately 225,000 dunams in the Emek Yizrael and about 65,000 dunams in the Plain of Acco – a total of 290,000 dunams, purchased at the price of £970,000.

It has often been asked why the Zionist Organization has chosen the Emek for settlement purposes, and has neglected the coastal plain, which is suitable for plantations of all sorts and for orange groves in particular. This question can best be answered by pointing out that the coastal plain has not been neglected at all. Since 1910 the Palestine Land Development Company alone has acquired 70,000 dunam in the coastal plain between Gaza and Haifa; and when we count the plain of Acco the total mounts to 135,000 dunams. This notwithstanding the Zionist public has heard much more of the purchases in the Emek Yizrael than of those in the coastal plain – largely because it was possible to buy large stretches of land at once in the Emek, while in the coastal plain only small parcels of a few hundred or a few thousand dunams could be bought at one time.

In addition to the above purchases on the part of the Palestine Land Development Company in the coastal plain we must also mention the 60,000 or 70,000 dunams near Binyamina which were partly bought by the ICA, and partly leased by it from the government on long-term leases. A few small parcels of land in the coastal plain have also been purchased by some private individuals and companies. When we consider also about 50,000 dunams for the purchase of which negotiations were begun several years ago by the Palestine Land Development Company, acting on behalf of the Jewish National Fund, and other companies, we see that approximately 250,000 dunams of land in the coastal plain (including the Plain of Acco) have become Jewish property – i.e., even more than in the Emek Yizrael.

It is, of course, true that in the first few years after the world war the Zionist Organization concentrated its colonization efforts upon the Emek; for only here could it hope to acquire, in a short time, extensive stretches of land for colonization on a large scale. Transactions corresponding to those which were completed in the Emek within a few months required many years where the coastal plain was concerned. But at that time it was absolutely necessary, in the interests of the entire Zionist movement, to begin colonization immediately, and not to postpone it for years. Furthermore, in the coastal region colonization must be based principally upon the cultivation of oranges; and orange plantations yield no profit for six years. Under uncertain financial conditions prevailing in the Zionist Organization in 1920 and 1921 such colonization in the coastal plain would have been attended by a great risk, for the living and working expenses of the settlers would have had to be drawn from the Zionist funds for at least six years. And at that time, when the Keren Hayesod was in its infancy, it was quite impossible to take over such an obligation for six years. It was necessary to find a form of colonization in which the settlers would be able to become self-supporting as soon as possible; and here general agriculture, with dairying as its most important branch, afforded the best opportunity.

None of the settlers of 1921 had the means to start orange plantations on their own account. For this was during the European inflation period, when the sum required for a Palestinian orange plantation amounted to millions and billions in European currency. Besides, orange growing was not very popular then. This branch of agriculture had been very unprofitable during the war and even in 1921 it was impossible to find a Jewish purchaser for one of the finest and best situated orange plantations in Palestine (although it was offered at an exceedingly low price), so that it had to be sold to an Arab.

Thus we may say that the Zionist Organization concentrated its land-purchasing efforts upon the two great plains of Palestine almost simultaneously. It is only in the mountainous country adjoining these plains that, recognizing the greater difficulties of colonization in the mountains, it bought nothing. One therefore receives a curious impression when one reads, in the report of the Jewish Agency Experts Commission, a detailed attack upon the Zionist mountain colonies. The colonies meant are Ataroth (Kalendie) and Kiriath Anavim, near Jerusalem. But these should be considered suburban rather than mountain colonies, for their very existence is due to the immediate proximity of the Jerusalem market. This proximity enables them to command such excellent prices for their milk, eggs, vegetables, and fruit that their financial situation is eminently satisfactory, and much better than that of many colonies in the plain.

When we look back upon the history of our acquisition of Palestinian land, we see clearly that the purchase of land in the Emek has been a deciding factor in the Jewish work in Palestine. This has been the first time that Jews have come to constitute the majority of the agricultural population of a considerable area, and that they have been able to establish themselves in the manner best adapted to their special requirements. The construction of the Port of Haifa and the growth of the city will bring out the significance of the Emek even more clearly. Next to the industrial development due to Nesher, Shemen and Grands Moulins, it is Jewish colonization in the Emek to which we must credit the increase of the Jewish population of Haifa from three thousand to fifteen thousand since the war, and the fact that the strong Jewish influence upon the city itself is evident to even the most casual observer.

Recommendations of the Palestine Royal Commission Report

(Lord Peel, 1937)

As with the Churchill white paper reprinted earlier in this volume, the Peel report was made in response to unrest in Palestine. Between April and October 1936 the Arabs took up a general strike in protest at the perceived oppressive nature of the British rule, and against continued Jewish immigration. A later phase of the rebellion turned violent, and was harshly suppressed by the British Army. In between the two phases came the Peel Commission paper which suggested the partition of the Land and the cessation of the British Mandate. **Summary extracts** of the ten main areas of recommendation are featured below.

1. A treaty system

4. The Mandate for Palestine should terminate and be replaced by a Treaty System in accordance with the precedent set in Iraq and Syria ...

2. The Holy Places

10. The partition of Palestine is subject to the overriding necessity of keeping the sanctity of Jerusalem and Bethlehem inviolate and of ensuring free and safe access to them for all the world. That, in the fullest sense of the mandatory phrase, is "a

sacred trust of civilization" – a trust on behalf not merely of the peoples of Palestine but of multitudes in other lands to whom those places, one or both, are Holy Places ...

3. The frontier

17. The natural principle for the Partition of Palestine is to separate the areas in which the Jews have acquired land and settled from those which are wholly or mainly occupied by Arabs ... The Jewish lands and colonies are mostly to be found in the Maritime Plain between Al Majdal and Mount Carmel, in the neighbourhood of Haifa, in the Plain of Esdraelon and the Valley of Jezreel, and in the east of Galilee; i.e., south of Tiberias, on the shores of the Lake, near Safad, and in the Huleh Basin. The rest of Galilee and the northern part of the plain of Acre are almost wholly in Arab occupation. So also is the central hill-country of old Samaria and Judaea except for Jerusalem and its vicinity. The towns of Nablus, Jenin and Tulkarm, the last an outpost on the edge of the Maritime Plain, are centres of Arab nationalism. Except in and near Jerusalem and at Hebron, there are practically no Jews between Jenin and Beersheba. This Arab block extends eastwards to the River Jordan between the Dead Sea and Beisan. In the area stretching south and south-east of Beersheba to the Egyptian frontier, the Jews have bought some isolated blocks of land but the population is entirely Arab ...

4. Inter-state subvention

23. As we have explained in an earlier chapter, the Jews contribute more per capita to the revenues of Palestine than the Arabs, and the Government has thereby been enabled to maintain public services for the Arabs at a higher level than would otherwise have been possible. Partition would mean, on the one hand, that the Arab Area would no longer profit from the taxable capacity of the Jewish Area. On the other hand, (1) the Jews would acquire a new right of sovereignty in the Jewish Area: (2) that Area, as we have defined it, would be larger than the existing area of

Jewish land and settlement: (3) the Jews would be freed from their present liability for helping to promote the welfare of Arabs outside that Area, It seems to us, therefore, not unreasonable to suggest that the Jewish State should pay a subvention to the Arab State when Partition comes into effect. There have been recent precedents for equitable financial arrangements of this kind in those connected with the separation of Sind from Bombay and of Burma from the Indian Empire; and in accordance with those precedents we recommend that a Finance Commission should be appointed to consider and report as to what the amount of the subvention should be ...

5. British subvention

26. The Mandate for Trans-Jordan ought not in our opinion to be relinquished without securing, as far as possible, that the standard of administration should not fall too low through lack of funds to maintain it; and it is in this matter, we submit, that the British people might fairly be asked to do their part in facilitating a settlement. The continuance of the present Mandate, as we have more than once pointed out, would almost inevitably involve a recurrent and increasing charge on the British Treasury. If peace can be promoted by Partition, money spent on helping to bring it about and making it more effective for its purpose would surely be well spent. And apart from any such considerations we think that the British people, great as their financial burdens now are, would agree to a capital payment in lieu of their present annual liability, as a means towards honouring their obligations and making peace in Palestine ...

6. Tariffs and ports

28. The Arab & Jewish States, being sovereign independent States, would determine their own tariffs. Subject to the terms of the Mandate, the same would apply to the Mandatory Government.

29. We recognize the crux arising from the fact that the tariff-policies of the Arab and Jewish States are likely to conflict.

The prevention of smuggling might be difficult. It would greatly ease the position and it would promote the interests of both the Arab and Jewish States if they could agree to impose identical customs-duties on as many articles as possible, and if the Mandatory Government, likewise, could assimilate its customs-duties as far as might be with those of one or both of the two States ...

7. Nationality

32. All persons domiciled in the Mandated Area (including Haifa, Tiberias, Safad, and the enclave on the Gulf of Aqaba, as long as they remain under Mandatory administration) who now possess the status of British protected persons would retain it; but apart from this all Palestinians would become the nationals of the States in which they are domiciled.

8. Civil services

33. It seems probable that, in the event of Partition, the services of the Arab and Jewish officials in the pre-existing Mandatory Administration would to a large extent be required by the Governments of the Arab and Jewish States respectively, whereas the number of British officials would be substantially reduced. The rights of all of them, including rights to pensions or gratuities, must be fully honoured in accordance with the provisions of Article 28 of the existing Mandate, it being borne in mind that, under any plan of Partition, there will be three Governments in place of the single Government of Palestine which is contemplated in that Article as being established in the event of the termination of the Mandate. This matter should be dealt with by the Finance Commission.

9. Industrial concessions

34. In the event of Partition agreements entered into by the Government of Palestine for the development and security of industries (e.g., the agreement with the Palestine Potash

Company) should be taken over and carried out by the Governments of the Arab and Jewish States. Guarantees to that effect should be given in the Treaties. The security of the Electric Power Station at Jisr el Majami should be similarly guaranteed.

10. Exchange of land and population

35. We have left to the last the two-fold question which, after that of the Frontier, is the most important and most difficult of all the questions which Partition in any shape involves.

36. If Partition is to be effective in promoting a final settlement it must mean more than drawing a frontier and establishing two States. Sooner or later there should be a transfer of land and, as far as possible, an exchange of population.

37. As regards land, the Jews on the one hand may wish to dispose of some or all of the lands now owned by them which lie within the boundaries of the Arab State, and their Jewish occupants may wish to move into the Jewish State and resume their life on the land therein. The Arabs on the other hand may likewise be willing to sell the land they own within the boundaries of the Jewish State. But what is to become, in that case, of its occupants, whether owners or tenants or labourers? Whether they remain in the Jewish State or move into the Arab State, where there is under present conditions no cultivable land to spare, there is a manifest risk of their becoming a "landless proletariat".

38. The Treaties should provide that, if Arab owners of land in the Jewish State or Jewish owners of land in the Arab State should wish to sell their land and any plantations or crops thereon, the Government of the State concerned should be responsible for the purchase of such land, plantations and crops at a price to be fixed, if required, by the Mandatory Administration. We suggest that for this purpose a loan should, if required, be guaranteed for a reasonable amount ...

13 |

An Extract from the speech 'On the Jewish Question'

(Adolf Hitler, January 30, 1939)

Adolf Hitler spent his early adulthood living a Bohemian lifestyle in the city of Vienna. At this time Vienna was a centre for the development of the pan-Germanic nationalist movement. In line with this, the city was also a hotbed of anti-Semitism. These ideas were particularly attractive to an impoverished idler like the young Hitler, who began to promote these ideas among his associates. Over time his anti-Semitism only increased, as did his standing in society. By 1939 he was Führer, and the menace of Europe. The following speech is one of his most infamous with regards to the Jews. He would return to the 'prophecy' within it throughout World War Two, particularly whenever he sought to escalate the persecution that would become the Holocaust. His prophecy proved false, he failed to annihilate European Jewry. He did, however, manage to force many Jews to leave Europe and head for Palestine, where they would form a refuge for the continuance of their nation – the State of Israel.

IN connection with the Jewish question I have this to say: it is a shameful spectacle to see how the whole democratic world is oozing sympathy for the poor tormented Jewish people, but remains hard-hearted and obdurate when it comes to helping them – which is surely, in view of its attitude, an obvious duty. The arguments that are brought up as an excuse for not helping them actually speak for us Germans and Italians.

For this is what they say:

1. "We", that is the democracies, "are not in a position to take in the Jews." Yet in these empires there are not ten people to the square kilometre. While Germany, with her 135 inhabitants to the square kilometre, is supposed to have room for them!

2. They assure us: We cannot take them unless Germany is prepared to allow them a certain amount of capital to bring with them as immigrants.

For hundreds of years Germany was good enough to receive these elements, although they possessed nothing except infectious political and physical diseases. What they possess today, they have by a very large extent gained at the cost of the less astute German nation by the most reprehensible manipulations.

Today we are merely paying this people what it deserves. When the German nation was, thanks to the inflation instigated and carried through by Jews, deprived of the entire savings which it had accumulated in years of honest work, when the rest of the world took away the German nation's foreign investments, when we were divested of the whole of our colonial possessions, these philanthropic considerations evidently carried little noticeable weight with democratic statesmen.

Today I can only assure these gentlemen that, thanks to the brutal education with which the democracies favoured us for fifteen years, we are completely hardened to all attacks of sentiment. After more than eight hundred thousand children of the nation had died of hunger and undernourishment at the close of the War, we witnessed almost one million head of milking cows being driven away from us in accordance with the cruel paragraphs of a dictate which the humane democratic apostles of the world forced upon us as a peace treaty. We witnessed over one million German prisoners of war being retained in confinement for no reason at all for a whole year after the War was ended. We witnessed over one and a half million Germans being torn away from all that they possessed in the territories lying on our frontiers, and being whipped out with practically only what they wore on their backs. We had to endure having millions of our fellow countrymen torn from us without their consent, and without their being afforded the slightest possibility of existence. I could supplement these examples with dozens of the cruellest kind. For this reason we ask to be spared all sentimental talk. The German nation does not wish its interests to be determined and controlled by any foreign nation. France to the French, England to the English, America to the Americans, and Germany to the Germans. We are resolved to prevent the settlement in our country of a strange people which was capable of snatching for itself all the leading positions in the land, and to oust it. For it is our will to educate our own nation for these leading positions. We have hundreds of thousands of very intelligent children of peasants and of the working classes. We shall have them educated – in fact we have already begun – and we wish that one day they, and not the representatives of an alien race, may hold the leading positions in the State together with our educated classes. Above all, German culture, as its name alone shows, is German and not Jewish, and therefore its management and care will be entrusted to members of our own nation. If the rest of the world cries out with a hypocritical mien against this barbaric expulsion from Germany of such an irreplaceable and culturally eminently valuable element, we can only be astonished at the conclusions they draw from this situation. For how thankful they must be that we are releasing these precious apostles of culture, and placing them at the disposal of the rest of the world. In accordance with their own declarations they cannot find a single reason to excuse themselves for refusing to receive this most valuable race in their own countries. Nor can I see a reason why the members of this race should be imposed upon the German nation, while in the States, which are so enthusiastic about these "splendid people", their settlement should suddenly be refused with every imaginable excuse. I think that the sooner this problem is solved the better; for Europe cannot settle down until the Jewish question is cleared up. It may very well be possible that sooner or later an agreement on this problem may be reached in Europe, even between those nations which otherwise do not so easily come together.

The world has sufficient space for settlements, but we must once and for all get rid of the opinion that the Jewish race was only created by God for the purpose of being in a certain percentage a parasite living on the body and the productive work of other nations. The Jewish race will have to adapt itself to sound constructive activity as other nations do, or sooner or later it will succumb to a crisis of an inconceivable magnitude.

One thing I should like to say on this day which may be memorable for others as well as for us Germans: In the course of my life I have very often been a prophet, and have usually been ridiculed for it. During the time of my struggle for power it was in the first instance the Jewish race which only received my prophecies with laughter when I said that I would one day take over the leadership of the State, and with it that of the whole nation and that I would then among many other things settle the Jewish problem. Their laughter was uproarious, but I think that for some time now they have been laughing on the other side of their face. Today I will once more be a prophet: If the international Jewish financiers in and outside Europe should succeed in plunging the nations once more into a world war, then the result will not be the Bolshevization of the earth, and thus the victory of Jewry, but the annihilation of the Jewish race in Europe! ... The nations are no longer willing to die on the battlefield so that this unstable international race may profiteer from a war or satisfy its Old Testament vengeance. The Jewish watchword "Workers of the world unite" will be conquered by a higher realization, namely "Workers of all classes and of all nations, recognize your common enemy!"

14 |

Extracts from 'UN General Assembly Resolution 181'

(November 29, 1947)

Resolution 181 recommended a partition of Mandatory Palestine at the end of the British Mandate, and is also known as the 'UN Partition Plan for Palestine', or simply 'the Partition Plan'. The resolution was passed with thirty-three countries in favour, thirteen against (largely Arab nations) and ten abstaining (including the United Kingdom).

The resolution proposed the creation of independent Jewish and Arab states (with borders pre-defined), but with the proviso that the two states should combine in a closely defined economic union. The city of Jerusalem was to be administered by the United Nations for a period of ten years, after which the residents of the city could modify its regime by means of a referendum.

PLAN OF PARTITION WITH ECONOMIC UNION

Part I. – Future Constitution and Government of Palestine

A. TERMINATION OF MANDATE, PARTITION AND INDEPENDENCE

1. The Mandate for Palestine shall terminate as soon as possible but in any case not later than 1 August 1948.
2. The armed forces of the mandatory Power shall be progressively withdrawn from Palestine, the withdrawal to

be completed as soon as possible but in any case not later than 1 August 1948. The mandatory Power shall advise the Commission, as far in advance as possible, of its intention to terminate the mandate and to evacuate each area. The mandatory Power shall use its best endeavours to ensure that an area situated in the territory of the Jewish State, including a seaport and hinterland adequate to provide facilities for a substantial immigration, shall be evacuated at the earliest possible date and in any event not later than 1 February 1948.

3. Independent Arab and Jewish States and the Special International Regime for the City of Jerusalem, set forth in Part III of this Plan, shall come into existence in Palestine two months after the evacuation of the armed forces of the mandatory Power has been completed but in any case not later than 1 October 1948. The boundaries of the Arab State, the Jewish State, and the City of Jerusalem shall be as described in Parts II and III below.

4. The period between the adoption by the General Assembly of its recommendation on the question of Palestine and the establishment of the independence of the Arab and Jewish States shall be a transitional period.

...

C. DECLARATION

A declaration shall be made to the United Nations by the Provisional Government of each proposed State before independence. It shall contain, inter alia, the following clauses:

General Provision

The stipulations contained in the Declaration are recognized as fundamental laws of the State and no law, regulation or official action shall conflict or interfere with these stipulations, nor shall any law, regulation or official action prevail over them.

Chapter 1: Holy Places, Religious Buildings and Sites

1. Existing rights in respect of Holy Places and religious buildings or sites shall not be denied or impaired.
2. In so far as Holy Places are concerned, the liberty of access, visit, and transit shall be guaranteed, in conformity with existing rights, to all residents and citizens of the other State and of the City of Jerusalem, as well as to aliens, without distinction as to nationality, subject to requirements of national security, public order and decorum. Similarly, freedom of worship shall be guaranteed in conformity with existing rights, subject to the maintenance of public order and decorum.
3. Holy Places and religious buildings or sites shall be preserved. No act shall be permitted which may in any way impair their sacred character. If at any time it appears to the Government that any particular Holy Place, religious, building or site is in need of urgent repair, the Government may call upon the community or communities concerned to carry out such repair. The Government may carry it out itself at the expense of the community or community concerned if no action is taken within a reasonable time.
4. No taxation shall be levied in respect of any Holy Place, religious building or site which was exempt from taxation on the date of the creation of the State. No change in the incidence of such taxation shall be made which would either discriminate between the owners or occupiers of Holy Places, religious buildings or sites, or would place such owners or occupiers in a position less favourable in relation to the general incidence of taxation than existed at the time of the adoption of the Assembly's recommendations.
5. The Governor of the City of Jerusalem shall have the right to determine whether the provisions of the Constitution of the State in relation to Holy Places, religious buildings and sites within the borders of the State and the religious rights appertaining thereto, are being properly applied and

respected, and to make decisions on the basis of existing rights in cases of disputes which may arise between the different religious communities or the rites of a religious community with respect to such places, buildings and sites. He shall receive full co-operation and such privileges and immunities as are necessary for the exercise of his functions in the State.

Chapter 2: Religious and Minority Rights

1. Freedom of conscience and the free exercise of all forms of worship, subject only to the maintenance of public order and morals, shall be ensured to all.
2. No discrimination of any kind shall be made between the inhabitants on the ground of race, religion, language or sex.
3. All persons within the jurisdiction of the State shall be entitled to equal protection of the laws.
4. The family law and personal status of the various minorities and their religious interests, including endowments, shall be respected.
5. Except as may be required for the maintenance of public order and good government, no measure shall be taken to obstruct or interfere with the enterprise of religious or charitable bodies of all faiths or to discriminate against any representative or member of these bodies on the ground of his religion or nationality.
6. The State shall ensure adequate primary and secondary education for the Arab and Jewish minority, respectively, in its own language and its cultural traditions. The right of each community to maintain its own schools for the education of its own members in its own language, while conforming to such educational requirements of a general nature as the State may impose, shall not be denied or impaired. Foreign educational establishments

shall continue their activity on the basis of their existing rights.
7. No restriction shall be imposed on the free use by any citizen of the State of any language in private intercourse, in commerce, in religion, in the Press or in publications of any kind, or at public meetings.
8. No expropriation of land owned by an Arab in the Jewish State, or by a Jew in the Arab State, shall be allowed except for public purposes. In all cases of expropriation full compensation as fixed by the Supreme Court shall be paid previous to dispossession.

...

The Economic Union of Palestine
1. The objectives of the Economic Union of Palestine shall be:
2. A customs union;
3. A joint currency system providing for a single foreign exchange rate;
4. Operation in the common interest of a non-discriminatory basis of railways; inter-State highways; postal, telephone and telegraphic services, and ports and airports involved in international trade and commerce;
5. Joint economic development, especially in respect of irrigation, land reclamation and soil conservation;
6. Access for both States and for the City of Jerusalem on a non-discriminatory basis to water and power facilities.

...

F. ADMISSION TO MEMBERSHIP IN THE UNITED NATIONS

When the independence of either the Arab or the Jewish State as envisaged in this plan has become effective and the declaration and undertaking, as envisaged in this plan, have been signed by either of them, sympathetic consideration should be given to its application for admission to membership in the

United Nations in accordance with article 4 of the Charter of the United Nations.

...

Part III. – City of Jerusalem

A. SPECIAL REGIME

The City of Jerusalem shall be established as a *corpus separatum* under a special international regime and shall be administered by the United Nations. The Trusteeship Council shall be designated to discharge the responsibilities of the Administering Authority on behalf of the United Nations ...

... D. DURATION OF THE SPECIAL REGIME

The Statute elaborated by the Trusteeship Council on the aforementioned principles shall come into force not later than 1 October 1948. It shall remain in force in the first instance for a period of ten years, unless the Trusteeship Council finds it necessary to undertake a re-examination of these provisions at an earlier date. After the expiration of this period the whole scheme shall be subject to examination by the Trusteeship Council in the light of the experience acquired with its functioning. The residents the City shall be then free to express by means of a referendum their wishes as to possible modifications of the regime of the City.

15 |

The Declaration of the Establishment of the State of Israel

(May 14, 1948)

On May 14, 1948, the day on which the British Mandate over Palestine expired, the Jewish People's Council gathered at the Tel Aviv Museum, and approved the following proclamation, declaring the establishment of the State of Israel. The new state was recognized that night by the United States and three days later by the USSR.

ERETZ-ISRAEL [(Hebrew) – the Land of Israel, Palestine] was the birthplace of the Jewish people. Here their spiritual, religious and political identity was shaped. Here they first attained to statehood, created cultural values of national and universal significance and gave to the world the eternal Book of Books.

After being forcibly exiled from their land, the people kept faith with it throughout their Dispersion and never ceased to pray and hope for their return to it and for the restoration in it of their political freedom.

Impelled by this historic and traditional attachment, Jews strove in every successive generation to re-establish themselves in their ancient homeland. In recent decades they returned in their masses. Pioneers, *ma'pilim* [(Hebrew) – immigrants coming to Eretz-Israel in defiance of restrictive legislation] and defenders, they made deserts bloom, revived the Hebrew language, built villages and towns, and created a thriving community controlling its own economy and culture, loving peace but knowing how to defend itself, bringing the blessings of progress to all the country's inhabitants, and aspiring towards independent nationhood.

In the year 5657 (1897), at the summons of the spiritual father of the Jewish State, Theodore Herzl, the First Zionist Congress convened and proclaimed the right of the Jewish people to national rebirth in its own country.

This right was recognized in the Balfour Declaration of the 2nd November, 1917, and re-affirmed in the Mandate of the League of Nations which, in particular, gave international sanction to the historic connection between the Jewish people and Eretz-Israel and to the right of the Jewish people to rebuild its National Home.

The catastrophe which recently befell the Jewish people – the massacre of millions of Jews in Europe – was another clear demonstration of the urgency of solving the problem of its homelessness by re-establishing in Eretz-Israel the Jewish State, which would open the gates of the homeland wide to every Jew and confer upon the Jewish people the status of a fully privileged member of the comity of nations.

Survivors of the Nazi holocaust in Europe, as well as Jews from other parts of the world, continued to migrate to Eretz-Israel, undaunted by difficulties, restrictions and dangers, and never ceased to assert their right to a life of dignity, freedom and honest toil in their national homeland.

In the Second World War, the Jewish community of this country contributed its full share to the struggle of the freedom- and peace-loving nations against the forces of Nazi wickedness and, by the blood of its soldiers and its war effort, gained the right to be reckoned among the peoples who founded the United Nations.

On the 29th November, 1947, the United Nations General Assembly passed a resolution calling for the establishment of a

Jewish State in Eretz-Israel; the General Assembly required the inhabitants of Eretz-Israel to take such steps as were necessary on their part for the implementation of that resolution. This recognition by the United Nations of the right of the Jewish people to establish their State is irrevocable.

This right is the natural right of the Jewish people to be masters of their own fate, like all other nations, in their own sovereign State.

ACCORDINGLY WE, MEMBERS OF THE PEOPLE'S COUNCIL, REPRESENTATIVES OF THE JEWISH COMMUNITY OF ERETZ-ISRAEL AND OF THE ZIONIST MOVEMENT, ARE HERE ASSEMBLED ON THE DAY OF THE TERMINATION OF THE BRITISH MANDATE OVER ERETZ-ISRAEL AND, BY VIRTUE OF OUR NATURAL AND HISTORIC RIGHT AND ON THE STRENGTH OF THE RESOLUTION OF THE UNITED NATIONS GENERAL ASSEMBLY, HEREBY DECLARE THE ESTABLISHMENT OF A JEWISH STATE IN ERETZ-ISRAEL, TO BE KNOWN AS THE STATE OF ISRAEL.

WE DECLARE that, with effect from the moment of the termination of the Mandate being tonight, the eve of Sabbath, the 6th Iyar, 5708 (15th May, 1948), until the establishment of the elected, regular authorities of the State in accordance with the Constitution which shall be adopted by the Elected Constituent Assembly not later than the 1st October 1948, the People's Council shall act as a Provisional Council of State, and its executive organ, the People's Administration, shall be the Provisional Government of the Jewish State, to be called "Israel".

THE STATE OF ISRAEL will be open for Jewish immigration and for the Ingathering of the Exiles; it will foster the development of the country for the benefit of all its inhabitants; it will be based on freedom, justice and peace as envisaged by the prophets of Israel; it will ensure complete equality of social and political rights to all its inhabitants irrespective of religion, race or sex; it will guarantee freedom of religion, conscience, language, education and culture; it will safeguard the Holy Places

15 – The Declaration of the Establishment of the State of Israel

of all religions; and it will be faithful to the principles of the Charter of the United Nations.

THE STATE OF ISRAEL is prepared to cooperate with the agencies and representatives of the United Nations in implementing the resolution of the General Assembly of the 29th November, 1947, and will take steps to bring about the economic union of the whole of Eretz-Israel.

WE APPEAL to the United Nations to assist the Jewish people in the building-up of its State and to receive the State of Israel into the comity of nations.

WE APPEAL – in the very midst of the onslaught launched against us now for months – to the Arab inhabitants of the State of Israel to preserve peace and participate in the upbuilding of the State on the basis of full and equal citizenship and due representation in all its provisional and permanent institutions.

WE EXTEND our hand to all neighbouring states and their peoples in an offer of peace and good neighbourliness, and appeal to them to establish bonds of cooperation and mutual help with the sovereign Jewish people settled in its own land. The State of Israel is prepared to do its share in a common effort for the advancement of the entire Middle East.

WE APPEAL to the Jewish people throughout the Diaspora to rally round the Jews of Eretz-Israel in the tasks of immigration and upbuilding and to stand by them in the great struggle for the realization of the age-old dream – the redemption of Israel.

PLACING OUR TRUST IN THE "ROCK OF ISRAEL", WE AFFIX OUR SIGNATURES TO THIS PROCLAMATION AT THIS SESSION OF THE PROVISIONAL COUNCIL OF STATE, ON THE SOIL OF THE HOMELAND, IN THE CITY OF TEL-AVIV, ON THIS SABBATH EVE, THE 5TH DAY OF IYAR, 5708 (14TH MAY, 1948).

David Ben-Gurion

Daniel Auster; Mordekhai Bentov; Yitzchak Ben Zvi; Eliyahu Berligne; Fritz Bernstein; Rabbi Wolf Gold; Meir Grabovsky; Yitzchak

Gruenbaum; Dr. Abraham Granovsky; Eliyahu Dobkin; Meir Wilner-Kovner; Zerach Wahrhaftig; Herzl Vardi; Rachel Cohen; Rabbi Kalman Kahana; Saadia Kobashi; Rabbi Yitzchak Meir Levin; Meir David Loewenstein; Zvi Luria; Golda Myerson; Nachum Nir; Zvi Segal; Rabbi Yehuda Leib Hacohen Fishman; David Zvi Pinkas; Aharon Zisling; Moshe Kolodny; Eliezer Kaplan; Abraham Katznelson; Felix Rosenblueth; David Remez; Berl Repetur; Mordekhai Shattner; Ben Zion Sternberg; Bekhor Shitreet; Moshe Shapira; Moshe Shertok.

Epilogue: Brother John Thomas and *Elpis Israel*

No book about the Christadelphians and the hope of Israel would be complete without a special reference to Brother John Thomas. In 1848 Europe was being turned upside-down by the many revolutions occurring across the continent. Brother Thomas had recently undertaken a highly successful preaching tour of Britain. His audiences demanded that he put his doctrinal and prophetic understandings into print. For this reason he confined himself to his London home until the task was done, and the end result was *Elpis Israel* (1849).

For over 165 years it has been a foundation work for the study and preaching of the Christadelphian community. The most often quoted chapter is the final chapter, in which Brother Thomas discussed the prophecies relating to the return of the Jews to the Promised Land, and all that would follow on from that momentous homecoming. Although one can never be sure of the route by which God's plan will be outworked, Brother Thomas' picture of the end-time has, piece-by-piece, slowly come to be vindicated, as a thorough reading of the following will show.

This printing includes a number of sub-headings. These did not form a part of Brother Thomas' original writing (with the exception of the sub-heading 'The Second Exodus'), but are included here as an aid to reference and a help for those who wish to study the chapter in sections.

On page 239, a paragraph has been printed in bold. This is the well-known quote about the pre-adventual return of the Jews under British protection. The quote has often proved useful for preaching purposes, and so it has been highlighted for easy reference. The rest of the chapter should be read to understand the quote in its context.

1|

The final chapter of *Elpis Israel*

(John Thomas, 1849)

IN the previous chapters the reader has been conducted to the crisis that awaits the world at the conclusion of the time of the end. The two great powers of the day – namely, Gogue, the lord of the earth, and the Lion of Tarshish, the king of the sea, have been brought up in battle array in the region of the Dead Sea. This state of things will have been created by the angel of the sixth vial, whose province it is to gather the kings of the earth and of the whole habitable, with their armies, into the land of Israel, which is "the great winepress of the wrath of God (Revelation 14:19,20) for a space of 200 miles. This will be brought about upon the same principles as the fulfilment of all other prophecies in ages past – namely, *through the policy of "the powers that be", controlled by God*. The insurrection of "the earth" in 1848 created a situation, in which the Roman question, the German question, and the Turco-Hungarian question, have become the elements of an inevitable war throughout Europe, which will terminate in the final destruction of the Austrian Empire and the Papacy, and the subjection of the Porte and the toe-kingdoms to the Autocrat.

But without some other element to complicate affairs, things might settle down into a mere substitution of one gigantic despotism for the many lesser ones that now exist. It is necessary, therefore, that some other ingredient be introduced into the mess, in order that the course of events may be directed into an eastern channel, by which the crisis may be transferred from Europe to the Holy Land. This political element is found in the commercial interests of Britain in India; in the importance of Syria, Palestine, and Egypt being in the possession of a friendly people to the preservation of those interests; and in the policy of colonising Palestine with Jews, and so attaching them to the interests of the country by which they are protected. Thus the ascendancy of the Autocrat in Constantinople and the West, by the jeopardy in which it puts the commerce and dominion of the Lion-power, excites the British Government to the adoption of a policy which, in its application to emergencies as they arise, elaborates the restoration of the Jews, and the resuscitation of the East.

The kingdom of God is Israelitish in nature

The restoration of Israel is a most important feature in the divine economy. It is indispensable to the setting up of the kingdom of God; for they are the kingdom, having been constituted such by the covenant of Sinai, as it is written, "Ye shall be unto me a kingdom of priests, and a holy nation" (Exodus 19:6). The apostles understood this well enough, and so do all who understand the Gospel of the kingdom. After his resurrection, Jesus conversed with them during forty days, "speaking of the things pertaining to the kingdom of God". This was certainly long enough, under the instruction of such a teacher, to enable them to understand the subject well. It took possession of their minds and hearts, and created in them a desire for its immediate establishment. Hence, they put the question to him, saying, "Lord, wilt thou **at this time** *restore* **again** the kingdom to Israel?" (Acts 1:3,6).

It is evident from this, that they regarded Israel as having once possessed the kingdom, and expected the same Israel to possess it again. No other meaning can be put upon their words: for to restore a thing *"again"* to a party implies that they had once possessed it before. When Israel had the kingdom, they were ruled by Israelites, and not by Gentiles, for a foreigner could hold no office under their law. This was not the case in the days of the apostles, for they were ruled by the Roman Senate, and kings of its appointment. But it will not be so when the kingdom is restored to them again. The horns of the Gentiles will then be cast out of the land, and they will be ruled by "Israelites indeed" who will have become *Jews by adoption*; for no Jews or Gentiles after the flesh can have any part in the government of Israel and the Israelitish empire, which will embrace all nations, unless their Jewish citizenship is based upon a higher principle than natural birth. The flesh constitutes a Jew a *subject* of the kingdom, but confers on him no right to sit and rule upon the thrones of the house of David. This is reserved for Christ and his apostles, who "shall sit upon twelve thrones of his glory"; and for all other Jews and Gentiles who shall have become "*Jews inwardly*", for whom the dominion under the whole heaven is decreed in the benevolence of God.

There are several strange fancies in the world concerning the restoration of the Jews. Some deny it *in toto*, and yet impose upon themselves the imagination that they believe the gospel of the kingdom! If any such have followed me through this work, they will, I think, long since have concluded that they have been in error. Others advance a little further, and regard it as an "open question" – a position that may be disputed, but for which more may be said than against it, but concerning which they are not able to decide. This is tantamount to saying that the gospel is an open question, and that they really cannot say whether the kingdom of God will have subjects or not. There are others who believe that Israel will certainly be restored, but they clog it with a condition which in effect makes its fulfilment impossible, or eternally remote. They tell us that they will not be restored until they are converted to Christianity!

By Christianity they mean the inanity preached from the "sacred desks" of the apostasy – the pulpit-gospels of the day; "for", say they, "if they abide not in unbelief they shall be grafted into their own olive again". This is quite true; but the fallacy consists in construing this to mean that their restoration is predicated on their believing what the Gentiles teach. The Gentiles themselves are in unbelief. How, then, can they convert the Jews? "Because of unbelief they were broken off, and thou, Gentile, standest by *faith*. Be not high-minded, but fear: for if God spared not the natural branches, take heed lest he also spare not thee"; for "thou also shalt be cut off if thou continue not in his goodness" (Romans 11:20-23). Both Jews and Gentiles are faithless in the gospel of the kingdom in the name of Jesus. The Jews believe one part of it, and the Gentiles another part of it, but even these several parts they adulterate with so many traditions, that neither Jews nor Gentiles believe anything as they ought. Therefore, as He broke off Israel by the instrumentality of the Romans, so He is now about to break off the Gentiles by the judgments soon to be poured out upon them.

The grafting-in of Israel: a two-stage process

The work of grafting Israel into their own olive belongs to God, who, as the scripture saith, "is able to graft them in again". No one, I presume, will dispute His ability. As I have shown elsewhere, He has assigned the work of restoration to the Lord Jesus, who will graft them in again upon a principle of faith. He will bring their unbelief to an end in a way peculiar to the emergency of the case. When the fulness of the Gentiles is come in, then Israel's blindness will be done away.

The restoration of the Jews is a work of time, and will require between fifty and sixty years to accomplish. When Gogue comes to be lord of Europe, like Pharaoh of old he will not permit Israel to remove themselves and their wealth beyond his reach. His dominion must, therefore, be broken before the north will obey the command to "give up", and the south to "keep not back"; and even then Israel must fight their way to Palestine as in the days of old.

The truth is, there are two stages in the restoration of the Jews, the first is before the battle of Armageddon; and the second, after it; but both pre-millennial. God has said, "*I will save the tents of Judah first*". This is the first stage of restoration. Jesus has already been "a stone of stumbling and rock of offence" to Judah and his companions for forty years, that is from the day of Pentecost to the destruction of the temple, so that they need not to be subjected to a like process any more. But the word saith, "He shall be a stone of stumbling and a rock of offence to *both* the houses of Israel" (Isaiah 8:14); now it is well known that this has not been fulfilled in relation to the ten tribes. They did not inhabit Canaan at the time Jesus sojourned and ministered there. The gospel of the kingdom has never been preached to them in his name; hence, they are only acquainted with him as they have heard of him by the report of Jesuits, and the priests of Gentile superstitions – a report which is incapable of making men responsible for not believing.

It remains, then, after Judah's tents are saved, to make use of them as apostles to their brethren of the other tribes, to preach to them a word from Jerusalem (Isaiah 2:2), inviting them to come out from the nations, and to rendezvous in "the wilderness of the people", preparatory to a return to a land flowing with milk and honey, in which Judah is dwelling safely under the sceptre of the Seed promised to their fathers. Judah's submission to the Lord Jesus, as the result of seeing him, will give them no right to eternal life, or to the glory and honour of the kingdom. It just entitles them to the blessedness of living in the land under the government of Messiah and the saints. So with the Ten Tribes; their faith in the word preached will entitle them to no more than a union into one kingdom and nation with Judah; and a participation in the blessings of Shiloh's reign during their natural lives. If any of them attain to eternal life and glory, it will be predicated on some other premises than those which precede their restoration.

There is, then, a partial and primary restoration of Jews before the manifestation, which is to serve as the nucleus, or basis, of future operations in the restoration

of the rest of the tribes after he has appeared in the kingdom. The pre-adventual colonisation of Palestine will be on purely political principles; and the Jewish colonists will return in unbelief of the Messiahship of Jesus, and of the truth as it is in him. They will emigrate thither as agriculturists and traders, in the hope of ultimately establishing their commonwealth, but more immediately of getting rich in silver and gold by commerce with India, and in cattle and goods by their industry at home under the efficient protection of the British power. And this their expectation will not be deceived; for, before Gogue invades their country, it is described by the prophet, as "a land of unwalled villages, whose inhabitants are at rest, and dwell safely, all of them dwelling without walls, and having neither bars nor gates; and possessed of silver and gold, cattle and goods, dwelling in the midst of the land" (Ezekiel 38:11-13). Now any person acquainted with the present insecure condition of Palestine under the Ottoman dominion must be satisfied from the testimony, that some other power friendly to Israel must then have become paramount over the land, which is able to guarantee protection to them, and to put the surrounding tribes in fear. This is all that is needed, namely, security for life and property, and Palestine would be as eligible for Jewish emigration as the United States have proved for the Gentiles.

Britain to facilitate the return of the Jews

But to what part of the world shall we look for a power whose interests will make it willing, as it is able, to plant the ensign of civilisation upon the mountains of Israel? The reader will, doubtless, anticipate my reply from what has gone before. I know not whether the men, who at present contrive the foreign policy of Britain, entertain the idea of assuming the sovereignty of the Holy Land, and of promoting its colonization by the Jews; their present intentions, however, are of no importance one way or the other, because they will be compelled, by events soon to happen, to do what, under existing circumstances, heaven and earth combined could not move them to attempt. The present decisions of "statesmen" are destitute of stability. A shooting star in the political firmament is sufficient to disturb all the forces of their system; and to stultify all the theories of their political astronomy. The finger of God has indicated a course to be pursued by Britain which cannot be evaded, and which her counsellors will not only be willing, but eager, to adopt when the crisis comes upon them.

The decree has long since gone forth which calls upon the Lion of Tarshish to protect the Jews. Upwards of a thousand years before the British were a nation, the prophet addresses them as the power which at *"evening-tide"* should interest themselves in behalf of Israel. In view of this, "the time of the end", he says, "The nations shall rush like the rushing of many waters: but God shall rebuke them, and they shall flee far *off*, and shall be chased as the chaff of the mountains before the wind, and like a rolling thing before the whirlwind"; or, as it is expressed by another, "and they became like the chaff of the summer threshing-floors; and the wind carried them away, that no place was found for them" (Daniel 2:35). "Behold", says the former prophet, concerning Israel at this time, "at evening-tide trouble; and before the morning *he* is not. This is the portion of them that *spoil us*, and the lot of them that rob us" (Isaiah 7:13,14) – referring, doubtless, to the overthrow and destruction of Gogue. Now, the invasion of their country by a spoiler at "evening-tide", who robs them, implies their previous return. This finished colonisation Isaiah styles, "a present unto the LORD of hosts of a people scattered and peeled"; for, speaking of "the time of the end", he says, "In that time shall the present be brought unto the LORD of hosts of a people scattered and peeled ... to the place of the name of the LORD of hosts, the Mount Zion" (Isaiah 18:7). But, then, the question returns upon us, by whom is the present to be made? The prophet answers this question in the first verse, saying, "Ho! to the land shadowing with wings, which is beyond the rivers of Khush: that sendeth ambassadors by sea, and on vessels of papyrus upon the waters, Go, ye swift messengers, to a nation scattered and peeled, to a people terrible from this and onward: a nation meted out and trodden down, whose land the rivers [invading armies, Isaiah 8:7] have spoiled". Now, the geography of this passage points to the Lion-power of Tarshish as "the land shadowing with wings". Taking Judaea, where the prediction was delivered, as the place of departure, the word *"beyond"* points to the east; that is, running a line from Judaea across the Euphrates and Tigris, "the rivers of Khushistan", it passes into Hindostan, where "the Merchants of Tarshish, and its young lions", rule the land.[1]

But the British power is still further indicated by the insular position of its seat of government; for the "sending of fleet messengers by the sea", implies that the shadowing power is an island-state. Ambassadors are sent from the residence of the Court, and if they proceed to their destination by sea, the throne of the power must be located in an island. The text, therefore, points to the north and east, to England and Hindostan, as the land shadowing Israel with its wings. To Britain, then, the prophet calls as the protector of the Jewish nation *in the evening-tide trouble*, and commands it to send its messengers in swift vessels because the crisis is urgent, and to plant Israel as "an ensign upon the mountains" (Isaiah 18:3); as it is written in another place, saying, "The Lord shall set an ensign for the nations, and shall assemble the outcasts of Israel, and gather together the dispersed of Judah from the four corners of the earth" (Isaiah 11:12).

When this is accomplished to the required extent it becomes a notable sign of the times. It will then be seen that the political Euphrates is evaporated to dryness, and that Israel is walking in the way of the kings of the east. In view of this, the prophet addresses mankind, saying, "All the inhabitants of the world and dwellers on the earth, tremble, when he lifteth up

---

1 The British ruled the land "beyond the rivers of Kush" or Ethiopia, in Africa, that is, Egypt, the Soudan, and the far South beyond the Atbara and the Blue and White Nile in 1849 when this publication was written.

an ensign on the mountains; and when he bloweth a trumpet, shall hear". The ensign being planted on the mountains of Israel by Britain, the Lord will cause the Assyrian Autocrat to "blow a trumpet", summoning the hosts of his nations to war; for He has said, "I will bring thee, O Gogue, against my land". They will "ascend and come like a storm from the north parts, and be like a cloud to cover the land" (Ezekiel 38:9,16); but "they shall be left together unto the fowls of the mountains, and to the beasts of the earth; and the fowls shall summer upon them, and all the beasts of the earth shall "winter upon them", for their carcases will lie exposed for "seven months" upon the field (Ezekiel 39:14). Then shall "the present" be brought in full of all the tribes of Israel not previously assembled by "the land shadowing with wings".

Britain to provide places of refuge during the Gogian invasion

But from the subjugation of the Jews for a short time after they have been colonised, the protection of the shadowing-power would seem to have been inefficient. So it will, as far as the mountainous parts of the land are concerned; but, then, it is testified by Daniel, that "Edom, and Moab, and the chief of the children of Ammon, shall escape out of the hand of the king of the north". These countries will be a place of refuge for those who fly from the face of the spoiler, as Turkey has recently been for the Hungarians, who have fled from the same power. The Lion-power of Tarshish being in military occupation of the countries that escape, is enabled to continue their protection efficiently. Hence, the prophet addresses it, saying, "Take counsel, execute judgment; make thy shadows as the night in the midst of the noon-day; hide the outcasts; bewray not him that wandereth. Let mine outcasts dwell with thee, Moab; be thou a covert to them from the face of the Spoiler". The context shows that this has reference to a future time; for, having shadowed them from the spoiler, who, during their coverture in Moab, has met with his overthrow at the hand of Michael, the great Prince of Israel, – the prophet goes on to announce the good news, saying, "The extortioner is at an end, the spoiler ceaseth, the oppressors are consumed out of the land".

This cannot be said of any period of Jewish history since the prophecy was delivered; nor can it be said of the land in its present state, for the extortioner and oppressor still keep it in subjection. But what follows shows conclusively that the time referred to is yet future; for, as soon as the deliverance of the land is declared, and the spoiler is no more, the prophet directs the reader's attention to the setting up of the kingdom, as the next event to come to pass, saying in these words, "*In mercy shall the throne be established: and* **he** *shall sit upon it in truth in the tabernacle of David*, judging, and seeking judgment, and hasting righteousness" (Isaiah 16:3-5; Jeremiah 23:5; 33:14,15). But Moab's population is vanished, and the country a mere wilderness, whose solitude is only disturbed by the howl of beasts, or the occasional tramp of the Bedouins. For Moab, therefore, to respond to the prophetic exhortation, a power must take possession of the country capable of outstretching its wings for the defence of a people, "whose land the rivers have spoiled", and that power, I believe, is Britain's, the Moab of the latter days.

As I have said elsewhere, the Lion-power will not interest itself in behalf of the subjects of God's kingdom, from pure generosity, piety towards God, or love of Israel; but upon the principles which actuate all the governments of the world – upon those, namely, of the lust of dominion, self-preservation, and self-aggrandisement. God, who rules the world, and marks out the bounds of habitation for the nations, will make Britain a gainer by the transaction. He will bring her rulers to see the desirableness of Egypt, Ethiopia, and Seba, which they will be induced, by the force of circumstances, probably, to take possession of. They will, however, before the battle of Armageddon, be compelled to retreat from Egypt and Ethiopia; for "the king of the north shall stretch forth his hand upon the land of Egypt, which shall not escape; and the Libyans and Ethiopians shall be at his steps". Hence, these will become the battle-ground for a time, until the seat of war is removed to the mountains of Israel, where, by the Autocrat's discomfiture, the war is brought to an end between the image-giant of Assyria and the Lion of the north and east.

Britain to conquer Egypt and its neighbours

The possession, or ascendancy of Britain in Egypt, Ethiopia, and Seba, will naturally lead to the colonization of Palestine by the Jews. Thus the proverb will be verified which saith, "The wicked shall be a ransom for the righteous, and the transgressor for the upright". Though generations of the Jews have been stiff-necked and perverse", yet their nation is a "holy nation" which other nations are not, inasmuch as Israel is the only nation God has separated to Himself for a peculiar people. In view of what I have been presenting, Jehovah saith to them, "Fear not, O Israel; for I have redeemed thee: I have called thee by thy name: thou art mine. When thou passest through the waters, I will be with thee; and through the rivers, they shall not overflow thee; when thou walkest through the fire, thou shalt not be burned; neither shall the flame kindle upon thee. For I am the LORD thy God, the Holy One of Israel, thy Saviour; *I gave Egypt for thy ransom, Ethiopia and Seba for thee*. Since thou wast precious in my sight, thou hast been honourable, and I have loved thee; *therefore will I give men for thee, and people for thy life*. Fear not; for I am with thee: I will bring thy seed from the east, and gather thee from the west; I will say to the north, Give up; and to the south, Keep not back: bring my sons from far, and my daughters from the ends of the earth; even every one that is called by my name; for *I have created Israel for my glory*, I have formed him; yea, I have made him" (Isaiah 43:1-7).

Thus the Lord disposes of nations and countries as it pleases Him. To "the land shadowing with wings", which shall proclaim their return to the dust of their fathers, He will give Egypt, Ethiopia, and Seba as their ransom; and enable them, through its power, "to lay their hands upon Edom and Moab"; and to obtain the ascendancy over "the children of Ammon".

Thus they will settle in these countries of the Red Sea; to which they will be attracted by the riches to be acquired through their connection with the commerce of the east; which will then resume its channel of the olden time, when Israel and the British, like Solomon's servants and the men of Tyre, will drive a thriving trade between the Indian and China seas, and the nations of the west.

Having thus brought my exposition of the sure prophetic word down to the termination of "the time of the end", I shall conclude my interpretations by exhibiting the truth revealed concerning the things of *the transition period* during which the God of heaven is setting up His kingdom, and breaking in pieces and consuming all the kingdoms of the world, and transferring their glory, honour, and dominion under the whole heaven to the saints of the Most High. These matters will be set forth in brief under the caption of –

The second Exodus
When the Lord has *"broken to pieces together"* all the parts of Nebuchadnezzar's Image – that is, destroyed that power which bound them all together as one dominion – the work next to be accomplished in relation to them is to subdue the gold, the silver, the brass, the iron, and the clay – in other words, the powers represented by them – that they may become "like the chaff of the summer threshing-floors"; so that, being carried away by the tempest of war, "no place may be found for them", and the subjugating power become as "a great mountain, and fill the whole earth".

But a question arises here which must be answered, or our exposition is at fault, and deficient of a very important link in the chain of testimony which connects the kingdom of God with the foundation of the world. It is, By what means are "the kingdoms of the world to become the kingdoms of our Lord and of his Christ", after he has dissolved the imperial bond of union among them by the glorious victory of Armageddon? Is it to be accomplished by sending missionaries of the tribe of Judah to the nations, preaching to them salvation from hell by Jesus Christ, as missionaries are now doing among the heathen, and inviting them to submit to the spiritual authority of the Lord, administered through men of like passions with themselves? Or is it to be brought about by burning up the wicked, and leaving none but the righteous to inherit the earth? Or are the existing orders of bishops, priests, ministers, and missionaries to be employed to bring the nations to the obedience of faith, that they may voluntarily surrender all political power into their hands, as the saints of the Most High God?

I answer unhesitatingly, that the conversion of the world to Christ's supremacy will be accomplished by no such fantastical schemes as are implied in these suppositions. The answer to the question is, that *the nations will be subdued to the sceptre of Shiloh by the sword, and that the tribes of Israel will be his soldiers in the war*. Besides punishing them for their idolatry, and subsequent unbelief of the gospel of the kingdom preached to Judah in the name of Jesus, Israel has been also scattered among all nations, that they may be ready for the work assigned them in "*the time of trouble*", which intervenes between the battle of Armageddon and their final and complete restoration at the end of forty years. Though the dominion of Gogue be broken, the kingdoms and states which acknowledge him as their imperial chief will not voluntarily surrender themselves to another lord, any more than the populations of the old Assyrian empire did when the power of Sennacherib was broken in one night. The effect of his overthrow was only to prepare them for subjection to a more civilized and powerful ruler. In this case, the Lord used the Chaldeans for their subjugation: but in the coming strife He will use the tribes of Israel.

The Lord Jesus Christ at his appearing in his kingdom finds Judah inhabiting the land. Not all the Jews, but a goodly number of them. Having gained the victory of Armageddon, he convenes the elders of the people, which as their deliverer he has a right to do. Thus "they look upon him whom they have pierced" (Zechariah 12:10) "and one shall say unto him, what are these wounds in thy hands? Then he shall answer, Those with which I was wounded in the house of my friends" (Zechariah 13:6). The effect of this information upon the people is to cause a national lamentation. They will then discover that he to whom they owe their deliverance from Gogue, is Jesus of Nazareth, whom their fathers crucified. They will therefore "mourn for him, as one mourneth for his only son, and will be in bitterness for him, as one that is in bitterness for his first-born. In that day, there will be a great mourning in Jerusalem, as the mourning of Hadadrimmon in the valley of Megiddo" (Zechariah 12:10-14). Two-thirds of the people will have been cut off by the war against Gogue, and the third which survives will have passed through a fiery ordeal. It will have been a refining process in which they will have been refined like silver, and tried as gold is tried. Thus prepared "a spirit of grace and supplications" will be poured upon them, and they will call on the name of the Lord, and He will hear them, (Zechariah 13:9) and open for them a fountain for sin and for uncleanness (Zechariah 13:1). He will say, "It is my people: and they shall say, The LORD (even Jesus) is my God" (Zechariah 13:9). Thus will Judah be grafted again into their own olive, and brought to acknowledge Jesus as King of the Jews, and to confess that "he is Lord, to the glory of God the Father".

Judah to deliver the Jews in bondage abroad

The New Covenant being made with the house of Judah, the kingdom is established. Not, however, to its full extent. It is but the kingdom in its small beginning, as when David reigned in Hebron over Judah only. The Lord Jesus, as King of Judah, will have to bring the ten tribes and the nations generally to acknowledge him as King of Israel and Lord of the whole earth. What would the reader think of the little kingdom of Greece undertaking to subdue the whole world? Yet when the Lord appears in his little kingdom of Judaea, he will undertake to deliver every Israelite in bondage, establish David's kingdom to its full extent, overturn all kingdoms and dominions among the Gentiles, abolish all their superstitions, enlighten them in the truth, and bring them to submit to him joyfully as their lawgiver, high priest, and king. He will begin this mighty enterprise with Judah; for "he hath made them as his goodly horse in the battle. And they shall be as mighty men, which tread down their enemies in the mire of the streets in the battle: and they shall fight, *because the* LORD *is with them*, and the riders on horses shall be confounded" (Zechariah 10:3-5). "And the governors of Judah shall say in their heart, The inhabitants of Jerusalem shall be my strength in the LORD of hosts their God. In that day", saith the Lord, "I will make the governors of Judah like a hearth of fire among the wood, and like a torch of fire in a sheaf; and they shall devour all the people round about, on the right hand and on the left" (Zechariah 12:5,6).

Such is the illustration of their prowess. The nations will be as wood, or as sheaves, subjected to the action of fire. They may resist, but they are certain to be subdued without further power of resistance. "They shall tread down the wicked; for they shall be ashes under the soles of their feet" (Malachi 4:3). Their conquests will begin with the countries contiguous to Judaea. For when the Assyrian shall invade their land, the Judge of Israel having caused him to fall, "Judah shall waste the land of Assyria with the sword, and the land of Nimrod in the entrances thereof: thus shall he" that is to be ruler in Israel "deliver them from the Assyrian when he cometh into their land, and when he treadeth within their borders. And *the remnant* of Jacob shall be in the midst of many people as a dew from the LORD" (Micah 5:1-7).

Having thus conquered the land which God promised to Abraham and his seed for an everlasting possession, and made Judah as a bent bow in the hand of the king, the next thing is for the Lord to fill it with Ephraim as His arrow-headed weapon of war (Zechariah 9:12-16). In other words, "the LORD will seek to destroy all the nations that come against Jerusalem (Zechariah 12:9) under the banner of Gogue; and to accomplish this so as at the same time to bring back the ten tribes to the land of Canaan, He will cause Judah to make war upon Greece, and blow the trumpet to war against the ten kingdoms of the habitable, and the populations of the West among whom "the remnant of Jacob" is dispersed. These scattered tribes will have been "hissed for" or invited to leave the lands of their oppressors, and to make common cause with Judah. They will respond to the invitation; and as "the arrow of the LORD they will go forth as lightning; and they shall devour and subdue" (Zechariah 9:12-16). "And they shall be like a mighty man, and their heart shall rejoice as through wine. And I will bring them, saith the LORD, again also *out of the land of Egypt*, and gather them out of Assyria; and I will bring them into the land of Gilead and Lebanon; and Ephraim shall *pass through the sea with affliction* and shall smite the waves in the sea, and all the deeps of the river shall dry up; and the pride of Assyria shall be brought down; and *the sceptre of Egypt shall depart away*" (Zechariah 10:7-11; Isaiah 11:15,16).

Let us, then, attend more particularly now to the relation subsisting between the king of Israel and his ten tribes, designated as *"Ephraim"* and *"the remnant of Jacob"* in the word. Addressing them, the Lord says by the prophet, "Thou art my battle-axe and weapons of war; for with thee will I break in pieces the nations, and with thee will I destroy kingdoms; with thee will I break in pieces captains and rulers". This has never been the case since the prophecy was delivered; it remains, therefore, to be fulfilled. With Judah as his goodly war horse and well-strung bow, filled with the Ephraim arrow, and wielding the Israel battle-axe, "The LORD will go forth with the whirlwinds of the south". "The remnant of Jacob will" then "be among the Gentiles in the midst of many people as a lion among the beasts of the forest, as a young lion among the flocks of sheep: who, if he go through, both treadeth down, and teareth in pieces, and none can deliver". By such a weapon as this, the Lord "will execute vengeance in anger and fury upon the heathen, such as they have not heard" (Micah 5:8,15).

The forty-year war against Gog's dominions

This belligerent state of things between the King of Israel and the nations of Gogue's dominion, styled "*the goats*", will continue for forty years. The subjugation will be gradual, as Israel is made to "go through" from kingdom to kingdom. "Feed thy people", saith the prophet, "with thy rod, the flock of thy heritage, which dwell solitarily in the wood; let them feed in Bashan and Gilead as in the days of old". In answer to this petition, the Lord replies, "*According* to *the days of thy coming out of the land of Egypt* will I show unto him (Israel) marvellous things". This is forty years; for so long were they in passing from Egypt to Canaan, which was the type of their coming out from among the nations to the Holy Land under the generalship of Elijah, the Lord's harbinger to the Ten Tribes. The "marvellous things" to be shown them will not be performed in private, but will be as notorious as the plagues of Egypt; for "the nations shall see and be confounded at all their might: they shall lay their hand upon their mouth, their ears shall be deaf. They shall lick the dust like a serpent, they shall move out of their holes like worms of the earth; they shall be afraid of the LORD the God of Israel, and shall fear because of thee" (Micah 7:14-17).

The more immediate consequence of these exterminating wars will be the cessation of all further resistance in the north, which will have been thus compelled to "*give up*" the Israelites among them, and to let them go and serve in "the wilderness of the people". They will not march directly into the Holy Land, because the generation of Israelites who leave the north will be no more fit for immediate settlement there than their fathers were who left Egypt under Moses. They would be as rebellious under the government of Shiloh as that generation whose carcases fell in the wilderness, and concerning whom "Jehovah sware in his wrath that they should not enter into his rest". They must, therefore, be subjected to discipline, and trained up under the divine admonition. But, notwithstanding all the "marvellous things" they will have witnessed, they will prove themselves true to the character of their fathers, who were stiff-necked and perverse, and resistant always of the Spirit of God; so that they will not be permitted to enter into the land of Israel. Their children, however, will come thither from "the land of the enemy", and attain to their own border (Jeremiah 31:15-17).

Not all of the Jews to be accepted into the kingdom

The reader will, doubtless, desire to know upon what ground I affirm these things. This is as it ought to be; for he should set his face like a flint, and refuse credence to anything and everything which is not sustained by "the testimony of God". Turn, then, to the prophet Ezekiel, where it is thus written, "As I live, saith the Lord GOD, surely with a mighty hand, and with a stretched-out arm, and with fury poured out, will I rule over you: and I will bring you out from the people, and will gather you out of the countries wherein ye are scattered, with a mighty hand, and with a stretched-out arm, and with fury poured out. And I will bring you into the wilderness of the people, and *there will I plead with you face to face; like as I pleaded with your fathers in the wilderness of the land of Egypt, so will I plead with you*, saith the Lord GOD. And I will cause you to pass under the rod; and will bring you into *a delivering of the covenant* and I will purge out from among you the rebels, and them that transgress against me. I will bring them forth out of the country where they sojourn, and *they shall not enter into the land of Israel*: and ye shall know that I am the LORD" (Ezekiel 20:33-38).

While they are in this wilderness it is, that the Lord Jesus becomes "a stone of stumbling and rock of offence to the house of Israel", as he had before been to Judah; and the consequence is that "the rebels among them" are excluded from the blessings of Shiloh's government, and eternal life and glory in the then world to come. Nothing can be plainer than Ezekiel's testimony. If the reader know how the Lord pleaded with Israel face to face in the wilderness by the hand of Moses, he will well understand the ordeal that yet awaits the tribes to qualify them for admission into the Holy Land. The Lord's power and the angel were with them in the wilderness of Arabia, but they saw not his person; so, I judge, will the Lord Jesus and some of the saints be with Israel in their Second Exodus, seen perhaps by their leaders, as the Elohim were by Moses, Aaron, the elders and by Joshua; but not visible to the multitude of the people, who must walk by faith and not by sight; for, though God is able to graft them in again, He can only do it upon a principle of faith; for the condition of their restoration laid down in His word, is, *"If they abide not in unbelief*, they shall be grafted in again".

It would seem from the testimony of Malachi, who prophesied concerning the ten tribes, that while they are in the wilderness of the people they will be disciplined by the law of Moses as their national code, while things concerning Jesus will be propounded to them as matter of faith; for it is testified by Hosea that they shall be gathered, and "shall sorrow a little for the burden of the King of princes" (Hosea 8:10). The person with whom they will have more immediately to do in their Second Exodus is Elijah. There would seem to be a fitness in this. In the days of their fathers, when they forsook the Lord and abolished the law of Moses, Elijah was the person whose ministerial life was occupied in endeavouring to "restore all things". Though he did much to vindicate the name and law of Jehovah, he was taken away in the midst of his labours. For what purpose? That he might at a future period resume his work and perfect it by restoring all things among the ten tribes according to the law of Moses, preparatory to their being planted in their land under a new covenant to be made with them there (Malachi 4:4-6).

But it may be objected that Elijah has come already, and that John the Baptist was he (Luke 1:17). True, in a certain sense he was. John was Elijah to the House of Judah in the sense of his having come "in the spirit and power of Elijah" (Luke 1:17). But John was not the Elijah who talked with Moses on the Mount of Transfiguration. The latter is Elijah to the house of Israel. The scribes taught that Elijah must precede Christ; which Jesus approved, saying, "Elijah truly shall first come, *and restore all things*". He said this after John was put to death. John did not restore all things; but Elijah will, and that too before the Lord Jesus makes himself known to the ten tribes, whom he will meet in Egypt.

The returning Jews to gather in Egypt once more

The period of Israel's probation drawing to a close, they will have advanced as far as Egypt on their return to Canaan, as it is written, "They shall return to Egypt" (Hosea 8:13). This is necessary, for it is written also in more senses than one, "Out of Egypt have I called my son". As they are to be gathered from the west, north, and east they will have gone through the countries by a circuitous route to Egypt. They are to be gathered from Assyria, or the countries of Gogue's dominion; but I have not yet discovered in the word the line of march they are to follow in arriving at Egypt. But that they are to be assembled there is certain; for it is written, "I will bring them *again* also out of the land of Egypt". This was spoken some two hundred years after the overthrow of Samaria; and it is indisputable that neither Israel nor Judah have been again brought out of Egypt to inhabit their land: the exodus from Egypt is therefore still in the future.

The singing of the Song of the Lamb

But in coming out of Egypt they will have to cross both the Nile and the Red Sea; and although their march hither will have been one of conquest, it will not have been unattended with defeat, because of their own rebelliousness. The hearts of their enemies will be hardened to their own destruction to the last conflict. The south will still be disposed to *"keep back"* Israel from their country. Therefore, leaving Egypt, "Ephraim shall pass through the sea of affliction, and shall smite the waves in the sea, and all the deeps of the river shall dry up: and the pride of Assyria shall be brought down, and the sceptre of Egypt shall depart away" (Zechariah 10:10,11). The combined forces of Egypt and

Assyria shall be broken as the hosts of Pharaoh, and the horse and his rider be drowned in the depths of the sea. For "the LORD shall utterly destroy the tongue of the Egyptian sea; and with his mighty wind shall he shake his hand over the river, and shall smite it in the seven streams, and make (Israel) go over dry shod ... like as it was to Israel in the day that he came up out of the land of Egypt" (Isaiah 11:15,16).

They will now sing the song of Moses, and the song of the Lamb, who will have given them such a mighty deliverance from all their enemies. Being now "the ransomed of the LORD, they shall return, and come to Zion with songs, and everlasting joy shall be upon their heads". The prophet "like unto Moses", mightier than Joshua, and "greater than Solomon", will conduct them into the Holy Land, and, having delivered to them the New Covenant, will "settle them after their old estates". Having "wrought with them for his own name's sake", and by them as his "battle-axe and weapons of war", subdued the nations, and brought them to his holy mountain, he will "accept them there", and "there shall all the house of Israel, *all of them* in the land", as one nation and one kingdom under Shiloh "serve the Lord GOD" (Ezekiel 37:21,28; 20:40; 34:22-31).

Israel to be the praise of the entire world

Thus the little kingdom of Judaea will become "a great mountain", or empire, "filling the whole earth". The "Economy of the Fulness of Times" will now have fairly commenced, and the Day of Christ in all the glory of the Sun of Righteousness have opened in all its blessedness upon the nations of the earth. The gospel preached to Abraham, saying, "In thee shall all families of the earth be blessed", will be a reality. The Lord with Judah as his bended bow and Israel for his arrow, having subdued the nations, and "bound their kings with chains, and their nobles with fetters of iron" as his conquests progressed, will have transferred their much-abused power to his saints (Revelation 2:26,27), who shall rule them with a rod of iron which cannot be broken.

Having received his law (Isaiah 42:4), and experienced the justice of its administration, "all nations will call him blessed", and "daily will he be praised". A universal jubilee will celebrate the admiration of mankind, and their devotion to the King of all the earth. The world will no more resound with war's alarms for a thousand years; and among the highest there will be glory to God, on the earth there will be peace, and good-will among men (Luke 2:14). The mission of the Lord Christ will have been gloriously fulfilled. He will have raised up the tribes of Jacob, restored the preserved of Israel, and been the salvation of Jehovah to the end of the earth (Isaiah 49:6). In his days there will be abundance of peace; for the nations will beat their swords into ploughshares, and their spears into scythes, and practice war no more. "At that time they shall call Jerusalem the throne of the LORD; and all the nations shall be gathered to it, to the name of the LORD, to Jerusalem" as the metropolis of the world: *"neither shall they walk any more after the imagination of their evil heart"* (Jeremiah 3:17). The things they now delight in will then be an abomination to them; for "the Gentiles shall come unto the LORD from the ends of the earth, and shall say, *Surely our fathers have inherited lies, vanity, and things in which there is no profit"* (Jeremiah 16:19).

When enlightened by the Lord, this will be their judgment of the "nations and denominations", Pagan, Mohammedan, Papal, and Protestant, which now as a covering spread over all nations (Isaiah 25:7), darkens their understandings, and alienates them from the life of God. But when the King of Israel and his Saints shall rule the world, all these superstitions will be for ever abolished, and mankind will be of one faith and practice. They will speak one religious language, and serve Jehovah with unanimity; for, says He, "Then will I turn to the people a pure language, that they may all call upon the name of the LORD with one consent" (Zephaniah 3:9). This must, indeed, be the Lord's doing, for who among men has the wisdom, knowledge, and power to bring the nations to speak intelligibly on religious subjects, and to be of one religion? The sword only, can prepare the way for this. Mankind must be made to lick the dust like a serpent, before they will consent to change their creeds for eternal truth. Judgment will bring them to reason, and they will say at length, "Come, let us go up to the mountain of the LORD, to the temple of the God of Jacob; and *He* will teach us of his ways, and we will walk in his paths: for out of Zion shall go forth the law, and the word of the LORD from Jerusalem" (Isaiah 2:3). Under such teachings as this the work will be accomplished.

As to Israel, the Lord will have gotten them praise and fame in every land where they have been put to shame; and have made them a name and a praise among all the people of the earth (Zephaniah 3:19,20). "All nations shall call them blessed, for they shall be a delightsome land, saith the LORD of hosts" (Malachi 3:12). Instead of being a by-word and a reproach, as at this day, the Gentiles will glory in their patronage; for "in those days it shall come to pass that ten men shall take hold out of all the languages of the nations, even shall take hold of the skirt of him that is a Jew, saying, We will go with you; for we have heard that *God is with you*" (Zechariah 8:23). Yes, the kingdom, and throne of David will then be in their midst again, and Christ the Lord God, and Holy One of Israel, sitting upon it in power and great glory. The gospel of the kingdom will be no longer a matter of hope, but a reality; and those who have believed it, and submitted cheerfully and lovingly to the law of faith in the obedience it requires, and have perfected their faith by works meet for repentance, will be shining "as the brightness of the firmament and as the stars for ever and ever". This is the Hope of Israel which is set before men in the Gospel, and for which Paul was bound with a chain. It is a very different one from that exhibited in pulpit-theology; yet it is that which must be embraced as the soul's anchorage, if a man would be saved, and inherit the kingdom of God.

The final rebellion

Such will be the order of things for a thousand years. But though truth and righteousness will have gained the ascendancy and have prevailed for so long a period, sin will still exist in the flesh, and in some instances reveal itself in overt acts of disobedience. This is implied by the sayings: "The sinner shall die accursed" (Isaiah 65:20) and, "Whoso will not come up of all the families of the earth unto Jerusalem to worship the King, the LORD of Hosts, even upon them shall be no rain" (Zechariah 14:16-19). There will be no occasion to march an army into a country to put down rebellion; it will be quite effectual, to bring it back to its allegiance, to withhold from it the fruits of the earth. This spirit of insubordination will, however, smoulder among the nations until at the end of the thousand years the *"enmity"* against the Woman's Seed bursts forth again into a flame. If the apostle felt the workings of "the law of sin" within him, though obedient to "the law of the spirit of life"; need we wonder that the same "law of nature" should gather force in the hearts of nations subdued by fire and sword to the sovereignty of Israel's King? Man, unrenewed man, is essentially ungrateful and rebellious. The whole history of his race attests it. A thousand years of peace and blessedness will fail to bind him, by the bonds of love and a willing fealty, to the glorious and benevolent, yet just and powerful, emancipator and enlightener of the world.

Some new demon, who would rather reign as Satan than serve in heaven, will arise among the nations, and unfurl the old satanic standard of the Dragon empire, which will be known to the generation of that remote future as the past existence of the Assyrian, Persian, Macedonian, and Roman empires is known to us; that is, historically. A giant will this rebel be in presumption and crime, and surpassing in hardihood the pre-millennial Autocrat, whom Michael bound with a great chain and cast into the abyss. But what will not a man adventure inspired with the pride of life! Enchanted thus, he becomes the *Adversary* (Satan) of the King of Glory; and goes forth to the remotest nations, to Gogue's Magogian people, and falsely *accuses* his administration, by which means he succeeds in detaching them from their allegiance, and in *deceiving* them into a vain attempt to recover their ancient dominion (Revelation 20:7-10).

The King, instead of nipping the insurrection in the bud, permits the Adversary and Seducer (the Satan and the Devil) to mature his plans, marshal his hosts, and lead them on to an invasion of the land of Israel. The King permits him to come up on the breadth of the land", and to "compass the camp of the saints about, and the beloved city". Having enclosed the Governor of the world and his ancients in the metropolis, and so hemmed them in as to prevent all escape, with no army in the rear to raise the siege, the sceptre of universal dominion would seem once more to be within the grasp of the Head of the Old Serpent Empire. Like our contemporaries, professing to believe the past, but denying that its scenes will ever be repeated, he remembers the overthrow of the former Gogue, as the Autocrat of Russia now remembers that of Sennacherib in the days of Hezekiah, but believes not in the repetition of so terrible a destruction. He will know, doubtless – and who after that the knowledge of the Lord shall have covered the earth for a thousand years will not know? – that "he must reign till he have put all his enemies under his feet": but he will no more believe that it will be so than the Old Serpent, the founder of his dominion, believed that God would subject Adam to death in the day of his transgression though He had declared it. He will persuade the nations that the King of Israel shall not reign for ever, and that the overthrow of his government is possible.

Thus deceived, we find them enrolled under Satan, or the Adversary, and "encompassing the camp of the saints, and the beloved city", full of savage exultation at the expected destruction of the best of kings. But fallacious will be the hopes of the rebel multitude, and dreadful the vengeance to burst upon them. The trembling earth and the blackening heavens warn them of a coming tempest. The dark vapours and thick clouds of the sky, curling in dense and lowering masses, suddenly hiss forth the forked lightning, and the heaven is rent by the deafening roar of the voice of God. Hail, and fire mingled with hail, pour down upon them, and they are destroyed from the face of the land.

Thus God will deliver His King; for "fire shall come down from God out of heaven, and shall devour them".

'The end'

Thus, though corruption of the flesh, *nationally expressed*, was restrained by the overthrow of Gogue, the Dragon-chief, at the pre-millennial advent of the King of Israel, it is finally subdued only when the head of the Serpent-power is crushed at the end of the thousand years. After this victory, another enemy remains to be destroyed to perfect the work of the Son of Man. Death is the last enemy. The power of death is the corruption of the flesh, which is the consequence of sin. But, the wicked all being destroyed by fire, there remain upon the earth only the faithful and true, who are rewarded for their fidelity with the inheritance of the ages. The "law of sin", or law of their flesh, is abolished in the change they undergo from corruption to incorruptibility and life. This is the abolishing of death from the earth, so that its inhabitants can die no more. This being brought to pass, the saying will be fulfilled, and the work accomplished, that "the Son of God was manifested that he might destroy the works of the Devil" and "him that hath the power of death, that is the Devil".

Such is "the end, when the Son shall deliver up the kingdom to the Father, that God may be all and in all" (1 Corinthians 15:24-28; Revelation 21:3). The separation between God and Man began with the transgression of the first Adam; it continues till the end of the 7,000 years, when sin and death are utterly eradicated, and harmony again established in this orb of His glorious universe. Earth will have been delivered from moral and physical evil by His power administered and displayed through the Lord Jesus Christ, who, though "subjected to the Father", will have the pre-eminence over all "his brethren through the endless duration of ages. The last resurrection, which is employed in the development of "the end" (Revelation 20:6), will bring up from the dust the sleeping dead of the previous thousand years. Those who are accounted worthy of eternal life will receive it, and be added to the saints of the "first resurrection".

Thus a population will have been provided for the earth, which, instead of being destroyed, will be renovated, and all things belonging to it made new (Revelation 21:5). The earth and its inhabitants will be incorruptible, undefiled, and unfading. God, according to His word, will have made "a full end of all nations", except that of Israel; which will be the sole occupant of the globe, and every Israelite, "an Israelite indeed", "equal to the Elohim", and crowned with glory and honour throughout all ages. During the thousand years their nation will consist of three classes, Christ and the saints, righteous Israelites in the flesh, and those who die "accursed": but when perfection comes there will be but one class, and all will be immortal. The purpose of God, in the formation of the earth, will be accomplished; and "the headstone of the creation will be brought forth with shoutings, crying Grace, grace unto it".

Scripture index

Genesis

3:15.................... 157
12:1.................... 168
    :1-3................. 149
    :3.... 155, 159, 172
13:14-17............. 125
15:1.................... 146
    :18..................... 171
17:4,8.................. 171
    :7...................... 168
    :7,8.................. 125
22:17,18............. 125

Exodus

2:23,24................. 24
3:10..................... 24
4:22....................... 7
    :22,23................ 24
5:1........................ 24
9:16..................... 56
14:7..................... 45
19:6................... 236
20 45
23:23................... 46
34:7................... 168

Leviticus

19 119
20 119
25:23...................... 8
26 133
    :3,4,14,16.......... 47
    :31...................... 16
    :40-42................ 16
    :42...................... 66

Numbers

24:14..................... 96
32:13................... 151

Deuteronomy

4:2.......................... 8
    :5-8................... 125
    :13...................... 45
    :30...................... 96
    :32-35................ 56
7:6....................... 25
11:2-4,7,8............. 57
    :12........................ 8
14:2....................... 7
17:18,19................ 8
18:15................... 13

28 133
    :13...................... 91
    :15,43,44........... 90
    :15-68.................. 9
    :28,29,37,47,48
    133
30:1-10............... 147
    :3,9..................... 17
    :4........................ 64
    :6........................ 17
    :15-18................. 47
    :15,19............... 133
31:29................... 96
32:7,8.................. 171
    :23-27................ 19
    :35,36,43........... 19
    :43.................... 169
33:29................. 170

Joshua

4:23,24................ 56

1 Samuel

8:7........................ 6
12:12..................... 6

Scripture index

2 Samuel

7:10 39
:14-16 39
:23,24 .... 25, 39
23:1-7 39
:3,4 126

1 Kings

2:12 5
10:18 5

2 Kings

17:6,24 77

1 Chronicles

28:5 126
29:23 6

2 Chronicles

9:8 6
11:13-16 79
29:36 176
36:22,23 171

Ezra

2:70 77
3:1 77
9:15–10:3 147

Nehemiah

1:2,4 176
7:1 77
:7 78

Psalms

11:6 58
21:9 58

32:1,2 149
45:6 168
50:3-6 58
51:17 136
68:16 126
89:3,4 126
:19-37 39
:38,39,44 9
102:13-16 126
110:1 37
:2 126
:3 169
122:6 169
:6,7 93
132 39
:11 3
:13 126
149:7-9 67

Proverbs

8:15 168

Isaiah

1:2 7
:10 171
:18 169
:26 .... 3, 93
2:1-4 30
:2 239
:3 .... 92, 126, 257
5:7 7
7:1 76
:13,14 241
8:1 82
:7 242
:14 239
9:6,7 4
:7 10
10:17-33 99

11:1-12 37
:10-14 70
:12 242
:15,16 ..... 250, 255
16:3-5 244
17:13,14 101
18 171
:2 133
:3 242
:7 .... 69, 169, 241
25:6-8 92
:7 .... 170, 256
26:9 59
:20,21 63
27:6 86
:12 64
29 101
:7 101
30:27,28 58
34:34 41
35:1 136
:10 128
41:14-16 70
:17-20 75
42:4 256
:24 26
43:1-7 245
:6 171
:10 137
:18-21 75
:19 169
:21 27
:22-24 27
44:28 171
48:6 61
49 94
:5 34
:5,6,8 148
:6 .... 19, 34, 64,
168, 256
:8 35

:12 171	**23** :5 244	:22-31 255
:22,23 62	:7,8 171	:25-27 88
:23 168	:20 96	**36** :16-24 28
:24-26 61	**25** :15-33 58	:21 27
:25 .... 66, 172	**30** :7,8 60	:22 137
51 :11 128	:10,11 33	:22,23 18
:22,23 169	:11 .... 12, 137	:24-28 18
52 :4 93	:18-21 87	:25-31 53
:11,12 68	:23,24 58	:31 18
57 :12 148	**31** :6,9 171	:33-35 88
59 :19,20 101	:9 136	**37** 100
60 :2 58	:10 ..... 42, 128, 171	:1-14 128
:9 68	:12 136	:15 82
:12 91	:15-17 252	:21-28 29
:18-23 88	:18-28 85	:21,28 255
:21 .... 20, 53	:31 82	:22 82
61 :1-9 36	:31-34 44	:22,28 128
62 :2 93	**33** :5 36	**38** 95, 100, 121
:3 93	:8,9 87	:8-12 100
:5 136	:14,15 244	:9,16 243
:6,7 .... 93, 176	:24-26 33	:11-13 240
63 :15,16,20 170	**40** :11,12 78	:13 121
65 :18 93	**43** :5 79	:16 96
:20 258	**48** :47 96	:18,22 96
66 63	**49** :39 96	:18-23 99
:10-13 93	**51** :20-23 71	:21 8
:15,16 58		**39** 95, 100
:18-20 62	**Ezekiel**	:6,7 97
:19 63	**7** :24 9	:8 98
	16 82	:12 98
Jeremiah	**20** :13 170	:14 243
2 :2 7	:33-38 252	:21-29 53
3 :12 171	:34-38 51	:22-29 30
:17 .... 92, 256	:40 255	:23 96
:18 81	:40,41 87	:26 97
14 147	:42-44 53	**43** :2-4 40
:7-9 147	**21** :26,27 127	:7 41
:8 147	:27 9	**44** :2 40
16 :19 .... 91, 256	**28** :25,26 87	**45** :1 41
17 :12-14 147	**34** :11,23,31 128	**47** :13,14 41
22 :2 5	:12,13,23,24 36	:13,21 42
		48 :29 .... 42, 82

Scripture index

Daniel
2:28 96
:35 241
4:32 168
5:23 171
7:14 168
:20 169
:22 66
:27 170
10:14 96
11 121
:45 98

Hosea
2:17-19 89
3:4,5 86
:5 96
8:10 253
:13 254
9:11 10
11:1,8,9 135
13:9,10 85
14:4-7 86

Joel
2:16 169
3 101
:1,2 59
:9-15 59
:16 101
:18-21 89

Amos
3:2 .... 8, 12, 25
9:7-15 118
:11 37
:13-15 89

Micah
3:12 129
4:1 129
:2-4 130
:7 129
:8 .... 91, 129, 170
:11-13 70
5:1-7 249
:8,9 70
:8,15 250
7:14-17 251
:15 51
:16,17 62

Habakkuk
2:3 27

Zephaniah
3:2 51
:9 256
:12-15 53
:16-20 31
:19,20 .... 91, 257

Haggai
2:6 171

Zechariah
1:11,15 175
4:6 146
6:12,13 41
8:20-23 31
:22 92
:23 ..... 92, 137, 257
9:12-16 ...... 69, 249, 250
10:3-5 249
:7-11 250
:10,11 254
12 121

Malachi
:1-14 133
:2 170
:3 98
:5,6 249
:9 249
:10 .... 16, 37, 74, 136, 170, 248
:10-14 248
13 121
:1 .... 136, 248
:6 248
:9 248
14 .... 101, 121
:1,2 98
:3-6 100
:9,16 130
:16 92
:16-19 258

Malachi
3:5 51
:6 169
:12 257
4:1,2 58
:3 249
:4-6 253
:5,6 72

Matthew
3:8 169
5:35 41
10:5 34
:5,6 63
:6 14
15:24 34
17:11 72
:12 72
19 53
23:4 153
:38,39 170
:39 15

24:14 168
:32-34 151
26:32 168
28:19 168

Mark

6:34,38-42 128

Luke

1:17 .... 72, 73, 253
:23 4
:33 130
2:14 256
13:35 37
19:13 168
21:24 9
:36 63
24:27,44 34

John

1:11 14
:29 73
4:22 .... 13, 43, 138
11:51 35
12:32 127

Acts

1:3,6 236
:6 .... 10, 129, 147
2:5,9 79
:30 .... 3, 38
3:20-22 14
:21 .... 129, 147
7:5 138
:53 47
8:12 141
9:31 168
15 56

:10 45
:16 10
23:6 143
26:6 144
:26 127
28:28 168

Romans

1:1 158
2:20 48
9:4 43
:4,5 138
11:1 12
:2 .... 34, 159
:12 165
:15 .... 138, 169
:20-23 238
:21 170
:25,26 .... 34, 138
:25-27 viii
15:8 145
:16 158

1 Corinthians

15:24-28 260

2 Corinthians

3:15 170
11:7 158

Galatians

1:6-9 148
3:8 142
:14 155
:16 125
:19 48
:21 48
:24 48
:26-29 138

Colossians

2:14 45

1 Thessalonians

2:2,8,9 158
5:4 168

2 Thessalonians

1:7-9 58
2 64
3:5 168

1 Timothy

2:2 170

2 Timothy

2:2 64
:8 146

Hebrews

1 38
2:2 47
11:12 7
:19,39,40 138

James

2:10 48

1 Peter

1:10 145
2:5 169
4:17 158

Jude

:14,15 67

Revelation

- **1**:3 171
- :7 168
- **2**:26,27 .... 67, 255
- **3**:2 168
- :11 168
- **4** 63
- **11** 161
- :17,18 58
- **12**:16 168
- **13**:2,7 169
- **14**:7 61
- **16** 95
- :12 170
- :13 170
- :13-16 100
- **17**:5 169
- :6 169
- :14 63
- **18**:5 169
- :7 169
- :21 169
- **19** 100
- :11,16 58
- **20** 96
- :6 260
- :7-10 258
- **21**:3 260
- :5 261
- **22**:20 168